Get the eBook FREE!

(PDF, ePub, Kindle, and liveBook all included)

We believe that once you buy a book from us, you should be able to read it in any format we have available. To get electronic versions of this book at no additional cost to you, purchase and then register this book at the Manning website.

Go to https://www.manning.com/freebook and follow the instructions to complete your pBook registration.

That's it!
Thanks from Manning!

Learn C++ by Example

Learn C++ by Example
COVERS VERSIONS 11 TO 23

FRANCES BUONTEMPO
FOREWORD BY MATT GODBOLT

MANNING
SHELTER ISLAND

For online information and ordering of this and other Manning books, please visit
www.manning.com. The publisher offers discounts on this book when ordered in quantity.
For more information, please contact

> Special Sales Department
> Manning Publications Co.
> 20 Baldwin Road
> PO Box 761
> Shelter Island, NY 11964
> Email: orders@manning.com

©2024 by Manning Publications Co. All rights reserved.

No part of this publication may be reproduced, stored in a retrieval system, or transmitted, in
any form or by means electronic, mechanical, photocopying, or otherwise, without prior
written permission of the publisher.

Many of the designations used by manufacturers and sellers to distinguish their products are
claimed as trademarks. Where those designations appear in the book, and Manning
Publications was aware of a trademark claim, the designations have been printed in initial caps
or all caps.

♾ Recognizing the importance of preserving what has been written, it is Manning's policy to have
the books we publish printed on acid-free paper, and we exert our best efforts to that end.
Recognizing also our responsibility to conserve the resources of our planet, Manning books
are printed on paper that is at least 15 percent recycled and processed without the use of
elemental chlorine.

The author and publisher have made every effort to ensure that the information in this book
was correct at press time. The author and publisher do not assume and hereby disclaim any
liability to any party for any loss, damage, or disruption caused by errors or omissions, whether
such errors or omissions result from negligence, accident, or any other cause, or from any
usage of the information herein.

 Manning Publications Co.
20 Baldwin Road
PO Box 761
Shelter Island, NY 11964

Development editor:	Doug Rudder
Review editor:	Adriana Sabo/Dunja Nikitović
Technical editor:	Timothy Jaap van Deurzen
Production editor:	Keri Hales
Copy editor:	Lana Todorovic-Arndt
Proofreader:	Melody Dolab
Typesetter and cover designer:	Marija Tudor

ISBN 9781633438330
Printed in the United States of America

To my husband, Steve Love,
for supporting me and chatting about possible
examples and approaches used in this book
when he wasn't busy writing his own.

brief contents

contents

foreword

C++ is an ever-improving language used in almost every corner of computing, from embedded systems, operating systems, browsers, games, and trading systems to the ebook reader you may be using to read this book. A new C++ standard comes out every three years, and compiler vendors are quick to pick up on the latest features. I've been writing C++ professionally for over 20 years in the seemingly disparate games and finance industries. I have mostly worried about the performance of my code, which led to me creating Compiler Explorer, and not about every little change to the language.

All the while, at the back of my mind, I was concerned I was missing something. When I heard Fran was writing this book, I was excited to have the opportunity to catch up on the newer parts of the language I'd been ignoring for so long.

I first met Fran at the C++ on Sea conference. She was running the lightning talks—each speaker gets 5 minutes to present, one after another in rapid succession. As the compère of the talks, Fran had to cover while one person got up on stage and the previous left, and in doing so, she invited the audience to play various guessing games, such the higher-or-lower card game or smash quiz, getting us to guess various conference speaker names mixed up with C++ keywords. Little did we know she was trying out some of the games she uses as examples in this book!

In this book, Fran covers many of the latest C++ features, including smart pointers, ranges, optional types, variant types, improved string formatting, constexpr, concepts, and coroutines. If any of those sound unfamiliar to you, then you're in for a treat. As I mentioned, I haven't always kept up to date with the newer features, and reading this book was a fun way of picking them up. And I finally learned the difference between aggregate initializers and initializer lists!

The continued evolution of the language means C++ today is not the bug-prone tangle of memory leaks you might remember from the 1990s and 2000s. Unfortunately, online resources are slow to catch up and often show the old, deprecated ways of doing things. This book clears up a lot of misconceptions and will set you up on the right track.

The examples are playful and fun but show real-world nontrivial code. Each section shows the journey of development, iterating on the code as Fran introduces new concepts one by one. I encourage you to play along and compile and run the code as you read each section. At least for me, learning by doing works better than just reading alone, and by tinkering with the code, you can get a better sense of how easy it is to make changes.

Along the way, there's great general development advice on the tradeoffs we all have to make when writing code. There are tests that explore the edge cases and how to handle them, and even examples of how to write code that won't compile if used incorrectly, with helpful error messages.

Each section has relevant links to online resources such as blog posts, reference sites, and online tools (not just Compiler Explorer) that can help you understand the matter more deeply. The links complement the book perfectly, not distracting from the flow of the examples but giving you an opportunity to explore further if you're so inclined.

Learn C++ by Example is a fun and pragmatic way to learn the newest features of C++. If, like me, you've been worrying you're missing out, or if you're returning to C++ after an absence, then let Fran take you on a journey of what's possible with modern C++ and learn how to code your way out of a paper bag too!

—MATT GODBOLT

preface

I first encountered C++ when asked to write a C++ parser to emulate code for an embedded device on a PC back in the 1990s. I only knew C at the time, so this was a baptism by fire. The C++ was predominantly C with classes, like many early versions of C++ were. Over time, I learned more and fell in love with the language. As a long-standing member of ACCU (https://accu.org/), I volunteered to become editor of its *Overload* magazine, which means I have to write an editorial every other month, as well as encourage people to write and collate feedback from the review team. *Overload* has a mix of articles from newcomers and seasoned professionals, covering C++ in depth, as well as broader programming topics, so as the editor, I need to try to keep up to date with everything. This is a challenge, and I still have lots to learn.

I have used C++ for personal projects, and you can find many of my talks on YouTube. I have also used C++ professionally, predominantly in investment banks and other financial institutions. I know other languages too, and often act as an intermediary between the quant teams writing C++ libraries and the frontend teams using them. I do understand a lot of the under-the-hood mathematics that rocket scientists use in their coding. To be honest, I've only worked with two rocket scientists, but you can do clever things with C++. The important part is understanding what you are doing and knowing how to test your code.

C++ is an evolving language, so I will never be up to date with all the changes. However, being aware of what I don't know means I can pick specific parts to practice. In this book, I share various small projects designed to help you learn a variety of newer C++ features. Over the years, I have met many people who used to know C++ but stepped away to use another language for a while, and they were overwhelmed by the number of new features and approaches when they considered picking up C++ again. It's disheartening to spend time learning something and then find it difficult to reacquaint oneself. I want to encourage anyone in such a situation to focus on key elements to get back up to speed. I hope this book fills that need.

This book does not cover everything that has changed from C++11 onward. As I wrote this book, C++23 was finalized, so I have included a few of the newest features at the time of writing. C++ will continue to change, but having a few small projects to play with means you can use them for practice as the language continues to evolve. For instance, this book uses various containers, from `std::vector` to `std::unordered_map`, and more. The containers have been a fundamental part of C++ for a long time, but recent changes make them easier to use. This book uses a variety of new features, without trying to be a reference book for the whole language. The "About this book" section gives further details.

acknowledgments

This book has been fun and challenging to write. I've learned loads as I've tried to explain various aspects of C++. I frequently asked others for help or ideas, while aiming to find simple but correct ways to describe the language. Thanks to everyone who argued with me to ensure I was correct.

I would like to thank Matt Godbolt for writing a foreword for me. I'm delighted you enjoyed reading this book.

At Manning, I'd like to thank my development editor Doug Rudder and my technical editor Tim van Deurzen for their feedback, help, and encouragement while writing this book. In addition, thanks to the entire staff who helped produce this book.

I would also like to thank everyone who has taken the time to give me feedback, in particular Howard Hinnant, Andreas Fertig, Nina Ranns, Silas Brown, and Seb Rose, who all took time out of their busy schedules to comment in detail on various chapters, calling me out where I was unclear or incorrect. I'm also grateful to ACCU and those in the general email group who explained interesting edge cases I discovered as I wrote. Any remaining mistakes are my own.

I thank everyone involved in C++, including Matt Godbolt for his Compiler Explorer, Andreas Fertig for C++ Insights, and all those who spend time and money on developing new standards or engaging in various discussion groups.

Finally, thanks to all the reviewers: Amit Lamba, Arun Saha, Aryan Maurya, Balbir Singh, Clifford Thurber, David Racey, Frédéric Flayol, Jean-François Morin, Johannes Lochmann, John Donoghue, Jonathan R. Choate, Jonathan Reeves, Joseph Perenia, Juan José Durillo Barrionuevo, Keith Kim, Kent Spillner, Matteo Battista, Mattia Antonino Di Gangi, Maurizio Tomasi, Michael Kolesidis, Mitchell Fox, Partha Pratim Mukherjee, Patrick Regan, Raushan Jha, Rich Yonts, Samson Hailu, Satej Kumar

Sahu, Srikar Vedantam, Sriram Macharla, Timothy Moore, Vimal Upadhyay, and William Walsh. Your suggestions helped make this a better book.

about this book

C++ has changed a lot over the last decade or so. Some people who used to know the language well might now be put off by how many new things they will have to learn. It doesn't have to be so hard. Getting up to speed now will make it easier to keep track as C++ continues to change and evolve. This book focuses on small projects using various parts of C++, rather than an exposition of the entire language. You will try out some ideas and learn language features on the journey, rather than plow through each part of the language's syntax and standard libraries using one-line examples. The first chapter is an introduction, and from chapter 2 until the last chapter, you will create small projects and games to help you learn. You might even have fun!

Who should read this book

If you have used C++ before but have failed to keep up with recent changes, this book is for you. If you used to be an expert, but your knowledge has gone hazy, and you want to get back up to speed, this book will help you. If you have never been an expert but have previously used some C++ and want to learn more, in particular newer approaches and features, this book will also be valuable.

How this book is organized: A road map

This book has nine chapters. The first chapter provides an introduction, and the remaining chapters focus on a puzzle or game to code. In some cases, we make a simplified version first before improving the game. In all cases, we focus on one or more main features of C++ and learn a variety of other ideas and approaches on the way:

- Chapter 1 provides background on C++, showing why it is relevant and useful and introducing some recent changes.

- Chapter 2 uses an `std::vector` to create Pascal's triangle. It also covers move semantics, using `std::format`, ranges, and lambdas.
- Chapter 3 uses random numbers to make a number-guessing game. It also introduces `std::optional`, `std::function`, and handling user input.
- Chapter 4 uses time points and duration from `std::chrono` to write a countdown. We also meet user literals and learn about `std::ratio`.
- Chapter 5 covers writing classes to build a deck of cards and play the higher-or-lower card game. It also covers scoped enums, `std::array`, the three-way comparison operator, and `std::variant`.
- Chapter 6 uses classes again to make some blobs race out of a paper bag, this time revising inheritance and detailing the new special member functions now available in C++. In addition, it covers the rule of zero, type traits, and smart pointers.
- Chapter 7 uses `std::map` and `std::multimap` to build a game of answer smash. These containers are not new, but we see how to use `std::pair` and `std::tuple` with structured bindings, allowing us to query the maps neatly. Furthermore, we also read data from a file.
- Chapter 8 uses the newer `std::unordered_map` and describes `std::hash` to build a mind-reading machine, or at least a program that guesses if you will pick heads or tails based on previous outcomes. It also shows how to turn the mind-reading machine into a coroutine.
- Chapter 9 rounds things out by going into detail on parameter packs and `std::visit`, showing us how to make a slot machine game. The chapter encourages you to practice more with various algorithms, `std::format`, and lambdas.

Start by reading the first chapter, and then get your chosen compiler ready. You *can* read the chapters in any order; however, they build on each other to some extent, even though each creates a self-contained project. When a feature is used again, the first mention is signposted, so you can skip back if you need to. Reading the chapters in order might be easier, though, as you gradually add new approaches to your repertoire. However you decide to read this book, do stop and try out some code. Then play the games you created, or play with the projects. Keep your brain in gear, ask questions, experiment, and above all, have fun!

About the code

This book contains many examples of source code, both in numbered listings and in line with normal text. In both cases, the source code is formatted in a fixed-width font to separate it from ordinary text. Sometimes, code is also in bold to highlight code that has changed from previous steps in the chapter, such as when a new feature adds to an existing line of code.

In many cases, the original source code has been reformatted; we've added line breaks and reworked indentation to accommodate the available page space in the book. Additionally, comments in the source code have often been removed from the listings when the code is described in the text. Code annotations accompany many of the listings, highlighting important concepts.

This book has code in all nine chapters. The code is all in the book but can be cloned from https://github.com/doctorlove/BootstrapCpp.git. The first chapter is a short `main` function used to discuss modern approaches in C++, while the fun and games start from chapter 2. You will need a compiler, and https://isocpp.org/get -started provides links to several good free ones. Some features, such as `std::format`, are not supported on all compilers, but the book calls this out, and the source code has comments showing what to do instead.

You can get executable snippets of code from the liveBook (online) version of this book at https://livebook.manning.com/book/learn-c-plus-plus-by-example. The complete code for the examples in the book is available for download from the Manning website at https://www.manning.com/books/learn-c-plus-plus-by-example.

liveBook discussion forum

Purchase of *Learn C++ by Example* includes free access to liveBook, Manning's online reading platform. Using liveBook's exclusive discussion features, you can attach comments to the book globally or to specific sections or paragraphs. It's a snap to make notes for yourself, ask and answer technical questions, and receive help from the author and other users. To access the forum, go to https://livebook.manning.com/book/learn-c-plus-plus-by-example/discussion. You can also learn more about Manning's forums and the rules of conduct at https://livebook.manning.com/discussion.

Manning's commitment to our readers is to provide a venue where a meaningful dialogue between individual readers and between readers and the author can take place. It is not a commitment to any specific amount of participation on the part of the author, whose contribution to the forum remains voluntary (and unpaid). We suggest you try asking the author some challenging questions lest their interest stray! The forum and the archives of previous discussions will be accessible from the publisher's website as long as the book is in print.

Other resources

Each chapter mentions further resources, and these are collated into an appendix at the end of this book, so you can easily look back without having to keep notes.

about the author

FRANCES BUONTEMPO has many years of C++ experience. She has worked as a programmer at various companies, mostly in London, with a focus on finance. She enjoys testing and deleting code and tries to keep on learning. She has given talks on C++ and more, which you can find on YouTube. She is the editor of ACCU's *Overload* magazine and will happily consider articles from readers who want to share what they learned from this book.

about the cover illustration

The figure on the cover of *Learn C++ by Example* is "Femme de l'Isle de Lemnos," or "Woman of Lemnos Island," taken from a collection by Jacques Grasset de Saint-Sauveur, published in 1788. Each illustration is finely drawn and colored by hand.

In those days, it was easy to identify where people lived and what their trade or station in life was just by their dress. Manning celebrates the inventiveness and initiative of the computer business with book covers based on the rich diversity of regional culture centuries ago, brought back to life by pictures from collections such as this one.

Hello again, C++!

This chapter covers

- Why C++ is relevant
- When C++ is useful
- What you need to know before reading this book
- How this book will bootstrap your knowledge of C++
- What you'll learn in this book

C++ is an old but evolving language. In programming, you can use it for almost anything and will find its application in many places. In fact, C++'s inventor, Bjarne Stroustrup, described it as the invisible foundation of everything. Sometimes, C++ might be present deep inside a library of another language because it can be used for performance-critical paths. Furthermore, it can run in small, embedded systems, or it can power video games. Even your browser might be using the language. C++ is almost everywhere.

The language is compiled and targeted at specific architectures such as a PC, mainframe, embedded devices, bespoke hardware, or anything else you can think of. If you need your code to run on different types of machines, you need to recompile it. This has pros and cons. Different configurations give you more to maintain, but compiling to a specific architecture gets you down to the metal, allowing the speed advantage. Whatever platform you target, you will need a compiler. You will also need an editor or integrated development environment (IDE) to write code in C++.

C++ stems from C, which has similar advantages but is a lower-level language. If you recognize ++ as the increment operator, you'll realize that the language's very name suggests it is a successor to C. You can avoid the depths of pointers and memory allocations with C++ by writing higher-level code. You can equally drop down to C or even assembly language in C++ code. Although C++ was never intended to take over the world or even replace C, it does provide many new ways to approach coding. For example, you can do a surprising number of things at compile time, using type-safe features rather than preprocessor macros often used in C.

This language underpins diverse technologies, including compilers or interpreters for other languages, and even C++ compilers themselves. You can develop libraries for use in other languages, write games, price financial instruments, and do much more. If you ever typed make at a prompt, you were probably using C++ without knowing it. C++ may power your browser or e-reader if you are reading this book in digital form, or it may have been used to write device drivers for your machine.

This book will give you a firm grounding in a handful of C++ language and library features. Each chapter walks through a small, self-contained project, focusing on one area. Along with each chapter's main feature, other parts of the language will be covered. For example, if you fill a container, such as a vector or an array, you may also want a way to display and manipulate its contents. Thus, the next chapter focuses on vectors but also introduces ranges and lambdas, as well as using format to display output. By gradually building up your repertoire, you will gain confidence, which will allow you to rediscover the joy of C++. This book will focus on several fundamental parts, showing you various ways in which the language is easier now than it used to be. You will end up with a firm grounding, ready to use and learn more C++.

1.1   Why does C++ matter?

C++ is designed by a committee. Some languages are introduced and developed by a company or an individual. C++ is not. Originally invented by Bjarne Stroustrup, Working Group 21 (WG21) of the International Organization for Standardization (ISO) is now responsible for its new versions. You can find more details at https://isocpp.org/std. There's been a new ratified standard every three years since 2011, each adding new features and sometimes simplifying ways of doing things. This means there is a lot to learn. Some documentation and descriptions sound as if they were written in legalese, which can be overwhelming. This book will use a few precise definitions to help you get the hang of parsing such explanations. Members of the committee make suggestions, write papers to explain their ideas, and demonstrate how to implement new features or small improvements, which leads to innovations that influence other programming languages too. For example, Java and C# would not have generics if C++

hadn't introduced templates. Ideas do flow in both directions. C++ also takes on board ideas from other languages, including functional programming idioms, such as lambdas.

These recent standards injected new life into C++, causing lots of excitement. Companies that have been using C++ for years may previously have relied on in-house libraries to support features that are now part of the core language. Upgrading to a newer standard can be hard work, but it means more people will be able to work on the code base without spending time getting up to speed with a niche implementation. In addition to changes in the technology stack in businesses, there are now several conferences devoted to C++, along with podcasts and blogs, as a new cohort gets involved. C++ has a reputation for being very hard-core, with geeks arguing about difficult stuff and being mean to newbies (and each other). This is partially unfair, but the IncludeCpp group (https://www.includecpp.org/) tries to be inclusive and welcoming. They have a discord group and tend to have a stall at C++ conferences, so if you go alone, you can head straight to them and say hi. Recent changes have made several parts of C++ easier to explain and use but have introduced more edge cases and complications. This book will tend to stick with commonly available features that make your life easier, but it's worth knowing a bit about some new, less widely supported features.

If you knew C++ before C++11, you might be intimidated by the changes. In fact, if you spent time catching up and blinked, you've still missed a lot. Fear not. Although C++ may resemble riding a bicycle (it hurts if you fall off), C++ doesn't have to be painful. This book will stop you from falling down the rabbit hole. You can have fun and learn many approaches and paradigms, from object-oriented programming to functional approaches. A grounding in C++ will make other languages and approaches easier to understand too. Furthermore, C++ is so pervasive that it will never go away, so it's useful to understand a little. You'll never know all of it. Even Bjarne himself is reputed to have said he'd rate himself at seven out of ten on C++ knowledge, so fear not. To be a good programmer, you don't have to know every detail of the language. Knowing enough as a basis to learn more is important. If you bootstrap your understanding now, you will also find it easier to keep up.

C++ has grown over time. Initially, C++ was C with classes, introducing the keyword `new` (along with `delete` and `class`) and the idea of constructors and destructors. These are functions that run automatically when an object is created and when it goes out of scope or is deleted. Unlike garbage-collected languages, such as C# and Java, you have control over an object's lifetime. Proponents of garbage-collected languages sometimes deride C++, claiming it's all too easy to end up with memory leaks. Now, you don't need to use `new` and `delete`, and C++ has smart pointers to help with memory management. The language evolved over time, adding various new features. It still remains relatively compact, although it has grown since it began. The language, like all others, is what you make of it. You can write terrible code in any language. You can also write beautiful code in any language, but you need to learn how. By trying out code as you read this book, you will end up with some small programs to play with.

They will cover various aspects of the language, giving you a firm grounding. You will see how C++ can be awesome.

There are many rivals to C++, yet C++ has staying power. It consistently remains at the top of the TIOBE index (https://www.tiobe.com/tiobe-index/#2022) and was ranked among the top three in 2022. You could use C instead, but you will see stars (pointers being represented with an * character). If you want a data structure beyond an array, you'll have to roll your own. You could use High Performance Fortran for extremely fast computation. The UK Met Office uses Fortran for their weather modeling because they have a vast amount of data to crunch in a very short time. Fortran also loiters in many academic institutions, so you may have seen or used it if you are an academic or student. However, it is a little niche. You are more likely to come across some C++ code in the wider world.

Various new languages have been invented, aiming to deal with C++ defects or annoyances. D feels similar to C++ because of the C-like syntax and high-level constructs, and it was invented to deal with the aspects of C++ the creators didn't like. Meanwhile, C++ continues to evolve, but it always aims to remain backward compatible, so it is constrained by historical decisions. New languages don't have a legacy and thus have more freedom. Go, Objective C, Swift, Rust, and recently Carbon also rival C++ in some areas. That's fine, and learning several languages and thinking about what might make a programmer's life easier is a good thing. Many times, new ideas introduced into the latest C++ standards are based on insights from other languages. As new languages have been introduced, C++ still remains prevalent and often takes on board any challenges they present. C++ isn't going away anytime soon. You can get involved and submit bug reports or suggestions too if you like. The committee consists of volunteers, who work hard to improve the language. ISOCpp provides details on how to get involved (https://isocpp.org/std/meetings-and-participation).

If you learn C++, you will have a solid foundation for other languages. The similarity to other languages can help you quickly pick up how to use them. You will get familiar with some data structures and algorithms, as well as various paradigms ranging from functional programming to object-oriented code. Even if you don't end up on the standards committee or inventing your own programming language, you will be well placed to continue a journey of lifelong learning and understand what is happening under the hood.

1.2   *When should you use C++?*

You can use C++ for anything, but some use cases are more sensible than others. To prototype some machine learning or run a statistics calculation, it might be quickest to start in Python and use existing libraries. Of course, those libraries may include some C++. If you feel confident enough to look at the source for a library to figure out why a bug happens, you have a head start on other programmers. If someone needs a program with a frontend, be that a website or local program with a graphical user interface (GUI), you could build the whole thing in C++, but it might be easier to split up the software. C++ doesn't support GUIs in the core language, unlike, say, C#, so the frontend would require an external library, such as the cross-platform C++ library Qt (https://www.qt.io/). You could also write the frontend in something completely different and call the C++ code as a service or library. So, given that you might start in another language to try out an idea or build part of your application in another tool chain, when should you use C++?

If you want a first-person shooter-style game, you could try to write it in JavaScript, but using a language that compiles to the hardware is more sensible. An interpreted language will be slower than a compiled language. C++ is therefore frequently used to write the game engine, render the graphics, work out the physics, detect collisions, and provide sound and artificial intelligence for bots. A scripting language might call into this engine, but the engine's power and speed often come from C++, squeezing every inch of power out of a top-end graphics card or another component of an expensive gaming rig. This also makes C++ suitable for high-performance computing (HPC), financial applications, embedded devices, and robotics.

Because C++ takes you close to the metal, you can break things. It's possible to brick an embedded device if you are not careful, rendering the machine inoperable. You're unlikely to manage that if you write a program to run on your laptop or computer. It might crash, proudly announcing a segmentation fault or similar on the way out. An embedded device without an operating system is different. If it's only running one program without an operating system, and that goes wrong, bad things can happen. That's okay too. Bjarne Stroustrup once said, "If you never fail, you aren't trying hard enough" (https://www.stroustrup.com/quotes.html). Although the language allows you to use raw pointers and potentially step over memory bounds or invoke undefined behavior, this book will steer you away from danger. Just remember, it has been said that with great power comes great responsibility. With enough of a solid foundation, you can program responsibly, learn lots, and have fun.

Although C++ doesn't support several things natively, such as unit testing, GUI coding, or even networking (that nearly made it into C++23 and might make it into a future standard), you can do these things using a suitable third-party library. What the core C++ language does provide is a large and thought-through standard library. If you were using C and wanted a normal distribution of random numbers, you'd need to dust off a mathematics book or read what Donald Knuth has to say on the matter. If you need a lookup table, you can use C++'s standard map. In C, you'd have to write your own. In fact, you get stacks, queues, heaps, and almost every data structure you can think of in C++ out of the box, along with a vast number of algorithms. This means learning C++ provides a solid foundation for understanding other languages.

If you need to do a lot of number crunching quickly, C++ is a great choice. Modern language versions also support a variety of random number distributions, as you will see in this book, making it relatively easy to set up a variety of complicated simulations. Even without using the latest and greatest parts of the language, you can build some serious applications in C++. For example, the MRC Centre for Global Infectious

Disease Analysis, affiliated with Imperial College in the United Kingdom, open sourced their COVID-19 simulation model (https://github.com/mrc-ide/covid-sim). These models were used to decide public policy in the United Kingdom during the pandemic. C++ does the heavy lifting, and some scripts, written in R, are provided to display the results.

C++ is often described as a multi-paradigm language. It supports object-oriented programming, but you are allowed to write free functions too. You can write low-level procedural code if you want, but you can also use generics (i.e., templates) and functional-style programming. You can even do template meta-programming (TMP), making the compiler do calculations for you. This was an accidental discovery, presented by Erwin Unruh at a C++ committee meeting in 1994. He demonstrated a program that didn't compile but rather printed out the prime numbers in the compiler error messages. Playing with TMP can be fun to explore and push to extremes, but simpler cases can give faster runtimes with type-safe, compiler-evaluated constants. If you learn how to use some C++, you will have a stable foundation for many other languages and know a great variety of different programming paradigms.

1.3   *Why read this book?*

As the language evolves, people are writing books for each new standard and more general-purpose style guides. The style guides won't make any sense if you don't know the new features, and the new features build on previous changes, so the full details can be overwhelming. Where do you start in the face of a moving target? Where you are. You need a way to bootstrap your learning. This book will take you through some central changes via small projects so you have something to experiment with. By using some of the new features, you'll be better able to recognize what modern C++ code is doing and know where to keep an eye out for further changes and developments.

Instead of reading a list of all the changes you may have missed, the ISOCpp website has a FAQ section (https://isocpp.org/wiki/faq) that provides an overview of some recent changes and big-picture questions. This website is run by the Standard C++ Foundation, a not-for-profit organization whose purpose is to support the C++ software developer community and promote the understanding and use of modern Standard C++. The site even has a section for people with a background in other languages who want to learn C++. It doesn't have a section for "Learning C++ if you already knew C++ a while ago." This book plugs that gap. You don't need a long list of every feature that's been introduced over the years. You need just enough to get your confidence back.

You can keep an eye on the myriad and excellent resources online to stay aware of what has been and is changing in the language. ISOCpp will help you do this. However, you do need to stop and try things out to learn. Spending time experimenting will pay off, and this book will guide you through some useful experiments. Trying out features in bite-sized chunks will help you crystalize ideas and concepts. You will see alternative approaches from time to time. By seeing two ways to put items in a `vector`, you will learn a new feature (the `emplace` methods) and recall an old feature (`push_back`). This will help you read other people's code and not be wrong-footed by unfamiliar approaches. You will learn how to think through alternatives, becoming aware of advice from different places, which sometimes conflicts. This book will take a pragmatic approach while encouraging you to think about alternatives.

1.4 How does this book teach C++?

This book covers a subset of features introduced into C++, from C++11 onward. At the time of writing, C++23 is in feature-freeze, making it ready for a new standard. Each chapter focuses on one main feature, although it introduces and uses other modern features and idioms as well. Some people who used to know C++ well are put off by how many new things they will have to learn to start using it again, and beginners often get frightened off quickly. It doesn't have to be so hard. Getting up to speed now will make it easier to keep track as C++ continues to change and evolve. If you haven't used C++ for a long time and have seen other books going through an extensive list of all the new features and idioms, but you don't know where to start or how to use them, this book will help you focus on some important parts, enabling you to dive into gnarly edge cases and thorough explanations elsewhere afterward.

This book focuses on self-contained projects using various parts of C++. You will try out some ideas and learn language features on the ride, rather than plow through each part of the language's syntax and standard libraries using one-line examples. If you have gone rusty, this book will give you a chance to practice and rediscover the joy of using C++. As you probably realize, writing a whole program gives you more practice than playing around with one or two lines. This book will therefore help you teach yourself.

1.4.1 Who this book is for

This book is aimed at people who have used a little, or even a lot, of the language and lost track of recent changes. If you recognize the syntax and want to try to learn more, you will gain something from this book. If you know what `int x = 5; int & y=x;` do, have used an `std::vector<int>` before, and recognize `std::cout << x`, you will be able to follow. If you've seen `int x{1};` before, you're part way there. If not, don't panic. The curly braces are a new way to initialize almost everything, which you'll soon get the hang of. If you used to know all the gnarly edge cases and quote chapter and verse of a previous standard, this book will help you focus on a handful of new features to get you back in the driving seat. Once you've finished reading this book, you will know where to get an up-to-date compiler and how to keep an eye on upcoming changes, and you'll be able to read and write modern C++. Let's look at some code now to get a feel for a few new ways of writing the language.

1.4.2 Hello, again, C++!

It's conventional to start learning a language with a "Hello, World!" program, so let's do just that. The following code prints a greeting onscreen.

Listing 1.1   Hello, World

```
#include <iostream>        ⟵─┤ Includes a header
                                            ┌─────────── Trailing
auto main() -> int {           ⟵────────────┘           return type
    std::cout << "Hello, world!\n";    ⟵─┤ Operators :: and <<
}
```

If you save this to a file called `hello_world.cpp`, you can compile it. For example, using the GNU compiler collection (gcc; see https://gcc.gnu.org/), use g++ supporting C++11 with

```
g++ hello_world.cpp -o ./hello.out
```

This book assumes you recognize the `include` statement, the scope resolution `operator::`, and the stream insertion `operator <<`. The code inserts the greeting to standard (std) `cout` inside the `main` function, the usual entry point for executable code. You knew that, however, the *trailing return type* `->` at the end of a function name may be unfamiliar, together with the keyword *auto* at the start of the line. You can write `int main()` here instead, as you always used to, but when C++11 introduced this feature, many people started using it everywhere for consistency. It becomes useful when you want to deduce the type a function returns. Our hello program doesn't need the trailing return. Furthermore, `main` is special in that it returns 0 by default, so it does not need a return statement even though it returns an `int`. Without a trailing return type, some template functions can be very tricky to specify. Let's consider an example that uses a template function.

You can use the + operator easily enough to add numbers. For example, `auto x = 1 + 1.23`. There's our friend `auto` again. We're trying to sum an integer (1) and a double (1.23), so the result is a double due to *integer promotion*. If you want a general-purpose addition function, you could attempt to write overloads for every possible pair of parameters or, more sensibly, write a template function. Even better, you can use one that is already written for you. The `functional` header includes a definition of `plus`. In fact, this header contains two definitions, one of which sums two parameters of the same type, which we create by saying `std::plus<int>` to add two integers. Since C++14, a version that deduces the template argument types was introduced. Using `std::plus<>` picks the new specialization, which works out the types for us. If you try the first version, 1.23 gets converted to an `int`, so you get 1 + 1, which some compilers warn about, whereas the second version adds the `int` 1 and the `double` 1.23 to get 2.23. Try it out!

Listing 1.2   Adding two numbers

```
#include <iostream>
#include <functional>

auto main() -> int {                                      ┌─ Enforces a sum of
    std::cout << std::plus<int>{}(1, 1.23) << '\n';    ⟵─┘  two ints, so returns 2
```

```
    std::cout << std::plus<>{}(1, 1.23) << '\n';        ◁┐  Figures out the
}                                                        │  different types
```

You are used to functions starting with the return type and then having a name and parameters, such as `int main()`. The return type is given first. To specify the return type, `plus` needs to express the addition operation of the two function arguments. This is much easier to do with parameter names, but those are not visible to the usual return type. The trailing return type makes using parameter names to specify the return type possible. You need to say `auto` at the start and indicate what type is returned after the trailing `->`.

Let's look at a simplified version of the `operator()` for the `plus<>` specialization. Remember, we want to declare a function that takes two things and returns the sum of them. We're going to use a template with two typenames, allowing two different types to be summed. The addition itself is the easy part and simply uses the + operator. The declaration has `auto` at the start and a type at the end.

Listing 1.3   A function to add two different types

```
template<typename T, typename U>
auto simple_plus(T lhs, U rhs) -> decltype(lhs + rhs)
{
    return lhs + rhs;
}
```

The operator function is a template using two different types, `T` and `U`, for the left-hand side (`lhs`) and right-hand side (`rhs`) of the binary operation, respectively. The return type is declared using `decltype` specifier and the expression `lhs + rhs`. If you squint, you can see how that's similar to the syntax for the `main` function we saw earlier. Put them side by side and have a look:

```
auto main() -> int
auto simple_plus(T& lhs, U& rhs ) -> decltype(lhs + rhs)
```

You can see the `auto` followed by the function name and parameters, then the arrow and the trailing return type in both cases. When we add 1 and 1.23, the parameter types are deduced to be an integer and a double. The trailing return type uses the expression (1 + 1.23) to get the return type of a double.

If you already recognize these new features, great. There are plenty more new things to learn. If you've never seen any of them before, concentrate on the main point here, which you saw when you tried out "Hello, World!": the trailing return type. You've learned something already.

1.4.3   What you'll learn from reading this book

You'll learn how to use some new elements of the language, from ranges to random numbers, and learn several other simpler ways of doing things on the journey. This book starts with a vector and builds up from there. Vectors are a good way to revise and then learn new features, including ranges, views, functors, and lambdas. Once you're comfortable filling, displaying, querying, and manipulating a vector using ranges and algorithms, you'll be ready to use other parts of the standard library, including time (`chrono`), random numbers, and, finally, coroutines.

Range-based `for` loops introduced in C++11 made the language simpler. You can use them to walk over a container without needing to dive into iterators first. Over time, full-blown ranges have become standard too, providing convenience and avoiding the direct use of iterators, as well as offering more unified lookup and extra safety. Previously, it was possible to pass the start of one container and the end of another to an algorithm and not realize this until something horrible happened at runtime. Ranges avoid that problem. You'll become familiar with using ranges to view and copy the contents of a container.

You'll find out how and why you don't need so much boilerplate code in a class by using the `default` keyword for constructors and operators. You'll learn how to use the new random number distributions. If you're used to calling C's `rand` function, the new approach might seem complicated at first, but it's powerful, and when used properly, it helps you avoid mistakes people often make, for example, when simulating rolling dice or shuffling a deck of cards.

By using self-contained projects in each chapter, you'll get the chance to use all kinds of new and old features. You'll get to the point where you understand new features, knowing when and why to use them in an idiomatic way. Sometimes opinions on the best way to do things differ. You saw the trailing return type early: `auto main() -> int`. Some people love it and use it everywhere, but some people hate it. The language's evolution has taken us beyond arguing about brace placement (sorry in advance if you don't like my approach) and given us lots more to argue about. This book will give alternatives, firmly sitting on the fence when it comes to such discussions so that you can concentrate on trying to write some code and experiment with new ways of expressing yourself.

1.5   *Some pro tips*

It's possible to get lost or overwhelmed when learning, especially if you are trying to tackle a big topic. If you bear in mind the following few tips, you'll be able to find your way.

First, many of the new features are *syntactic sugar*, and second, many elements of code use punctuation, which is hard to look up. If you wanted to find out what the `->` symbol was doing in the main function given previously, where would you start? One very useful tool is Andreas Fertig's C++ Insights (https://cppinsights.io/) website. C++ Insights transforms code to show the details behind some newer C++ features. It is based on Clang (https://clang.llvm.org/) and Andreas' understanding of C++ (https://cppinsights.io/about.html). If you type in the `plus` code we looked at in listing 1.2, C++ Insights will transform the code for you.

Listing 1.4   C++ Insights output

```
#include <iostream>
#include <functional>

int main()                  ⟵┐  The trailing return
{                             │  has been rewritten.
  std::operator<<
    (
        std::cout.operator<<
        (
        std::plus<int>{{}}.operator()(1, static_cast<const int>(1.23))
        ),
        '\n'               ┐  Spelling out << and () are operators
    );                   ⟵┘  and convert 1.23 to an int.
  std::operator<<
    (
        std::cout.operator<<
        (
        std::plus<void>{}.operator()(1, 1.23)
        ),
        '\n'               ┐  Spelling out <<
    );                   ⟵┘  and () are operators.
  return 0;              ⟵┐  We didn't explicitly return
}                          │  0, but it happens for us.
```

Try it out directly (https://cppinsights.io/s/508b2063). The insight may show lots of details, and the generated code is based on Clang, so it may not always work on other compilers, but listing 1.4 shows the transformed trailing return symbol `->`, along with the `std::plus<int>` and `std::plus<void>` structures being used. If you can't understand a function you come across, try out C++ Insights for clues.

The next thing to bear in mind is that not all compilers support all the new features, so you might need more than one. At the very least, you might need to use the option `/std:c++latest` in Visual Studio or `--std=c++20` for g++. If you can't face having to set up another tool, you can always try out C++ code in various compilers online via Matt Godbolt's Compiler Explorer (https://godbolt.org/). It supports a huge variety of different compilers, allowing you to see how each behaves. This book will try to stick to common parts, but if you want to explore more, this is a great resource, along with C++ Insights. Each has a link to the other, so why not use both? Before spending time getting a toolchain setup, CppReference has a list of compiler support for each of the new features (https://en.cppreference.com/w/cpp/compiler_support) to help you decide which version you need. This is another great resource for checking function signatures or simply finding which standard header file you need to include to use a feature.

Finally, if you get stuck, don't panic. The compiler may well still give you several errors if you forget a semicolon deep inside some template code. Newer compilers might pinpoint the actual problem, though, rather than giving pages of errors to wade through. Most modern compilers do try to be slightly more helpful, so if you had pain previously and gave up, things might be easier now. Nonetheless, you will get incomprehensible errors from time to time. If you can't figure them out, ask someone for help or try starting at the first error. If that doesn't work, try starting at the last error, or at least find one pointing at your code, rather than library code. If that doesn't work either, comment it all out and add your code back in slowly. Or, even better, consider using version control and reverting to what worked. This book won't take you through all the details of how to set up a sensible working environment but will point you to useful tools and things to consider along the way.

Summary

- C++ is everywhere and can be used for almost anything.
- C++ is evolving, with a new standard every three years, decided on by WG21 of ISO.
- C++ is a multi-paradigm language.
- You need a compiler that supports your chosen platform.
- Other similar languages are available, but C++ gives you a solid grounding in a variety of techniques and idioms.
- No single compiler currently supports every feature of the latest version of the language, but you can use Godbolt and C++ Insights to try out short snippets to check whether they compile.
- Coding a whole program is a great way to learn, and you'll do just that in the rest of this book.

Containers, iterators, and ranges 2

This chapter covers

- Filling and using containers, with a focus on a vector of numbers
- Range-based `for` loops and `auto`
- Using a container with standard algorithms
- Using `format` to display output
- Ranges, views, and lambdas

Containers and algorithms have been a fundamental part of C++ for a long time. Containers have included sequences (e.g., `vector`), associative containers (e.g., `map`), and, since C++ 11, unordered associative containers (e.g., `unordered_map`). The containers manage the storage for their elements. The separation of data structures and algorithms offers great flexibility, allowing one algorithm to be applied to various containers. The addition of ranges to the core language provides simplified ways to access and manipulate containers. To explore these features, in this chapter, we are going to construct Pascal's triangle, which is made by adding up adjacent numbers from the preceding row, starting with a single 1 in the first row. The entries can be used to count the number of event combinations and more. We will use vectors to store the values, starting with the first row, to practice using a vector and writing out to the screen. We'll then generate and display more rows, learning how to use vectors differently. Finally, we'll discuss some of the triangle's properties. This will help us think about testing our code later.

You'll need a compiler and editor or an IDE if you want to code along. A list of free resources is available at https://isocpp.org/get-started. I'm using a mixture of Vim with GNU Compiler Collection (GCC) in the Windows Subsystem for Linux (WSL) and Visual Studio 2022 community edition, with `/std:c++latest` in the C++ command line properties.

2.1 *Creating and displaying a vector*

First, we will create a vector containing a single number and display it. This will be the first row of the triangle. Vectors are the most commonly used containers, so starting with them is handy. We can then practice putting different elements in vectors, including other vectors, and using them with algorithms. We will also employ several other C++ features as we code.

It's a good idea to keep your code outside the `main` entry point function so you can add tests easily or build a library to make reusing the code straightforward. That said, we'll put everything in one file, called `main.cpp`, to keep things simple, and we'll make a function that we'll call from `main`. We start by making a vector containing a number and displaying the contents as follows.

Listing 2.1   Filling and displaying a container

```cpp
#include <iostream>          Includes headers for output
#include <vector>            and the vector itself

void generate_triangle()
{
    std::vector<int> data{ 1 };     ◁──┘  Defines a vector, initialized
                                           with a single number 1
    for (auto number : data)        ◁──┐
    {                                      Uses a range-based for loop
        std::cout << number << ' ';        to walk over the vector
    }
    std::cout << '\n';
}

int main()
{
    generate_triangle();
}
```

If you're playing along, compile and run your code. For the GCC tools, compile like this:

```
g++ -Wall --std=c++2a -o main.out main.cpp
```

We don't need to say which `std` we are using here, as long as the compiler supports at least C++11, and we are checking for any warnings, with `all` to the warning flag `-W`. The `-o` flag names our output, which we can run by typing `./main.out` once it has built the single `main.cpp` file. If you are using an IDE, find your Build button, and then find the Run button. You should get a single digit on your screen.

The code contains a few newer C++ features. At the top, we've included two headers: `iostream` for input and output streams and `vector`. This should be familiar. We then have a function to generate and display the first line of our triangle using a `vector` for storage. The `vector` is initialized with the single number 1:

```
std::vector<int> data{ 1 };
```

Notice we're using curly braces, called the *uniform initialization syntax*. If we say

```
std::vector<int> data( 1 );
```

instead, we get a vector with one value, which is 0. A vector has various constructors. The second version using `(1)` treats the number 1 as a count of elements. The first version, using curly braces `{1}`, is using an *initializer list*. The list can have more than one item, and the vector is created with the contents of the initializer list. Trying to use an initializer list of `{1, 2.3}` would generate a compiler error. This requires a *narrowing conversion* because `2.3` is a double, and we want a `vector` of int. We can even use `{}` to initialize a single number: `int x{ 42 }`. As the brace initialization can be used in many places, it is called *uniform initialization*. ISOCpp suggests preferring brace initialization (http://mng.bz/n1m5) because it avoids narrowing and allows consistency. Initialization is a big topic and can get complicated. For example, Nicolai Josuttis has talked about "The Nightmare of Initialization in C++" (https://www .youtube.com/watch?v=7DTlWPgX6zs). The important thing to note here is that we can use an initializer list to construct a vector.

Armed with our container of data, we can show its contents on the standard output stream (`cout`). We employ a *range-based* `for` *loop* to walk over the container, using the insertion `operator <<` to stream out elements from the container. Generally, a range-based `for` loop has the `for`, parentheses, and a colon, as we saw in listing 2.1:

```
for (auto number : data)
```

This is a more succinct syntax than traditional `for` loops. On the left side of the colon, there are a type and a variable name. We can be lazy and get the compiler to figure out the type by using `auto`. To the right of the colon, there is a container, array, or similar. We can think of the range-based `for` loop as syntactic sugar to make our lives easier. We do not need to spell out the stopping conditions or how to step through the items. The range-based `for` loop does this for us.

If we try the code out in C++ Insights (https://cppinsights.io/), we see the loop transformed into a traditional C-style `for` loop with three parts: a beginning, a stopping condition, and an increment. Every container has a beginning and an end, and the range-based `for` loop uses these to walk through the elements. C++ Insights shows all the gory details but gives code equivalent to

```
for (auto position = data.begin(); position!=data.end(); ++position)
```

With the C-style `for` loop, we use a position that is an *iterator* into the vector, which we need to *dereference*, using `operator *`, when we want to print the value:

```
std::cout << *position << ' ';
```

The range-based `for` loop is much easier to use and means we can code at a higher level without having to think about iterators.

Let's look at `auto` in more detail. The keyword tells the compiler to deduce the type. If you're using an IDE, a mouse hover over the word `auto` might tell you the number's deduced type. Visual Studio says it's using `std::vector<int>>::iterator::value_type`, which is `int`. Typing `int` instead of `auto` makes little apparent difference in our case, but there are advantages to almost always using auto (AAA). This phrase was coined by Herb Sutter on his Guru of the Week blog (http://mng.bz/vPpp). In more complicated cases, `auto` will save a lot of typing, while tending to keep the code type safe. If we change the container's type to use `double` instead, we do not need to change the loop as well, so the code is less brittle when we use `auto`. Using `auto` can also pick up subtleties that can be easily missed. If we make the data constant

```
const std::vector<int> data{ 1 };
```

the loop variable's type automatically changes to a `const_iterator`, so we do not need to remember to make the change there. In fact, we can even declare our container using `auto`:

```
auto data = std::vector<int>{ 1 };
```

Because `data` is a vector of `int` constructed with an initializer list containing an `int`, it is deduced to be `vector<int>`.

More significantly, `auto` can help us avoid implicit conversions, including narrowing conversions, and force us to initialize our variables. We can say `auto variable = init`, or if we want a specific type, we can say `auto variable = type{init}`. In both cases, we are forced to spell out how to initialize the variable. We cannot say `auto variable;` because we will get a compiler error. If we try something like `auto x = int{ 1.5 }`, we will also get a compiler error because we are trying to use a narrowing conversion. If we say `int x = 1.5` instead, we might get a warning, but some people ignore warnings. Not a good idea, but it happens. Using `auto` would stop the potential error.

Back to our vector. We can make one more small change to how we create our vector. We told the compiler to put an integer in the vector, so surely it can figure out the type of the elements in the vector. Yes, it can now. Since C++17, we can simply say `std::vector data{ 1 }`. Notice we haven't specified the template type. Instead, we are relying on *class template argument deduction* (CTAD). If we decided to use `auto` (almost) everywhere, we could even change our declaration to `auto data = std::vector{ 1 }`. Now, if we want an empty vector, the type cannot be deduced because `auto data = std::vector{}` does not have a way to deduce the type of the elements, so it fails to compile. CTAD is another new feature that saves us some typing.

We can now display the first row of Pascal's triangle. This may seem like a small step, but we have seen a handful of C++ features and can build on this. Next, we will add more rows to the triangle and learn more C++ along the way.

2.2   Creating and displaying Pascal's triangle

We now have the first row and will use it to make the next few rows, displaying what we get. We will use C++20's range library to print out the results. Ranges are one of the bigger features introduced in C++20 that go beyond shorter syntax. Once we have several rows, we will then think about some properties of Pascal's triangle, which will help us test our code and practice using our vectors. Let's start with a recap of how to build Pascal's triangle.

2.2.1   A reminder of Pascal's triangle

Pascal's triangle contains several useful number sequences. One common use is to find the number of ways events can combine. If you toss a coin once, you can get either heads or tails. If you toss it twice, you can get heads twice, tails twice, or one of each, in two ways: heads and then tails or tails and then heads. For three tosses, you might get all heads, two heads, one heads, or none, but how many combinations are there for a given number of heads? Pascal's triangle will tell us.

The triangle starts with a number 1, by definition. If we are looking for the number of possible combinations when tossing a coin, there is one result for zero coin tosses. Each subsequent row then starts and ends with 1, by definition. This corresponds to the combination of events. For one coin toss, we can get a single heads in one way or a single tails, again in one way. The second row is therefore two 1s. For the third row, again, we start and end with a 1 because we can get all heads in one way or all tails in one way. The next number is the sum of the two numbers in the preceding row, laying out the rows as shown in figure 2.1.

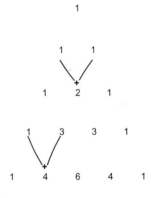

To generate the fourth row, we start with a 1, then sum the first two numbers from the last row, getting $1 + 2 = 3$; next, we sum the second and the third number, getting $2 + 1 = 3$. We have used up the previous row, so we add a final

Figure 2.1   The figure shows the first few rows of Pascal's triangle.

1. For three coin tosses, the fourth row is telling us how many combinations we can have: 1, 3, 3, 1. In other words, there is one way to get all heads; three ways to get two heads (HHT, HTH, THH); three ways to get one heads (HTT, THT, TTH); and finally, one way to get no heads (TTT).

We continue with the next row, starting with 1, adding adjacent pairs in the previous row, and ending with a final 1. We could do this forever on paper, but code is a different matter. An integer will have a maximum value, which will vary between machines and compilers. If we include the numeric header, we can find out what a platform gives by calling `std::numeric_limits<int>::max()`. I get 2,147,483,647, which is 1 less than 2 to the power of 31, $2^{31} - 1$. That's plenty of space for a few rows.

2.2.2   *Coding Pascal's triangle*

There are several equivalent ways to generate the triangle; however, let's write code based on the definition we just looked at. We saw how to build a new row using numbers from the previous row, so let's build a function taking the last row and returning the next row. In the last section, we sent data straight to the screen, but that made code difficult to test, so it makes sense to return the data instead and write a separate display function. Single-responsibility functions are sensible after all. We made a `vector` of integers for the first row, so we will continue using a `vector<int>` for each row. The next listing shows our function, adding a 1 at the start and end of the next row and doing some adding in between.

Listing 2.2   The next row of Pascal's triangle using the previous row

```cpp
std::vector<int> get_next_row(const std::vector<int> & last_row)
{
    std::vector next_row{ 1 };          ◁——  CTAD used to deduce that our
    if (last_row.empty())                     template contains integers
    {
        return next_row;
    }
    for (size_t idx = 0; idx+1 < last_row.size(); ++idx)
    {
        next_row.emplace_back(last_row[idx] + last_row[idx + 1]);   ◁——┐
    }
    next_row.emplace_back(1);                              Stores the sum of the two
    return next_row;                                      numbers in the row above
}
```

We initialized our first row using curly braces because there was a specific value. Now we want to calculate values and add them to a `vector`. There is more than one way to do this. To add to the end of the vector, we can use `push_back` or `emplace_back`. To add items inside elsewhere, we can use `insert` or `emplace`. The `emplace` versions send in data to create the item in place, while `push_back` or `insert` take a fully formed item that they copy, as illustrated in figure 2.2.

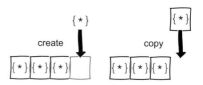

Figure 2.2   `emplace` (left) takes parameters to construct an item in place, while `push_back` takes a fully constructed item copied into the vector.

For our integers, both methods amount to the same. Sometimes, the `emplace` version is quicker because it constructs the element directly in place in the vector; however, `push_back` can be safer sometimes. The `emplace` version will find a constructor for us, which might not be what we would have chosen ourselves. Jason Turner discusses the pros and cons on C++ Weekly (https://www.youtube.com/watch?v=jKS9dSHkAZY). The bottom line is that we are likely to see both being used.

We can now calculate the values in each row, but we need to store them somewhere. A vector is a sensible choice, giving us an `std::vector<std::vector<int>>`. That's a mouthful, and the compiler can figure this out for us. This means we can use `auto` as the return type when we write a function to create the triangle to save typing out `std::vector<std::vector<int>>` in full. For a more complicated function, we might need to help the compiler figure out what type is being returned, but the compiler can cope in this example. How many rows do we want? We can postpone that decision if we accept the required number as a parameter. All we need to do is call our `get_next_row` function to populate the vector we return, starting with an empty data row.

> **Listing 2.3   Generating several rows of Pascal's triangle**

```
auto generate_triangle(int rows)        ◁───┐  auto shorthand for
{                                            │  deduced return type
    std::vector<int> data;
    std::vector<std::vector<int>> triangle;
    for (int row = 0; row < rows; ++row)
    {                                        ┌─  Generates the next row
        data = get_next_row(data);      ◁───┘   from the previous row
        triangle.push_back(data);   ◁───┐  Adds it to
    }                                   │  the triangle
    return triangle;
}
```

We could stop here, display our triangle, and move on to a new chapter. However, this approach is not particularly efficient. We can do better.

2.2.3   *Move semantics and perfect forwarding*

A vector has many different constructors. We used the version taking an initializer list in listing 2.1 when we made the first row of our triangle:

```
std::vector<int> data{ 1 };
```

To generate the triangle, we *default construct* each data row as

```
std::vector<int> data;
```

and assign it after the function call:

```
data = get_next_row(data);
```

We then push the data to the back of the triangle:

```
triangle.push_back(data);
```

This is not as efficient as it could be. We create the row data, and a copy is pushed back to the vector of vectors. If we make a couple of small changes, in effect by using a different constructor, we can avoid the copy. Let's see how to do this using what is referred to as *perfect forwarding*.

We saw earlier that `vector` supports `push_back` and `emplace_back`. The former takes a fully formed item, which we have here, while the latter constructs an object in place. There are two versions of `push_back`. The first takes an item by reference:

```
void push_back( const T& value );
```

That version will be called by our code. It takes our `data` and makes a copy at the end of the triangle. We can avoid that copy if we use the second overload of `push_back`. The signature uses `&&` to indicate an *rvalue reference*.

```
void push_back( T&& value );
```

What is an rvalue reference? Any expression has a *value category*, such as an rvalue or an lvalue. There are other categories too, but we will not go into all of them here. Instead, we will concentrate on avoiding the copy. CppReference gives the full details (http://mng.bz/468R) in case you want to take a deeper dive.

C uses the idea of lvalues and rvalues. If we say

```
int x = 42;
```

the variable `x` is on the left of an expression and is therefore called an lvalue, whereas `42` is on the right and is called an rvalue. The lvalue has a name, while the rvalue does not. When we call `get_next_row`, we have an rvalue. This is a temporary unnamed vector, which we copied previously to the lvalue `data`. This is wasteful. Rather than keeping a copy of the data, we can use the `back` method to get the last row of the triangle. Thus, we need to initialize the triangle with the first row so that there is an element at the back. We can now write our function as shown in the next listing.

Listing 2.4   Moving a temporary

```
auto generate_triangle(int rows)
{
    std::vector<std::vector<int>> triangle{ {1} };    ◁──  Adds first row so
    for (int row = 1; row < rows; ++row)        ◁─────  we can call back
    {                                                   Starts at 1 because we
        triangle.push_back(get_next_row(triangle.back()));   already have a row
    }
    return triangle;
}
```

We no longer have a copy of data. The `push_back( const T& value )` version initializes a new element with a copy of the value, but the version taking an rvalue reference, `push_back( T&& value )`, can move the temporary into the triangle for us, avoiding the copy. The vector has various constructors, including one taking an rvalue reference, called a *move constructor*. Its signature has the `&&` we saw earlier:

```
vector( vector&& other );
```

The `push_back` method taking `T &&` value can utilize this constructor by calling `std::move`, referred to as *move semantics*. The `push_back &&` overload can be, and often is, implemented as

```
void push_back( T&& value ) {
    emplace_back(std::move(value));
}
```

Inside the `push_back` method, the rvalue has a name (`value`), so it becomes an lvalue. By calling `std::move(value)`, the value is cast back to an rvalue so that the rvalue constructor is picked. In effect, C++'s `move` operation does not actually move anything. It casts a value to an rvalue. This allows an overload taking an rvalue to be called, referred to as *perfect forwarding*. Once `move` has been called and an rvalue passed to a function, the value is in a valid but unspecified state. Since it's been moved, it's not of much use to us anymore. Without the move, the other vector would be passed as an lvalue, and the copy constructor would be called. This involves unnecessary copies, so it would forward the value imperfectly.

Move semantics and perfect forwarding are big topics, and we have only scratched the surface. Thomas Becker wrote an excellent blog post back in 2013 that walks through the details (http://mng.bz/QRE6). An rvalue reference, `&&`, might be an lvalue or an rvalue. If it has a name, it is an lvalue, but calling `std::move` casts it to an rvalue, allowing perfect forwarding. In fact, we could call `emplace_back` directly ourselves with the rvalue or temporary:

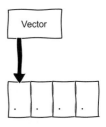

```
triangle.emplace_back(get_next_row(triangle.back()));
```

How does the move constructor avoid a copy? A vector stores items contiguously, so we can access elements using iterators as well as indexing. We don't need to know the number of elements at compile time because a vector can resize dynamically. When a vector runs out of space, it allocates more memory. We can think of it as a container pointing to some items, as shown in figure 2.3.

Figure 2.3   A vector is pointing to its elements.

There's more to a vector than a pointer to its elements, but focusing on this will reveal how the move constructor avoids copying. A copy constructor or assignment will need to copy over each element, so we would have the original vector of, say, four elements, as shown in figure 2.3, along with an identical copy, also pointing at four elements. A move constructor can effectively steal the elements from the rvalue by pointing to the rvalue's items, rather than allocating copies, as shown in figure 2.4.

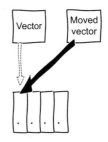

Nothing else can try to use the nameless temporary's elements afterwards, so this is fine. Furthermore, nothing has actually moved, but rather, the move constructor took ownership of the temporary's data, and no elements needed copying.

Figure 2.4   A move-constructed vector can steal the rvalue's elements.

We've seen two ways to generate the vector. The second version is more efficient because it doesn't make unnecessary copies. We now need a way to display our triangle.

2.2.4   *Using ranges to display the vector*

Previously, we sent our vector with a single element straight to the screen, but if we write something more general, we can send it to a file or any other stream. We do this by overloading the `operator <<` for our triangle. We have a row, which is a `vector`, which contains a `vector` of integers. Rather than writing a `for` loop within a `for` loop to write out each element, we can use the `ranges` library to copy the elements to the provided stream. If your compiler doesn't support `ranges::copy` yet, you can use `std::copy` instead. We can use an output stream iterator (`std::ostream_iterator`) to copy to and indicate we want a space between each number; otherwise, they will be unreadable. Include `<algorithm>` for `std::copy` and the `<iterator>` header for `std::ostream_iterator`. Then add a new function as indicated in the following listing.

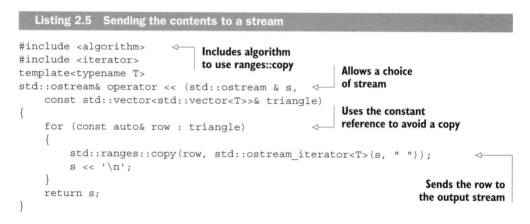

> **Listing 2.5   Sending the contents to a stream**

```
#include <algorithm>              ◁──┐ Includes algorithm
#include <iterator>                  │ to use ranges::copy
template<typename T>
std::ostream& operator << (std::ostream & s,    ◁──┐ Allows a choice
    const std::vector<std::vector<T>>& triangle)        of stream
{
                                             ┌─ Uses the constant
    for (const auto& row : triangle)   ◁──────  reference to avoid a copy
    {
        std::ranges::copy(row, std::ostream_iterator<T>(s, " "));   ◁────┐
        s << '\n';
    }                                                          Sends the row to
    return s;                                                  the output stream
}
```

Note we are now using a constant reference to each row in the triangle by using `const auto& row` in the `for` loop. This should be familiar. If we used `auto row: v` instead, we would copy the entire contents of the row into `data`. The reference avoids the copy, and `const` means we cannot change the contents. The CPP core guidelines (http://mng.bz/Xqn9) encourage us not to make expensive copies of a loop variable in a range based `for` loop, as pointed out in the expressions and statements (ES) section, "ES.71: Prefer a range-for-statement to a for-statement when there is a choice." These guidelines are curated by Bjarne Stroustrup and Herb Sutter, along with many other contributors, and contain lots of sensible advice. You will see more of them from time to time in this book.

The `for` loop gives us a reference to each row. We send this to the stream using a range algorithm. As with the range-based `for` loop we used in listing 2.1, the range's copy figures out where to start and end from our data vector. A range is conceptually anything that allows iteration by providing a `start` iterator and `end` sentinel. The older algorithms took a `begin` and an `end` of the same type. A sentinel is a recent addition generalizing the idea of the `end` iterator, similar to the idea of using a null character to indicate the end of a `char` array. We could write our own sentinel to stop when a negative number is encountered or any other custom logic. However, our vector has a `begin` and `end`, which is all we need here. We could use the non-range copy algorithm from the same header, but we'd need to specify `begin` and `end` ourselves:

```
std::copy(data.begin(), data.end(), std::ostream_iterator<T>(s, " "));
```

Either version of `copy` is fine, but the range version is a little less wordy. This is one of many range versions of standard algorithms. Ranges provide considerably more than succinct syntax. We can also take views of ranges, allowing composition and filtering without copying data. Views are evaluated on demand; in other words, they support lazy evaluation. We will use a few more ranges later in this chapter.

Now we can call our code to generate the triangle and see what we get. If we ask for a large number of rows, it won't fit on the screen, and we might overflow our `int`, so let's try 16.

Listing 2.6 Main code to generate and display the triangle

```
int main()
{
    auto triangle = generate_triangle(16);
    std::cout << triangle;
}
```

The `<<` operator finds our new function and generates a left-justified triangle, as shown in figure 2.5.

> **WARNING** Defining `operator <<` for common types, such as `vector<vector< int>>`, is generally a bad idea because a large system may end up with clashes if two different libraries or components try to do the same thing. It's okay for your own classes. Writing a named function is better. We'll do that shortly.

```
1
1 1
1 2 1
1 3 3 1
1 4 6 4 1
1 5 10 10 5 1
1 6 15 20 15 6 1
1 7 21 35 35 21 7 1
1 8 28 56 70 56 28 8 1
1 9 36 84 126 126 84 36 9 1
1 10 45 120 210 252 210 120 45 10 1
1 11 55 165 330 462 462 330 165 55 11 1
1 12 66 220 495 792 924 792 495 220 66 12 1
1 13 78 286 715 1287 1716 1716 1287 715 286 78 13 1
1 14 91 364 1001 2002 3003 3432 3003 2002 1001 364 91 14 1
1 15 105 455 1365 3003 5005 6435 6435 5005 3003 1365 455 105 15 1
```

Figure 2.5 The first few rows of Pascal's triangle

If we try generating many rows, say, 36, the last few rows won't fit on the screen, and we'll start seeing the integer wrap around and become negative. Printing each row out starting at the left was easy enough, but it gives us an unconventional output. We can do better if we center-justify the output. This also gives us the opportunity to learn about the new format library.

2.2.5   *Using format to display output*

When we saw how to generate the triangle, figure 2.1 showed the rows center-justified, which is the conventional way to show the triangle. Sticking with 16 rows gives numbers up to four digits long, so if we center each number in six spaces and add enough spaces at the start of each line, we will have what we want. We can use the std::format tools to do this by including the format header. format started life as the Victor Zverovich's open source fmt library (https://fmt.dev/latest/index.html). Some compilers do not fully support format yet, so you may need to use this library instead. There are various ways to install the library, but the simplest is to download from the main page and unzip the download. Instead of including the standard format header in the code that follows, use fmt/core.h; it is simplest to use the header only:

```
#define FMT_HEADER_ONLY
#include <fmt/core.h>
```

You also need to use fmt::format instead of std::format in the code, and you need to tell the compiler the additional include path, using the -I switch:

```
-I/[path_to_unzipped_fmt_download]/include
```

At the time of writing, the open source library contained more features than currently supported in standard C++, but we will stick with commonly supported features here.

> **TIP**   If your compiler doesn't support format yet, you can use the open source fmt library (https://fmt.dev/latest/index.html). Alternatively, the fmt library includes a link to Godbolt (https://godbolt.org/z/Eq5763), which includes the fmt library so you can try out code in the compiler explorer.

The format library is similar to C's printf function but is often faster, simpler, and safer to use. The syntax uses curly braces inside a string as placeholders. The placeholder can be empty, take a format specifier (such as d for decimal), or give the index of an argument from the values. If we don't specify which value to use where via an index, they are placed in order. The format specifiers are very similar to Python's. If we asked for a number with the d format specifier but passed a string

```
auto does_not_compile = std::format("I am not a number {:d}", "ten");
```

we would get a compiler error, making format safer to use than printf. For numbers, we might want a plus or minus signs shown, so we can indicate that after the colon by using {:+d}. If we don't specify it, we get the default of a minus sign for negative numbers and no sign otherwise. After the colon, we say if we want decimal (d), binary (b), and so on.

Looking back at figure 2.5, the largest number in the last row is 6435. Because our numbers are therefore no more than four digits long, we can center each element in a block of six, giving at least one space on each side. The specifier for center is ^, for left is <, and for right is >, so we format the elements using

```
std::format("{: ^6}", element);
```

Notice the placeholder {} with a colon. We aren't using an index, so put nothing before the colon. We then have " ^6", meaning pad with spaces to a length of 6, and center the value. In fact, we could vary the length by adding more curly braces inside the placeholder to send the 6 to, inside the placeholder, like this:

```
std::format("{: ^{}}", element, 6);
```

This gives us a *nested replacement field*. This way, we can calculate how much space each number needs. We will not do that here, but take time to experiment with format.

We also need spaces at the start of each row to get a symmetric triangle. If we work out how long the last row is, we can halve its length to determine where to put the 1 from the first row. Let's think this through for a couple of rows. We noted that the largest number on the last row is 6435, and it has four digits. If we add a space on each side, we need a block of six for each number. The second row will require two blocks of 6, giving twelve characters. To place our first number in the middle, we need three spaces at the start to make the first block sit on the two numbers in the next row. Because we told format to center the values, the first one will be in the middle of that block. Figure 2.6 shows this for the first two rows, using 1234 to indicate any four digits.

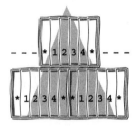

Figure 2.6 If we add three spaces at the start of the first row, as indicated by the dashes, we can make the triangle more symmetrical.

Calling back().size() on the vector of rows tells us how many blocks of six we will use for a final row. To put the first row in the middle, we need three spaces per row that we add; thus, we need padding of three times back().size() initially. For each row, we also shrink our padding by three at each step to make the triangle shape.

Pulling together our format and spaces calculation, we can write the following function to display our triangle.

Listing 2.7 Center-justified output

```
void show_vectors(std::ostream& s,
    const std::vector<std::vector<int>>& v)
{
    size_t final_row_size = v.back().size();
    std::string spaces(final_row_size * 3, ' ');      ← Three spaces
    for (const auto& row : v)                            per row
    {
        s << spaces;
```

```
    if (spaces.size() > 3)
        spaces.resize(spaces.size()-3);        ◁──┐ Shrinks the spaces by
    for (const auto& data : row)                   │ three for each row
    {
        s << std::format("{: ^{}}", data, 6);  ◁──┐ Center-aligns each
    }                                              │ number in a block of six
    s << '\n';
}
}
```

We can then call our new function instead of our previous operator in the `main` function.

Listing 2.8   `main` **function to generate and display the triangle**

```
int main()
{
    auto triangle = generate_triangle(16);       ┐ Swaps the operator << from
    show_vectors(std::cout, triangle);        ◁──┘ listing 2.6 to show_vectors
}
```

This generates and displays our triangle center-justified, as shown in figure 2.7. The output looks about right, but we need to think about how to test our results. We will learn more C++ on the way.

```
                                      1
                                  1       1
                              1       2       1
                          1       3       3       1
                      1       4       6       4       1
                  1       5      10      10       5       1
              1       6      15      20      15       6       1
          1       7      21      35      35      21       7       1
      1       8      28      56      70      56      28       8       1
  1       9      36      84     126     126      84      36       9       1
1      10      45     120     210     252     210     120      45      10       1
    1      11      55     165     330     462     462     330     165      55      11       1
  1      12      66     220     495     792     924     792     495     220      66      12       1
 1      13      78     286     715    1287    1716    1716    1287     715     286      78      13       1
 1      14      91     364    1001    2002    3003    3432    3003    2002    1001     364      91      14       1
1      15     105     455    1365    3003    5005    6435    6435    5005    3003    1365     455     105      15       1
```

Figure 2.7   A center-justified triangle

2.3   *Properties of the triangle*

We have already seen some patterns in the triangle. We know each row starts and ends with a 1, so we can start by adding a check for this property. We will then consider the number of elements we expect in each row, as well as the sum of the elements. Finally, we will see how many rows we can safely generate before the numbers get too big to fit into an integer. We will build these properties into a suite of tests.

Unfortunately, C++ does not come with a testing framework. Rather than spending time setting up and learning such a framework, we will use the `assert` function defined in the `cassert` header. The letter c at the start tells us we are pulling in code from the C standard library. `assert` is a macro, so the preprocessor copies the contents verbatim. It will abort our program if the expression in the assertion is false. Some setups only use the `assert` in a debug build by determining whether the NDEBUG macro is defined. Without it, the assertions do something, but if NDEBUG is defined, they do nothing. Check your setup. The simplest way is to check whether `assert(0)` halts the program.

> **Listing 2.9 Starting with a failing test**

```
#include <cassert>
#include <vector>
void check_properties(const std::vector<std::vector<int>> & triangle)
{
    assert(0);          ◁─── Forces an assertion
}                            failure on line 5

int main()
{                            Calls function
    check_properties({});  ◁── with empty vector
}
```

Using g++ in Ubuntu on the WSL, we see the message `Aborted` along with a line number, function name, and the message

```
test.out: main_assert.cpp:5: void check_properties(const
    std::vector<std::vector<int> >&): Assertion `0' failed.
Aborted
```

If we run this from Visual Studio, we get a dialog box, with details including the line number where the assertion failed. Beginning with a failing test is a good way to start testing code. At the very least, it proves we will get some feedback if an assertion fails. This means we are ready to test our triangle generation.

> **NOTE** Using `assert` and checking properties from `main` is a pragmatic way to start testing; however, it's worth taking time to learn a proper unit-testing framework. Several C++ testing frameworks, including Catch2, Google Test, and Boost, are available.

Now we have a function to add properties to. Remove the `assert(0)`, and we are ready to add properties to check whether we have the right numbers in our triangle.

2.3.1 Checking the first and last elements of each row

We know the first and last numbers in each row must be 1, so we will test that first. We need to add two assertions to our `properties` function to test our expectations, passing in the rows as in the following listing.

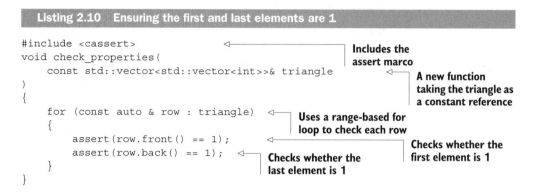

Listing 2.10   Ensuring the first and last elements are 1

```cpp
#include <cassert>                              ◁──────────   Includes the
void check_properties(                                        assert marco
    const std::vector<std::vector<int>>& triangle  ◁──   A new function
)                                                           taking the triangle as
{                                                           a constant reference
    for (const auto & row : triangle)   ◁──   Uses a range-based for
    {                                         loop to check each row
        assert(row.front() == 1);   ◁──                   Checks whether the
        assert(row.back() == 1);   ◁──                    first element is 1
    }                           Checks whether the
}                               last element is 1
```

We can call this from `main` after we have generated the triangle. Our single test was successful, so we are ready to add more. Be warned: because a failing assert calls `abort`, if one thing fails, we will not check any further properties. You can avoid this by stacking up failure messages and asserting the error messages are empty. Try this out, or even better, try to write the tests in a proper framework.

2.3.2 Checking the number of elements in each row

Pascal's triangle has several other properties. The *n*-th row has *n* numbers. Why? We know the first row is a solitary 1. The second row is two 1s. The third starts with 1, then sums the 1s from the previous row to get the number 2, then has another 1 at the end, giving us three numbers. There are four numbers in the fourth row, and this pattern continues. Look back at the triangle in figure 2.5 if you are not convinced. We can add another `assert` to check this if we keep track of the row number.

Listing 2.11   Ensuring each row has the expected number of elements

```cpp
size_t row_number = 1;                      ◁──   Tracks the row number
for (const auto & row : triangle)                 with a variable
{
    assert(row.front() == 1);
    assert(row.back() == 1);                      Checks whether each row
    assert(row.size() == row_number++);   ◁──     has the expected size
}
```

We should now check the contents. If we check each entry, we need to find another way to generate each number in the row; otherwise, we will duplicate the code we are trying to test. This trap is all too easy to fall into, and trying to think in terms of properties can help us avoid such problems.

2.3.3 Checking the sum of the elements in a row

The sum of the numbers in each row also follows a pattern. Table 2.1 demonstrates that these are powers of 2, starting with 0. Remember, anything to the power of 0 is 1. This gives us another property to check.

Table 2.1 The sum of the numbers in each row of the triangle is a power of 2.

Row numbers	Sum	Power of 2
1	1	0
1+1	2	1
1+2+1	4	2
1+3+3+1	8	3
1+4+6+4+1	16	4

We need to find the sum for the numbers in each row to check this property. Rather than writing out a `for` loop, we can use the *standard template library* (STL). Herb Sutter and Andrei Alexandrescu suggested preferring algorithm calls to handwritten loops in their book *C++ Coding Standard: 101 Rules, Guidelines and Best Practices* (Addison-Wesley Professional, 2004). The STL also contains many algorithms for use with generic containers, including an `accumulate` method that lives in the `numeric` header, which is exactly what we need. We noted earlier that some algorithms support ranges, but some, including `accumulate`, do not. We, therefore, need to explicitly find `begin` and `end` ourselves.

The `accumulate` function has two versions. They both take a first and last iterator of some range or container, along with an initial value. The first version applies the `operator+` to each element and the current accumulation value, starting with the provided initial value. If we use an initial value of 0, we will obtain the sum of all the elements, which is exactly what we need. The second version allows us to provide our own *binary* operator. That can be any function taking two arguments. The first argument starts with the given initial value, so it must be of the same type, or the initial value must be convertible to the type of this parameter. The second parameter takes the values from the iterator; thus, it also needs to be of a suitable type. CppReference (http://mng.bz/yZGp) gives full details, including the signatures. For the first version, which we will use, we have

```
template< class InputIt, class T >
T accumulate( InputIt first, InputIt last, T init);
```

Notice the initial value, `init`, has type T. So does the return value. If we use an `int`, we will get an `int` back, even for a container of doubles. Our container has `ints`, so we are fine, but we would need to use `0.0` if we were to use doubles. The `accumulate` function is very flexible. The second version takes a binary operator:

```
template< class InputIt, class T, class BinaryOperation >
T accumulate( InputIt first, InputIt last, T init, BinaryOperation op );
```

We could use `operator*` to find the product of all our numbers, provided we start with an initial value of 1. The more general second form is sometimes called a *left fold*. If you want to revise algorithms, looking through what is in the `algorithm` and `numeric` headers is a good starting point.

Now we can include the check for the sum of the rows in our property test function. Starting with an expected total of 1 and doubling each time, we can check that the sum of a row is the power of 2 we expect. Adding the expected total to our properties function and using the accumulate function, along with the `numeric` header, we have the following new check.

Listing 2.12   Ensuring each row has the expected sum of elements

```
int expected_total = 1;              ◁──┐ Our expected
for (const auto & row : triangle)       │ total starts at 1.
{
    assert(std::accumulate(row.begin(),
                    row.end(),                    ┐ Checks
                    0) == expected_total);  ◁──┘ the total
    expected_total *= 2;             ◁──┐ The expected total doubles
}                                       │ with each iteration.
```

If we run our code, all the assertions pass. These properties do not prove we are correct, but they do give us some confidence in the generation code. We will now look at one final property of the triangle and then round off with another pattern, just for fun. Again, we will practice more C++ on the way.

2.3.4   *How many rows can we generate correctly?*

As each number is the sum of two previous numbers and we started with positive numbers, we should never get negative numbers. To the uninitiated and mathematicians, adding positive numbers should always give positive numbers. However, numbers do surprising and sometimes annoying things on computers, such as overflowing. We will start by setting up a test and then see if we can break it. If we keep adding `int`s, we will eventually overflow the maximum possible size. The standard tells us this is undefined behavior:

> *If during the evaluation of an expression, the result is not mathematically defined or not in the range of representable values for its type, the behavior is undefined.* (https://eel.is/c++draft/expr)

We could do some mathematics to find the maximum number of rows we can fit into our chosen numeric type. However, if we see what happens when we try to keep adding rows, we can learn some more C++ on the way. Although we are relying on undefined behavior, in Visual Studio, an integer wraps around so we can find the maximum number of rows we can safely generate.

There are various ways to check that the values are not negative. We can check whether every number is positive or try to find any negative numbers. We could write our checks in a `for` loop, but we will heed the advice to use algorithms where we can. In fact, we will try a few approaches, getting a bit more practice with algorithms, and we will learn more about ranges too.

The `algorithm` header provides several *non-modifying sequence* operations. Many of these find or search for elements. We can use `all_of` to check that all elements are positive. We could also use either `none_of` or `any_of`, which do what we might expect. All three take a *unary predicate*, which is a function that takes a value and returns a `bool`. The values come from a container or range.

We want to check that all our numbers are greater than zero. This seems more positive than saying none of them are negative. We could write a function, but we can also use an anonymous function, known as a *lambda*. The syntax looks very much like a normal function, but it has no name and has a *capture list* at the start indicated by square brackets: `[]`. This allows us to capture local variables by reference or as a copy. We would say `[&]` to capture anything used in the body of the lambda expression by reference, and `[=]` to capture anything used by value. We could also specify specific variables by saying `[=, &x]`, so that x is captured as a reference, and anything else is captured by value. We could also explicitly name y as captured by value, in which case, we do not need the equals sign: `[y, &x]`. We don't need to capture anything in our case. We only need to check whether any integer is greater than or equal to zero:

```
[](int x) { return x >= 0; }
```

A named function would look like this:

```
bool non_negative(int x){ return x >= 0; }
```

The syntax for each is similar, with a parameter list and the body in curly braces. The named function must specify a return type. The lambda can use a trailing return type, which we saw in chapter 1, but the return type is deduced if none is provided. Lambda expressions construct *closures*, borrowing a term from functional programming. We will look at this in more detail in the next chapter.

We use our lambda in `std::all_of` like this:

```
std::all_of(row.begin(), row.end(), [](int x) { return x >= 0; })
```

Using a named function is absolutely fine too, but for small functions, it can be easier to see what is happening if everything is in one place. Now, we have explicitly stated `int` as the parameter type. We know our `vector` contains integers. However, we were told to almost always use `auto` earlier, and we can do that here too:

```
std::all_of(row.begin(), row.end(), [](auto x) { return x >= 0; })
```

If we were to change the type contained in the vector, we wouldn't need to change this code as well. In fact, we can also use a range to check all the rows like the following:

```
assert(std::ranges::all_of(row, [](auto x) { return x >= 0; }));
```

We've used a range-based `for` loop several times now and used `ranges::copy` in listing 2.5 to send a row to the screen. We know some of the standard algorithms, such as `all_of`, have a `ranges` equivalent, although not all of the algorithms have equivalents. Where they do exist, they save us from typing out `begin` and `end`. Ranges offer far more, though. Containers and algorithms are a part of the STL. The two abstractions are useful but rely on iterators. Writing your own can be cumbersome, and if you want to compose algorithms, you need to track where the end is after each call. Notoriously, the `remove_if` algorithm does not remove anything. Instead, it shunts the elements you do not want removed to the start of the collection and returns an iterator to the first of the unneeded elements, which you can use instead of `end` if you want to do something further without these elements. The following code shows what happens if we forget to track the new end.

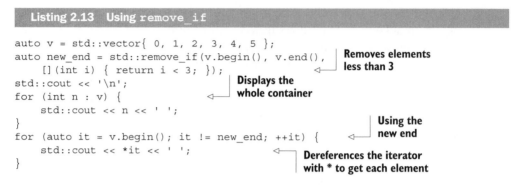

Listing 2.13 Using `remove_if`

```
auto v = std::vector{ 0, 1, 2, 3, 4, 5 };
auto new_end = std::remove_if(v.begin(), v.end(),        Removes elements
    [](int i) { return i < 3; });                        less than 3
std::cout << '\n';                        Displays the
for (int n : v) {                         whole container
    std::cout << n << ' ';
}
for (auto it = v.begin(); it != new_end; ++it) {         Using the
    std::cout << *it << ' ';                             new end
}                                         Dereferences the iterator
                                          with * to get each element
```

The first loop prints out 3, 4, 5, 3, 4, 5 in Visual Studio because the elements less than 3 have been removed. Other compilers might give different results. However, we now have three elements beyond the new end. The second loop displays 3, 4, 5 as required. Things get out of hand quickly if you need to filter and transform several times over.

Ranges avoid this problem. They allow us to take a read-only `view` of a container and filter or transform the elements in the view, without needing to keep track of iterators. We can access the `ranges` view using `std::view`. This is a convenient shorthand for `std::ranges::views`, defined in the `ranges` header. If we want to skip over initial elements less than 3, we can use `drop_while`, which may be familiar from various other programming languages:

```
for (int n : std::views::drop_while(v, [](int i) { return i < 3; })) {
    std::cout << n << ' ';
}
```

If your compiler does not support ranges yet, try this out on the Compiler Explorer (https://godbolt.org/z/YrnsTGbfx). We can also use the pipe character `'|'` to apply `drop_while` to our container. The pipe character is an operator allowing us to chain together multiple algorithms, which is neat and powerful. If we want to compose several views, the first approach would end up with several calls nested deeply inside brackets, whereas separating the steps with the pipe operator makes code easier to read. You may be familiar with the pipe characters used in Unix to send the output from one command to another. We only want one filter for this example. We can rewrite the version sending the vector to the `drop_while` function using the pipe operator like this:

```
for (int n : v | std::views::drop_while([](int i) { return i < 3; })) {
    std::cout << n << ' ';
}
```

If we run it, we see 3, 4, 5 without having to concentrate on remembering which iterator is pointing where.

We can use views to make sure that we have no negative numbers in our triangle's rows. Rather than skipping initial elements using `drop_while`, we want to filter out any negative numbers, so we use the `filter` function.

Listing 2.14   Making sure there are no negative numbers by using a view

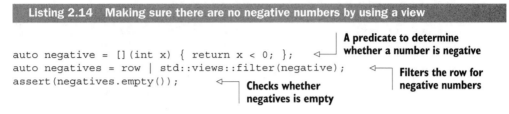

```
auto negative = [](int x) { return x < 0; };          A predicate to determine
                                                      whether a number is negative
auto negatives = row | std::views::filter(negative);  Filters the row for
assert(negatives.empty());        Checks whether      negative numbers
                                  negatives is empty
```

As with the `drop_while` example, we have the form

```
v | function(lambda)
```

which gives us a view of our container.

We can add this check to our tests for negative numbers. Everything is fine if we stick with generating 16 rows. If we try 35 rows, however, the assertion fails. When we learned how to generate rows in the triangle, we noted that we would run out of numbers eventually. We found our largest possible entry using `std::numeric_limits<int> ::max()`, which is likely to be 2,147,483,647, depending on your compiler. The maximum value in the 34th row is 1,166,803,110. We then get double this amount in the next row because we add adjacent values, which would give 2,333,606,220. This number overflows an `int`, and the behavior is undefined by the standard as we saw. On some systems, this wraps around to the minimum value, –2147483648, and then counts up again. That is why our test fails. An unsigned would give us more space: it would still wrap around after 4,294,967,295, but to 0. This would make the error harder to spot.

The core guidelines tell us we should not try to avoid negative values by using `unsigned` (http://mng.bz/M9VQ). We can assign a negative value to an unsigned, for example, `unsigned int u1 = -2`. Annoyingly, this compiles and gives us a large positive number. With a signed integer, we can check that the value is not negative. With an unsigned integer, we cannot check anymore. We know how many rows we can safely generate. Let's test one final property of the triangle.

2.3.5   *Checking whether each row is symmetric*

Every row is symmetric. The first and last numbers are both 1s, which is symmetric, and we checked this. We can go further and check all the entries for symmetry. This is like checking that a word is a palindrome, meaning that it reads the same backward as forward. CppReference uses checking for palindromes as an example of ranges' `equal` method (http://mng.bz/amej). We can repurpose this to check our vector. We need to make sure that the first half of a row matches the second half reversed.

Ranges provide a view of a container. Views have a `take` method, which walks over as many elements as we ask for. We need the first half, that is, `v.size()/2`. We compare this with the second half, reversed, using `ranges::equal` method.

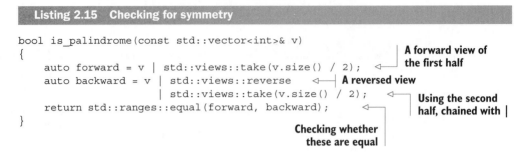

Listing 2.15 Checking for symmetry

```
bool is_palindrome(const std::vector<int>& v)
{
    auto forward = v | std::views::take(v.size() / 2);
    auto backward = v | std::views::reverse
                      | std::views::take(v.size() / 2);
    return std::ranges::equal(forward, backward);
}
```

A forward view of the first half

A reversed view

Using the second half, chained with |

Checking whether these are equal

Note that we have chained together views with the pipe operator and do not need to focus on which iterators are needed where. We can add one final assertion to our tests using the palindrome function:

```
assert(is_palindrome(row));
```

We now have a useful set of tests and have used a handful of methods in the ranges' library. There are many other patterns in the triangle, but as this chapter is nearly done, we will only look at one more pattern to pull together what we've learned.

2.3.6 *Highlighting odd numbers in a row*

If we highlight the odd numbers in the triangle, we will see another pattern. Looking back at our code to show the triangle in listing 2.7, we can transform each row before we print it using another tool from the `ranges` library. Every odd number is one more than a multiple of two, so we can check `x % 2` to find odd numbers. We will display them with a star to see the pattern. Otherwise, we display a single space. We will use the view's transform method to apply action to each row:

```
auto odds = row |
    std::views::transform([](int x) { return x % 2 ? '*' : ' '; });
```

We can use our transformation code to give something similar to listing 2.7, where we showed the actual values in the triangle. Figure 2.8 illustrates the resulting pattern.

Listing 2.16 Showing odd numbers as stars

```
void show_view(std::ostream& s,
    const std::vector<std::vector<int>>& v)
{
    std::string spaces(v.back().size(), ' ');
    for (const auto& row : v)
    {
        s << spaces;
        if (spaces.size())
```

```
        spaces.resize(spaces.size() - 1);
    auto odds = row | std::views::transform([](int x)
                        { return x % 2 ? '*' : ' '; });
    for (const auto& data : odds)
    {
        s << data << ' ';
    }
    s << '\n';
    }
}
```

Figure 2.8   An approximation to the Sierpinski triangle obtained by printing an * for an odd number and a blank space for an even number

We expected the symmetry. The repeating triangles might be a nice surprise. This approximates the Sierpinski triangle, which is a triangle shape recursively divided into smaller triangles. If we made an equilateral triangle, folded the corners over each other, and drew lines where we made the folds, we would get the blank triangle in the middle of figure 2.6, along with a triangle at the top, one on the bottom left, and one on the bottom right. We can then do the same with the three triangles on the corners. This triangle is fractal because it repeats as you zoom in. We could keep dividing up the triangles forever in theory, showing this fractal property. We could also try out even numbers instead or a different modulus, and we would see other patterns.

In this chapter, we have learned a fair bit about how to use vectors. We have not covered everything, but we have done enough to recognize various C++ features and test our code.

Summary

- Containers are part of the STL, and the compiler can sometimes deduce the type of expressions for us.

- We can initialize objects using an initializer list {`value1`, `value2`, ...} when we want to provide values directly.
- We can use `emplace_back` or `emplace` when we want to create an object in place directly in a container, or `push_back` or insert when we already have an object.
- The range-based `for` loop is a common way to walk over a container, avoiding iterators or indices.
- Use `auto` almost always, including relying on class template argument deduction when using containers.
- `std::move` casts a value to an rvalue, allowing perfect forwarding.
- Some versions of standard algorithms take `begin` and `end`, while others in the `std::ranges` namespace now support ranges.
- Views and filters can be chained with the pipe operator.
- Lambdas are unnamed functions that can capture variables and form closures.
- Use `format` to align text or set the width or precision of numbers for speed and type safety.

Input of strings and numbers

This chapter covers

- Input of numbers and strings
- Using `optional` when we may not have a value
- Working with random numbers
- Further practice with lambdas and `std::function`

In this chapter, we will write a number-guessing game to practice taking inputs by using strings and numbers. We need to generate a random number to guess, accept input from a player, and report whether the player's guess is correct. We will ensure the guess is actually a number, so we will learn about working with strings and numbers. We will give clues if the guess is wrong, starting with "too big" or "too small," and then add more clues, such as how many digits are correct. The brief introduction to random numbers will give us a foundation for later chapters, and we will learn several more C++ features along the way.

3.1 Guessing a predetermined number

We will start with a constant number to guess. Guessing a number that never changes is not much of a game, but it means we can concentrate on dealing with user input. If we put the predetermined number in a function, we can change it later.

Listing 3.1   A number to guess

```
unsigned some_const_number()
{
    return 42;
}
```

Feel free to pick another number. We don't need an entire function for this, but it might make the guessing-game code clearer than sending in a hard-coded or *magic* number. We will switch this out for a random number later. For now, all we need to do is take some user input and see if it matches.

3.1.1   *Accepting user input the hard way*

We used the stream insertion `operator <<` to send values to the screen in the last chapter. The `iostream` header also provides input via the stream extraction `operator >>`. We can use this operator to send input into a variable like this:

```
unsigned number;
std::cin >> number;
```

It's defined for all standard C++ types, as is `operator<<`. We are trying to stream anything typed into an `unsigned` because our number to guess is `unsigned`. If the user types in digits followed by Enter, the variable might contain a number. In the last chapter, we saw that we can assign a negative number to an `unsigned`. For a signed number, the high order bit indicates the sign of the number, whereas an unsigned number uses this bit as part of the value, so we can say `unsigned int number = -2`, and it will compile, but the number will have a large positive value, `4294967294`, in Visual Studio 2022. Furthermore, the input might not be a number or might even be too big to fit into our chosen numeric type. This suggests streaming straight into an `unsigned` is a bad idea, but we can persuade it to behave relatively well with some extra effort. We will try alternative approaches in the next section.

Let us see how far we can get if we stick with direct input to an `unsigned`. The operator skips over any initial whitespace and then consumes characters until Enter is pressed, as shown in figure 3.1. If there is only initial whitespace and a few digits, everything is fine. The whitespace is ignored, and the digits are transformed into a value stored in the `unsigned` variable. However, if the input is not suitable for an `unsigned`, two things happen: the input stream is in an error state, and it has unused characters that need clearing up.

As soon as an unsuitable character is encountered, a flag is set, which we could check directly by calling `std::cin` `.fail()`. We can also use the operator's explicit conversion to a `bool` by checking whether (`std::cin >> number`) is

Figure 3.1   Streaming into an `unsigned` skips over initial whitespace, accepts as many digits as fit into the `unsigned`, and then ignores anything else, leaving the unused characters in the stream.

true. The stream's conversion happens via an `explicit operator bool`, which means it can be *explicitly* converted to a `bool`. CppReference (http://mng.bz/W164) describes this check as idiomatic. The operator is marked as `explicit`, so we need to be in a context that expects a `bool`, such as an `if` or `while`, meaning we cannot accidentally convert the stream to a `bool`. If something fails, we need to clear the failed flag and mop up the bad characters using the `ignore` function. The function takes two parameters: the number of characters to extract and a delimiting character to stop at, so we want the maximum possible number of characters and to stop at a new line character, `'\n'`. Then we can loop until the user enters something sensible. Pulling this together and including the `limits` and `iostream` headers gives us the following.

Listing 3.2 Reading a number from standard input

```
unsigned input()
{
    unsigned number;
    while (!(std::cin >> number))          ◁──┐  Streams characters in and
    {                                              checks nothing failed
        std::cin.clear();   ◁──┤ Clears the fail flag
        std::cin.ignore(
            std::numeric_limits<std::streamsize>::max(), '\n');   ◁──┐
        std::cout << "Please enter a number.\n";
    }                                                              Mops up
    return number;   ◁──┐ Returns a number                        invalid input
}                        if we escape the loop
```

Armed with our initial predetermined number from listing 3.1, we can use the input function from listing 3.2 and create a guessing game.

Listing 3.3 A first attempt at a number-guessing game

```
void guess_number(unsigned number)
{
    std::cout << "Guess the number.\n";
    unsigned guess = input();
    while (guess != number)          ◁──┐  Loops while the
    {                                       guess is wrong
        std::cout << guess << " is wrong. Try again\n>";
        guess = input();
    }                                ┌ Only exits the loop
    std::cout << "Well done.\n";   ◁──┘ for a correct guess
}
int main()
{                                                        Calls our guessing function with
    guess_ number(some_const_number());   ◁──┐ our predetermined number
}
```

We can play the game, but we can also make several improvements. We are ensuring a number is entered. If we try some gibberish, we get told off over and over again until we enter a number, as shown in figure 3.2.

```
Guess the number.
>Hello
Please enter a number.
>I don't want to
Please enter a number.
>Why should I?
Please enter a number.
>Can I stop please?
Please enter a number.
>
```

Figure 3.2   We get stuck in a loop if we do not enter a number.

Now try a negative number, for example, -1. Figure 3.3 shows what happens.

```
Guess the number.
>-1
4294967295 is wrong. Try again
>
```

Figure 3.3   Guessing a negative number doesn't work as expected.

We know why this happened; when we assign -1 to an unsigned, it wraps around. We can fix this by changing the type to int. As shown in figure 3.4, if we try a few other nonnegative numbers and end with our not-very-random number, 42, we win.

We have a semblance of a number-guessing game, but it would be nice to give the user a way to indicate they give up. By changing the input function, we can make numeric input *optional* so the user can stop the game more easily.

```
Guess the number.
>0
0 is wrong. Try again
>100
100 is wrong. Try again
>42
Well done.
```

Figure 3.4   Provided we avoid bad input, we can play a rather predictable game.

3.1.2   Accepting optional numeric input

The c in cin stands for character. Instead of streaming directly into a numeric type, we could stream the characters into a string. If we include the string header, we can accept input this way:

```
std::string in;
std::cin >> in;
```

The string will contain the user input, but cin will stop on whitespace. If we type "Hello, World!," the string will only contain "Hello," leaving the remaining input behind to stream into another string or ignore. We can get the entire line instead like this:

```
std::string in;
std::getline(std::cin, in);
```

This will collect every character, including whitespace until the end of the line, leaving the characters before the end line for us in the `std::string in`. We can then choose what to do with the entire line.

Because we want to compare the input with a number, we will need to do something to convert the input. If we write an appropriate function, called `read_number`, taking a stream, we process the string we got from `getline` after including the `sstream` header:

```
std::istringstream in_stream(in);
auto number = read_number(in_stream);
```

How do we implement this `read_number` function? There are various ways to try to parse an integer from a string or stream. Working with `IOStreams` can get very gnarly very quickly. Angelika Langer and Klaus Kreft wrote a book called *Standard C++ IOStreams and Locales: Advanced Programmer's Guide and Reference* (Addison-Wesley Professional; 2000), which gives in-depth coverage. It is a huge book, which reflects the complexity of this topic. To keep things simple, we will use `std::optional` here, which will make our life easier.

The `optional` type was introduced in C++17 and lives in the `optional` header. It is sometimes described as a *vocabulary type*, along with `std::any` and `std::variant`. They are templates, so take a type as a parameter. After the response we saw in figure 3.3, we know we should use integers rather than unsigned integers, so we will use a signed integer for the template type:

```
std::optional<int> value;
```

This has no value. We can see if an `optional` has a value by checking the `has_value()` member function explicitly or using the `explicit operator bool`; in other words, using the `optional` in an `if` or `while` expression or similar. This is similar semantics to the stream used earlier. It's worth noticing patterns in the C++ language and library. They can inform our own code by showing us sensible approaches. Having no value might be legitimate, but we can initialize the value with an integer instead

```
std::optional<int> value = 101;
```

or change the value:

```
value = -2;
```

This allows `optional` to possibly contain a value. Some functional programming languages have the idea of a `maybe` type. We don't have to reserve values to indicate a variable is unset if we use an optional type. The `operator bool` will return `true` if the value is set. If we want to use the value, we call the `value` function:

```
int actual_value = value.value();
```

If the `optional` doesn't contain a value, we will get an exception. If it does, we get a number.

We can now write a function to read a number from a stream. We can either use `getline` outside the function to form a stream, having read the whole line of input, or tidy up nonnumeric input in our `read_number` function. If we do the latter, we don't need to remember to do this when we call the function. Our new function looks like this.

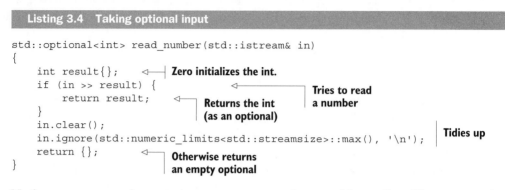

Listing 3.4   Taking optional input

```
std::optional<int> read_number(std::istream& in)
{
    int result{};    ◄─┤ Zero initializes the int.
    if (in >> result) {                    ◄─────
        return result;    ◄─┐               Tries to read
    }                       │ Returns the int  a number
    in.clear();             │ (as an optional)
    in.ignore(std::numeric_limits<std::streamsize>::max(), '\n');   │ Tidies up
    return {};    ◄─┐
}                   │ Otherwise returns
                    │ an empty optional
```

Notice we are returning an empty `optional` on the penultimate line. If we return the `result`, we are returning an `int`, so the `optional` will have a value, defeating the point of using the `optional` to indicate that the user wanted to stop guessing.

We have given ourselves options by sending the stream into the reading function, rather than pinning it down to standard input. For example, we could get the whole line of input using `std::stringstream in_stream(in)` outside the function and send that in instead. This would mean we still know what the user typed. We decided to clear the stream if it didn't contain a number, so we have lost the input if `cin` is sent in directly. That is good enough for our game, but we can see that we have choices here.

If the user enters a number, our new function will return an `optional` with a value; otherwise, an empty `optional` is returned. We can check for an empty optional in the `while` loop with

```
while (guess = read_number(std::cin))
```

so we can drop out of the loop and stop asking for guesses if the player doesn't enter a number. Note that a few compilers may issue a warning when we use the result of the assignment as a condition, especially if using clang or GCC with the warning flag `-Wparentheses`. Using a second set of parentheses indicates we do intend to check the value assigned and stops the warning:

```
while ((guess = read_number(std::cin)))
```

We could even say what the number is if the player gives up. Pulling this together, we have code for a slightly better game.

Listing 3.5   Allowing giving up

```
void guess_number_or_give_up(int number)
{
    std::cout << "Guess the number.\n>";
```

```
    std::optional<int> guess;
    while (guess = read_number(std::cin))          ◁─┐ Drops out of the loop if
    {                                                │ input is not a number
        if (guess.value() == number)
        {
            std::cout << "Well done.";          ┐ Stops if the
            return;                           ◁─┘ guess is correct
        }
        std::cout << guess.value() << " is wrong. Try again\n>";
    }
    std::cout << "The number was " << number << "\n";    ◁─┐ Tells the player
}                                                          │ the number

int main()
{
    guess_number_or_give_up(some_const_number());
}
```

If we play the game now, we can give up, by typing either "Give up" or any input other than a number (figure 3.5).

Our game works, but it would be nice to give the player clues when they are wrong. Once we have that in place, we will be ready to dive into using random numbers.

```
Guess the number.
>10
10 is wrong. Try again
>-4
-4 is wrong. Try again
>Give up
The number was 42
```

Figure 3.5   The player can now give up and find out the number.

3.1.3   *Validation and feedback using std::function and lambdas*

If the guess is wrong, it is either too big or too small. We could check that in place, but using a validation function gives us more flexibility. Although we will only report if a number is too big or too small here, we will add various other feedback in our final section when we create a prime number-guessing game. We will use a lambda again and see how to send it to our guessing game.

We want to change our function signature to say something like this:

```
void guess_number_or_give_up(int number, lambda message)
```

However, there is no lambda keyword. Every lambda has a unique type, so we need another way to express that we have something we can call, like a function or a lambda, known as a *callable*, as our second parameter. We could use a template:

```
template<typename T>
void guess_number_or_give_up(int number, T message)
```

However, this does not express that the message is callable. We could use a *concept* to constrain the template type, giving an alternative approach that we will look at in the next chapter. For now, we will use `std::function`. This will help us understand lambdas better.

`std::function` is a template providing a general-purpose wrapper for lambdas, named functions, or any callable object. We need to specify the return and parameter types in the template. For our game, we have a number and a guess, which are our inputs for the message function, and we want to return a message to display, which can be a `string`. For a named function, the signature would look like this:

```
std::string message(int, int);
```

The return type comes first, followed by the function name and the parameters (two `int`s in our case). To create an `std::function`, we include the `functional` header and declare a function wrapper with the same signature:

```
std::function<std::string(int, int)> callable;
```

The template parameters, `std::string(int, int)`, look like the named function, but without a name. We call `callable` as we would any function:

```
auto message = callable(1, 2);
```

Because we haven't specified what the `callable` should do, it is an *empty* function, so it throws an exception. This mirrors the behavior of `optional`. We can initialize `callable` with a lambda:

```
std::function<std::string(int, int)> callable = [](int number, int guess) {
    return std::format("Your guess was too {}\n",
        (guess < number ? "small" : "big"));
};
```

The function is no longer empty, and we can safely call it. Notice we are using `std::format` again. Section 2.2.5 gave instructions on how to use the `fmt` library instead if your compiler does not support `std::format` yet. Don't forget that you will need to change `std::format` to `fmt::format` and include the `fmt/core.h` header instead of the standard `format` header. We can now add an extra parameter for a message function to our game so we can give the player clues if their guess is wrong.

Listing 3.6 Providing clues if the guess is wrong

```
void guess_number_with_clues(unsigned number,
        std::function<std::string(int, int)> message)
{
    std::cout << "Guess the number.\n>";
    std::optional<int> guess;
    while (guess = read_number(std::cin))
    {
        if (guess.value() == number)
        {
            std::cout << "Well done.";
            return;
        }
        std::cout << message(number, guess.value());      ◁─┐  Shows a message if
        std::cout << '>';                    ◁──────────────┤  the guess is wrong
    }                                                       │
    std::cout << std::format("The number was {}\n", number); │  Adds a prompt
}                                                           │  after the message
```

We also need to change our `main` function, providing the message via a lambda function. We can either send it in directly or declare the lambda on a separate line using `auto`.

Listing 3.7 Improved number-guessing game

```
int main()
{
    auto make_message = [](int number, int guess) {
        return std::format("Your guess was too {}\n",
            (guess < number ? "small" : "big"));
    };
    guess_number_with_clues(some_const_number(), make_message);
}
```

Why do we declare the `message` as `auto` rather than specifying `std::function<std::string(int, int)>`? Although it is less typing, there is an important point to note here as well. The type of the lambda or *closure* is unnamable by us, but `auto` infers the exact type for us. Two lambdas taking the same parameters and having the same return type actually have different types. However, both lambdas could be assigned to the same `std::function`. This is useful for our purposes but has drawbacks. A lambda can be inlined, avoiding the overhead of a function call. If we copy a lambda into an `std::function`, it can no longer be inlined, so calling it might be slower. Copying our lambda to an `std::function` might also involve dynamic memory allocation. Scott Meyers gives full details in "Item 5: Prefer auto to explicit type declarations" in his book *Effective Modern C++* (O'Reilly Media, 2014), and we already know we should almost always use `auto`. If we declare the lambda as `auto`, we avoid the overheads, although it will be copied to an `std::function` in the method call. We could actually change the function signature in listing 3.6 to use `auto` as well:

```
void guess_number_with_clues(unsigned number, auto message);
```

We now have another reason to almost always use `auto`. We have lost the idea of the message generator being an invocable function, though. Once we know a bit about concepts, we can fix that. For the impatient, we can include the concepts header and say

```
void guess_number_with_clues(unsigned number,
    std::invocable<int, int> auto message)
```

to get helpful compiler errors if we pass something that is not able to be invoked with two integers. We will see more concepts in the next chapter. For the patient, there is a proposal to introduce an `std::function_ref` as an alternative to `std::function`, overcoming the performance problems (http://mng.bz/wjgg). C++ is continuing to evolve to make our lives easier. However we make our messages, we now get clues when we try to guess the number (figure 3.6).

```
Guess the number.
>17
Your guess was too small
>1000
Your guess was too big
>Give up
The number was 42
```

Figure 3.6   The game now gives clues and allows the player to give up.

We now have a functioning, if somewhat boring, number-guessing game. We can improve on that by picking a random number to guess.

3.2   *Guessing a random number*

C++11 introduced a random number library. It takes a bit more effort to use than C's `rand` function but provides lots of different ways to generate random numbers with various useful properties. This section will show how to get a random number from one of the many distributions. We need to pick a seed and choose an engine, as well as decide which distribution to use. We will look at the distributions in more detail in chapter 6. This section sets the groundwork.

3.2.1   *Setting up a random number generator*

For our guessing game, we want a random integer. Picking the random number from an interval would be nice, and any number should be equally likely, so we will use the *uniform* integer distribution, called `uniform_int_distribution`. This distribution is suitable for simulating dice rolling, which needs a number between one and six for each roll without bias toward any outcome. It is useful for any situation requiring equally likely whole numbers, such as picking a number for us to guess in our game.

Each distribution is a template taking a type of number to generate. The `uniform_int_distribution` is constrained to whole number types. There is a similar `uniform_real_distribution` for floats or doubles. We will use an integer and request numbers between 1 and 100 inclusive:

```
std::uniform_int_distribution<int> dist(1, 100);
```

The C `rand` function does not support intervals, which we often want with random numbers. For example, a dice roll needs a number between 1 and 6, or picking a card from a deck needs a number between 1 and 52. C++ helps us out here, allowing us to be explicit.

To provide numbers, the distribution needs an engine or generator. The engine provides random numbers. Yes, to generate random numbers, the distribution needs to be provided with random numbers. The distribution uses probability functions to ensure the numbers are uniform or follow whichever distribution is requested. For a uniform number in a range, the distribution squashes or transforms the numbers the engine provides to the requested interval. If we used C's `rand` instead, we would have to squash the numbers to the interval ourselves.

We cannot generate a genuinely random number from a function because a function returning a different value every time it is called would usually be regarded as a bug. So how can a random number engine work? What we can do is generate a *pseudo-random number* by writing a function that starts with a seed and does some arithmetic to generate a new number, while remembering that new number for the next call. Eventually, the numbers will start repeating if the number matches the original seed. Many pseudo-random number generators use a polynomial function combined with some modulo arithmetic. We could write a generator ourselves.

Listing 3.8   A terrible random number generator

```
int random_number(int seed = 0)
{
    static int x = 0;       ◁──┐  Static storage holding the
    if (seed)                  │  number for the next call
        x = seed;

    x = ++x % 2;            ◁──┐  Makes a new value from the
    return x;                  │  last value
}
```

This is a terrible random number generator because it will only return `0` or `1`, and these values alternate. We either get `0, 1, 0, 1, ...` or `1, 0, 1, 0, ...` depending on the seed. As it repeats every two numbers, it has a *period* of two. Fortunately, C++ provides several engines that do a much better job, including the tersely named `mt19937` engine. The `mt` stands for Mersenne Twister. These generators use prime numbers that are one less than a power of two, called Mersenne primes, in their modulus part and have a much better calculation step than our increment, `++x`. This engine provides a period of $2^{19937} - 1$. We could also use the `std::default_random_engine`, which may well be the `mt19937` engine.

There are various ways to seed the random number engine. If we stick with a specific number, we will get the same sequence of random numbers for each run. The ability to regenerate a sequence of pseudo-random numbers by supplying the same seed is useful for simulations and for testing, as the outcomes are then identical for each run. We could use the current time to get different numbers on each run, but we haven't learned about time in C++ yet. We will do that in the next chapter. The `random` header provides a `random_device`, which is itself a random number generator, producing *non-deterministic* random numbers. CppReference points out that it may generate the same number sequence every time it is called (http://mng.bz/84RZ). Some older implementations always returned `0`, so it is worth checking whether you get a different number if you call it a few times running. The random device might be using the state of your hard drive, or similar physical component, to generate a number. CppReference also warns us that even though it generates random numbers, it is designed to generate a seed because calling it repeatedly may start generating the same numbers over and over.

After including the `random` header, we use the random device to seed our random number generator:

```
std::random_device rd;
std::mt19937 engine(rd());
```

This gives us the engine or generator we need to use a distribution.

3.2.2   *Using the random number generator*

Armed with a seed and engine, we can now draw a single number from the distribution. We do this by calling the distribution's `operator()`.

Listing 3.9   Generating a single random number

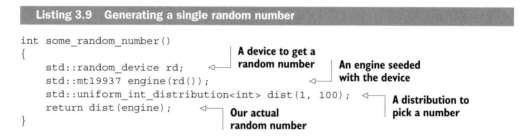

```
int some_random_number()
{
    std::random_device rd;
    std::mt19937 engine(rd());
    std::uniform_int_distribution<int> dist(1, 100);
    return dist(engine);
}
```

A device to get a
random number

An engine seeded
with the device

A distribution to
pick a number

Our actual
random number

That is quite a bit of code to generate one number, but we need a seed, an engine, and a distribution before we can request a random number. We cannot get away with less code here. We will use random numbers in future chapters too, so we will get more practice. Now, if we want several random numbers, we could make a class and set up the seed and distribution in a constructor, calling `dist(engine)` from a member function each time we need a new number. We will create a class in chapter 5 and only need one number here, so the function suits our needs.

Notice that C++ has given us more control than the C function. The engine can be switched out to another that repeats less often, although the `mt19937` is fine here because we only need one number. We have also specified the range the random number should come from. The first three lines are set up, which we only have to do once. If we wanted another random number, we would call `dist(engine)` again without the setup. If we called this several times and recorded the results, we would see the numbers for 0 to 100 generated in approximately equal or uniform proportions.

We can now make our game slightly more challenging by calling the new function instead of `some_const_number` in `main` function, leaving everything else the same.

Listing 3.10   A random number guessing game

```
int main()
{
    auto message = [](int number, int guess) {
        return std::format("Your guess was too {}\n",
            (guess < number ? "small" : "big"));
    };
```

```
    guess_number_with_clues(some_random_number(), message);
}
```
◁─┐ **Possibly not 42 for a change**

We could change the message to give different clues (e.g., whether the number is odd or even, or we could keep track of guesses to remind the user if they have already tried a number). We will not do that here, but we can see how passing in the message keeps the code relatively flexible. What we will do is generate a prime number to guess. We will therefore learn how to generate a random number with a required property, in this case, a prime number, and will provide clues if the number is wrong.

3.3 Guessing a prime number

For more practice with random numbers, we will generate a prime number to guess. If the player gets it wrong, we will say which digits are correct. That will give us a bit more practice with the lambdas for our messages too.

3.3.1 Checking whether the number is prime

We need to adapt our function generating the number to guess if we want a prime number. Instead of returning `dist(engine)` immediately like we did in listing 3.9, we can first check if the number is prime. If so, we return it; otherwise, we try another random number until we get something suitable. How do we check if a number is prime?

Prime numbers have two factors. One only has one factor, so we can special case this and return false. 2 is 1×2 (or 2×1), so it has precisely two factors. This is the first prime. 3 is the next prime, so we can return true immediately for either of these numbers. Any multiples of 2 or 3 after that are not prime. For example, 6 is divisible by 2 and 3 and is also divisible by 1 and 6. We can therefore check for these using `operator%`.

The number 4 gets caught in the check for multiples of 2. We therefore only need to check if the number is a multiple of any number from 5 upwards since we covered 2, 3, and 4. We could keep track of the primes we find, rather than only considering multiples of 2 or 3, and build what is known as the sieve of Eratosthenes. This would be more efficient, but it means we would need to keep track of the primes. We can stop checking at the square root of our number to save a bit of time. There is no point in checking beyond that. For example, the number 35 is 5×7. Starting to check from 5, we immediately find a factor, so we can say 35 is not prime. We found this before the square root of 35, something slightly less than 6. Having found the first factor, we do not need to check the 7 because we found the 5 already and returned. If a factor is larger than the square root, there will always be another factor smaller than the square root, which we will find first. We pull our checks for factors together into a function as follows.

> **Listing 3.11   Function to check whether a number is prime**

```
bool is_prime(int n)
{
    if (n == 2 || n == 3)
        return true;
```
◁─┐ **2 and 3 are prime.**

```
    if (n <= 1 || n % 2 == 0 || n % 3 == 0)
        return false;

    for (int i = 5; i * i <= n; ++i)
    {
        if (n % i == 0)
            return false;
    }

    return true;
}
```

◄── **1 and any multiple of 2 or 3 are not prime.**

◄── **Checks if 5 upwards is a factor**

◄── **We found a factor, so the number is not prime.**

◄── **If we get here, we have a prime.**

We could make other optimizations to make the function faster, but this is quick enough for our game. We have a way to check if a number is prime, but before we use it, we will add some tests for this function.

3.3.2 Checking properties with static_assert

We will add a function to test whether our `is_prime` function works. We can hard-code a few numbers for the test. This means we are not using any runtime input, so we can run our checks at compile time. We indicate that by adding the keyword `constexpr`, short for constant expression, at the start of our function signature:

```
constexpr bool is_prime(int n)
```

Saying a function or variable is a `constexpr` means it can be evaluated at compile time, in theory. It might not be. A `constexpr` variable is `const`, meaning we can't change its value. For a `constexpr` function, the arguments have to be constant expressions too. If they don't get set until runtime, for example, via user input, evaluation cannot happen at compile time. So `constexpr` indicates that a value, or return value, is both constant and computed at compile time, when possible. Using `constexpr` can therefore allow us to evaluate variables or functions at compile time. Let's see how.

We can still call our function at runtime, but we can now check the code at compile time too. Instead of using C's `assert` function like we did in the last chapter, we can use `static_assert` in a test function:

```
void check_properties()
{
    static_assert(is_prime(2));
}
```

The `static_assert` can be used in other places too, such as a namespace (see http://mng.bz/E97o), but making a function for our tests makes them easy to find. The `static_assert` needs a constant expression, such as our `constexpr` function, and generates a compiler error if the expression is false. We can add a call to the `check_properties` function at the start of the `main` function, and our single assertion passes at compile time, leaving nothing to do at runtime. If we use a non-prime number, such as 4, instead of 2, we get a compile error:

```
main.cpp(108,24): error C2607: static assertion failed
```

Finding and catching errors early is always a good thing. Furthermore, evaluation at compile time can speed up runtime. Both `static_assert` and `constexpr` were introduced back in C++11. The latter was made more flexible over time, allowing local variables and loops. Prior to that, we needed to use recursion. C++20 then introduced the specifiers `consteval` and `constinit`. `consteval` is applied to functions to ensure they are being evaluated at compile time, whereas a `constexpr` may or may not be evaluated at compile time. `constinit` is applied to variables, ensuring initialization at compile time. A `consteval` function is also called an *immediate function*, and we get a compile error if it cannot be evaluated at compile time.

We can also see variables declared as `constexpr`:

```
constexpr int x = 41 + 1;
constexpr bool x_prime = is_prime(42);
```

This makes the variables constant as well as calculated at compile time, so we cannot change them. Trying to do so by saying x = 43 results in a compile error. Compile time evaluation is a powerful tool. The important point for now is that `constexpr` function can run at compile time or runtime.

Now that we know how to test if a number is prime, we can use the check to generate a prime number to guess in our game.

3.3.3   Generating a random prime number

We saw how to generate a random number in listing 3.9. We used `random_device` to seed an engine and a distribution to pick a random number from a range. There aren't so many prime numbers between 1 and 100, so we will increase the range to 99,999, giving us more possible prime numbers and up to five digits. Instead of returning the first number generated, we need to check to see if it fulfills our requirements. We use our `is_prime` function and keep trying until we get a suitable number in an empty `while` loop. Let's use {} to initialize everything to remind ourselves about uniform initialization.

Listing 3.12   Generating a prime number

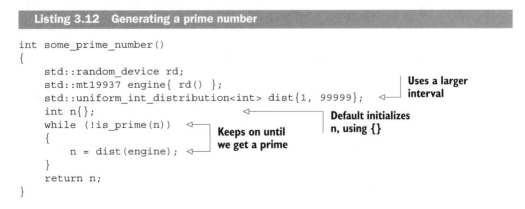

Filtering out random numbers that do not fulfill a criterion is known as *rejection sampling*. It's a simple way to generate random numbers that fulfill a property. Many of the distributions provide random numbers with properties required for simulations and games, but when the distribution is hard to encode mathematically, rejection sampling works well.

We can now amend our guessing game, using a randomly generated prime number, and adapting the call to the guessing game in listing 3.10 appropriately:

```
guess_number_with_clues(some_prime_number(), message);
```

This is all very well, but we can generate better clues. We could report if any of the digits are correct with a bit of thought. There are only 10 digits, so we could make two guesses with different digits. If a new clue tells us which are in the number, we know which digits to use. We may get them in the wrong place, and some may repeat, but it should be much easier to guess the number.

3.3.4   Deciding which digits are correct

We will use the character `^` to indicate a digit in the wrong place, `*` for a digit in the right place, and a dot for a digit that isn't present. If the number is 12347 and we guessed 23471, we have guessed all the digits, but they are in the wrong place. We would indicate this by displaying `"^^^^^"`. If the number is 78737 and we guess 87739, we would display `"^^**."`. Displaying this under the guess would give

```
87739
^^**.
```

The second 7 and the 3 are in the right place, so they get an `*`. The 7 and 8 at the start are in the wrong place, so each gets a `^`. The final digit, 9, is wrong, so it gets a dot.

To create the clue, we need a function taking the number and the guess and returning a string. If we convert the numbers to a string, we can check the digits one at a time. There are various ways to do this, and we will use `format`. We want to add leading zeros, so the number itself and the guess are both five digits long. We used the format specifier `"{: ^6}"` in the last chapter to pad a number with spaces ensuring it was six characters long. The `^` means center-justified. This time, we want right-justified, so use `>`, and we want 0 instead of space, giving us `"{:0>5}"`. If we set up a string filled with five dots, `std::string matches(5, '.')`, and put stars where the digits are correct, we are partway there.

Listing 3.13   Start of a function indicating which digits are correct

```
std::string check_which_digits_correct(int number, int guess)
{
    auto ns = std::format("{:0>5}", (number));      Converts numbers
    auto gs = std::format("{:0>5}", (guess));       to strings
    std::string matches(5, '.');                ◁──────  Starts with
    for (size_t i = 0, stop = gs.length(); i < stop; ++i)      five dots
    {
        char guess_char = gs[i];
        if (i < ns.length() && guess_char == ns[i])
```

```
        {
            matches[i] = '*';
        }
    }
    return matches;
}
```
◁── **Indicates correct digits with a star**

Now we need to find whether there are any digits in the wrong place. If the number is 78737 and we guess 87739, we have two 7s. One is correct, so it got an *, and the other is wrong. If we change the middle 7 in the number to an *, we won't use it in our check for misplaced digits. We can do that in the first loop; then we find digits that are in the wrong place in a second loop, indicating this with a ^. Once we have counted a digit as misplaced, we will change that to a ^ as well, so we don't report two misplaced digits when only one is in the number. For example, if the number is 12347 and the guess is 11779, both 7s are wrong, but we want to indicate we have one misplaced 7, rather than two:

```
11779
*.^..
```

If both 7s were to get the ^, indicating they are misplaced, that suggests the number contains two 7s. Our feedback makes it clear there is only one 7 in the number.

An `std::string` has a find method, which returns `npos` if there is no position matching. Some compilers also now support a `contains` function, which is more succinct, but we need the position if the digit is found to avoid using it again, so we need to use `find`. The `find` function takes a character to find and a starting position and returns an index. Because we want to search from the start, we need to use starting position `0`. If we get `npos` back, this means the character isn't there. We can do this in one `if` statement, using the `if` statements with initializer:

```
if (size_t idx = ns.find(guess_char, 0); idx != std::string::npos)
```

This was introduced in C++17. It looks like a normal `if`, but has an initialization followed by a semi-colon and then a condition: `if (init; condition)`. Without this, we would have to find the index and then check the value in separate statements. Either way is fine, but `if` statements with an initializer can keep code tighter, particularly by keeping the scope of the variable smaller because the variable is only in scope inside the `if` block. Adding the check for misplaced digits to the previous listing gives us the following.

> **Listing 3.14   Showing misplaced digits**

```
std::string check_which_digits_correct(int number, int guess)
{
    auto ns = std::format("{:0>5}", (number));
    auto gs = std::format("{:0>5}", (guess));
    std::string matches(5, '.');
    for (size_t i = 0, stop = gs.length(); i < stop; ++i)
```

```
    {
        char guess_char = gs[i];
        if (i < ns.length() && guess_char == ns[i])
        {
            matches[i] = '*';           Don't double
            ns[i] = '*';          ◄───  count this digit.
        }
    }
    for (size_t i = 0, stop = gs.length(); i < stop; ++i)  ◄───   Now checks
    {                                                              guesses that
        char guess_char = gs[i];                                   don't match
        if (i < ns.length() && matches[i] != '*')
        {
            if (size_t idx = ns.find(guess_char, 0);
                idx != std::string::npos)    ◄───   Looks for the
            {                                        guess character
                matches[i] = '^';
                ns[idx] = '^';      ◄───   Don't reuse
            }              ◄───             this digit either.
        }          idx has now gone
    }              out of scope.
    return matches;
}
```

We can and should add tests to our properties function. For example, after including the `cassert` header, we can add a check:

```
assert(check_which_digits_correct(12347, 23471) == "^^^^^");
```

The code provided with this book has several tests in the properties function, covering repeated and missing digits, omitted here for brevity.

We can now use our function to create a clue in the guessing game and call our properties test from `main`. While we are making that change, we will return the number formatted to five digits. This way, shorter numbers get leading zeros, so the ^ looks like it is pointing at any misplaced digits. For example, if the number is 17231 and we guess 1723, we would see

```
01723
.^^^^
```

This isn't required, but it will remind a player they can use a zero. The following listing shows what we have when we put things together.

Listing 3.15   A much better number-guessing game

```
void guess_number_with_clues(int number, auto message)
{
    std::cout << "Guess the number.\n";
    std::optional<int> guess;
    while (guess = read_number(std::cin))
    {
        if (guess.value() == number)
```

```
        {
            std::cout << "Well done.";
            return;
        }
        std::cout << guess.value() << " is wrong. Try again\n";   ⊣ Displays
        std::cout << message(number, guess.value());         ◁──    clues
    }
    std::cout <<
        std::format("The number was {:0>5}\n", (number));   ◁──┐ Shows the
}                                                               │ correct number
                                                                │ as five digits
int main()
{                                      ┌─ Calls the
    check_properties();   ◁──────────────┘ tests
    auto message = [](int number, int guess) {
        return std::format("{}\n",
            check_which_digits_correct(number, guess));   ─┐ Messages saying which
    };                                                  ◁──┘ digits are correct
    guess_number_with_clues(some_prime_number(), message);   ◁──┐ Plays
}                                                                │ the game
```

If we play the game, we can start with two prime numbers with different digits to narrow down possible numbers. 12347 and 56809 cover all the digits, so they are good starting guesses (figure 3.7).

```
Guess the number.
12347
12347 is wrong. Try again
^.^..
56809
56809 is wrong. Try again
...^^
90113
90113 is wrong. Try again
^^^**
01913
Well done.
```

Figure 3.7   **Start with two prime numbers with different digits to narrow down possible numbers.**

3.3.5   *Providing different clues using std::function*

Now, 90113, guessed in figure 3.7, is not a prime number. We can add this check to our message easily enough.

Listing 3.16   A longer message

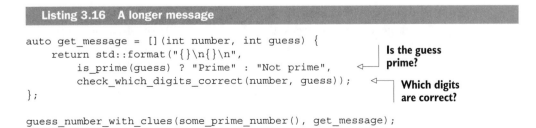

```
auto get_message = [](int number, int guess) {
    return std::format("{}\n{}\n",                        ┌─ Is the guess
        is_prime(guess) ? "Prime" : "Not prime",     ◁──────┘ prime?
        check_which_digits_correct(number, guess));   ◁──┐ Which digits
};                                                       │ are correct?

guess_number_with_clues(some_prime_number(), get_message);
```

We could extend this further, but adding lots of separate checks into the single lambda is a bad idea. Lambdas are good when we need a small function, but we should not let them get unwieldy. We need a different approach. We can add a check for the length as well because the number will not be more than five digits. We are therefore trying to check three things and return a message in each case. We can check the length and whether a number is prime with two separate lambdas, taking the guess and returning a string.

Listing 3.17   Check the length and whether the number is prime

```
auto check_prime = [](int guess) {
    return std::string((is_prime(guess)) ? "" : "Not prime\n");
};

auto check_length = [](int guess) {
    return std::string((guess < 100000) ? "" : "Too long\n");
};
```

Listing 3.14 gave clues about which digits were correct, but it requires the number as well as the guess. We can use the closure aspect of lambdas to make an anonymous function taking a single integer if we capture the number to guess. We saw [=] and [&] for captures by value and by reference in section 2.3 when we first met lambdas. We can say [number] to mean capture the variable number by value since we don't use the = sign when we capture a specific variable by value. We could use [&number] to mean capture number by reference. Either way, we have *enclosed* our function, taking two numbers with the number to guess to make a new function.

Listing 3.18   Capturing the number

```
int number = some_prime_number();
auto check_digits = [number](int guess) {          ◁─┐  Captures the
    return std::format("{}\n",                        │  number by copy
        check_which_digits_correct(number, guess));
};
```

We now have three lambdas that take an integer and return a string. It would be nice to put them in a container, like a vector, so the game can walk through the clues and possibly add more checks. What type would the vector contain, though? We know that each lambda has a different type, but we can wrestle them into an std::function and put them in a container if we include the functional and vector headers. The guessing game can then check the clues and show the first one only. If we check whether the number is prime first, we can enforce that the guess is prime and avoid giving further clues until another guess is made. We therefore need a slight change to our guessing function to call the messages.

Listing 3.19 Using all the clues

```
void guess_number_with_more_clues(int number, auto messages)
{
    std::cout << "Guess the number.\n>";
    std::optional<int> guess;
    while (guess = read_number(std::cin))
    {
        if (guess.value() == number)
        {
            std::cout << "Well done.";
            return;
        }
        std::cout << std::format("{:0>5} is wrong. Try again\n",
                                 guess.value());
        for (auto message : messages)            ⟵┐ Gets
        {                                          │ messages
            auto clue = message(guess.value());
            if (clue.length())
            {                            ┌ Only displays
                std::cout << clue;       │ first clue
                break;
            }
        }
    }
    std::cout << std::format("The number was {:0>5}\n", (number));
}
```

Now we can call our game after we call our test code in the main function.

Listing 3.20 Pulling it all together

```
int main()
{
    check_properties();
    auto check_prime = [](int guess) {
        return std::string((is_prime(guess)) ? "" : "Not prime\n");
    };

    auto check_length = [](int guess) {
        return std::string((guess < 100000) ? "" : "Too long\n");
    };

    const int number = some_prime_number();
    auto check_digits = [number](int guess) {
        return std::format("{}\n",
            check_which_digits_correct(number, guess));
    };
    std::vector<
        std::function<std::string(int)>
    > messages                    ⟵┐ Lines up checks
    {                              │ and clues
        check_length,
        check_prime,
```

```
        check_digits
    };
    guess_number_with_more_clues(number, messages);        ⟵┐ Plays
}                                                             └ the game
```

Having a handful of prime numbers to start off with will make playing easier. Try 12347 and 56809, as they use all the digits. We are free to ignore any clues, so we can try to find out which five digits we need first.

Wrestling the lambda into an `std::function` is not ideal, as we saw in section 3.1.3, because it can no longer be inlined. We will see another approach when we learn about parameter packs for templates in the final chapter. For now, we have learned about input and output, as well as strings, integers, and vectors. We can also generate random numbers. We will learn about handling time next and continue to build up our C++ knowledge.

Summary

- Character input comes from `std::cin` and can be streamed into specific types, but we need to check for errors and clean up unused input.
- Use `std::getline` to get an entire line of text, including whitespace.
- `std::optional` can be used for a value that may be unset.
- Both `std::cin` and `std::optional` have an `explicit operator bool`, allowing us to check for errors or missing values easily.
- Look for common patterns in the language and libraries to inform your own code.
- Random numbers in C++ require both an engine and a distribution.
- A random number engine can be seeded with `std::random_device`.
- Rejection sampling is a quick way to select random numbers fulfilling properties if a suitable distribution is not available.
- Some expressions can be calculated at compile time, so marking them with `constexpr` is a good idea.
- Use `static_assert` to check expressions at compile time.
- A lambda can be stored in `std::function`, but this may make code larger and slower.

Time points, duration, and literals

This chapter covers

- Using `std::chrono` time points and durations
- Using ratios
- Using literal suffixes
- Using the overloaded `operator/` to create dates
- Input and output of time points and durations
- Using different time zones

In this chapter, we will make a short program to create a countdown to an event. To do this, we will use time points and durations from the `chrono` header. This feature was introduced in C++11, and although the essence has remained the same, several useful additions have been made over time. Howard Hinnant is the main author and designer of this feature. In his Meeting C++ talk in 2019, he gave a lot of background to its design (https://www.youtube.com/watch?v=adSAN282YIw). As we use `chrono`, we will learn several important idioms and approaches applicable to many other situations.

We will build a simple countdown in the first section and then dig deeper into the types we used. We will discover how to use the ratio templates so that we can understand durations. We'll then learn how to read dates in so we can count down to any event and print out countdowns in various units. We will learn about literal suffixes to specify days, months, and so on and why they are useful. We will also encounter the idea of *requirements* and touch on concepts. Having covered these newer C++ features, we'll finish with a countdown using a zoned time.

4.1   *How long until the last day of the year?*

We will start by finding out how long it is until the end of a specific year to get a basic countdown. We only need a small amount of code, so this chapter's project is small in terms of lines of code. However, we will expand our knowledge as we code.

To find how far off a date is, such as New Year's Eve, we need to know the current time. The `chrono` header gives us a way to do this, providing us with date and time:

```
std::chrono::time_point now = std::chrono::system_clock::now();
```

Several details are hiding in there, which we will unpack further in this chapter. The `time_point` is a class template, using a clock and a duration. We have a choice of clocks, each able to work out the time and date for us. We will look at the duration details in the next section, but at a high level, it specifies the units of time, such as seconds or days. We have applied class template argument deduction (CTAD) to avoid specifying these template parameters, so we need to use at least C++17. Without it, we would need to spell out the full type, `std::chrono::time_point<std::chrono::system_clock>` or just use `auto`.

What is a clock? The `system_clock` we are using is based on the operating system's time. Now, an administrator can change the system's time, so calling `now` might appear to go back in time if the system time gets changed. That is not a problem, but it's worth knowing. Each clock provides a member variable called `is_steady`, which tells us if this might happen. We could use a `steady_clock` instead, although that is better suited for timing intervals. There are other clocks as well, for example, the `high_resolution_clock`, which provides the finest grain tick. Be warned that despite the name, this clock might be a `system_clock` or `steady_clock`, rather than a clock with a super-small tick size. There is also a `file_clock` for use with timestamps on files. Different file systems support different resolutions, so this provides a consistent way to access such information, regardless of the resolution used by the file system. We will stick with the `system_clock` in this chapter. It provides a systemwide real-time wall clock based on coordinated universal time (UTC) and maps easily to C's `time_t`, allowing us to interact with a C library if required.

Armed with another time point, we can find the difference between each to get a time interval or *duration*. For example, if we create a time point at the last day of the year, we can find how long it is until the last day of the year. New Year's Eve is always on the 31st of December, so we can specify a specific year, month, and day using C++20's `std::chrono::year_month_day`.

Listing 4.1 Creating a specific date

```
auto new_years_eve = std::chrono::year_month_day(
    std::chrono::year(2022),
    std::chrono::month(12),
    std::chrono::day(31)
);
```

We will see how to get the year from the `time_point` now shortly so we can write a more general and useful countdown. First, we will find the difference between the fixed date in listing 4.1 and the current `time_point`. Before we find the difference between our two dates, notice that `year_month_day` uses the *whole value idiom*. The whole value idiom has roots in Ward Cunningham's CHECKS pattern language (http://c2.com/ppr/checks.html), which mentions whole values to represent the meaningful quantities and is further explored by Martin Fowler's quantity pattern (https://martinfowler.com/eaaDev/Quantity.html) that represents dimensioned values with both their amount and unit. Rather than using integers for each parameter and trying to remember which order the constructor parameters are in, even though there is a big clue in the name, we have to explicitly pass an `std::chrono::year` to the year parameter and so on. The whole value idiom creates lightweight types to ensure parameters are passed correctly. A compiler error will ensue if we try to pass a month where a day is required, pinpointing a problem early and precisely.

To compare the `new_years_eve` with the current date time, we need to convert the date to another `time_point`. We only have days without a time, so we specify days as the duration of the `time_point` for the conversion:

```
auto event = std::chrono::time_point<std::chrono::system_clock,
                        std::chrono::days>(new_years_eve);
```

We could use one of two type aliases from `chrono` to make our `event` definition more succinct. First, whenever we need a time point based on a system clock, we can use `sys_time` and specify the duration. Thus, we could say

```
auto event = std::chrono::sys_time<std::chrono::days>(new_years_eve);
```

Second, if we need days specifically, we can use `sys_days` as a shorthand:

```
auto event = std::chrono::sys_days(new_years_eve);
```

Either way, we now have two `time_points`, so we can subtract them to find the difference and stream the value out, using `chrono`'s `operator<<`, which was introduced in C++20.

Listing 4.2 Duration between two time points

```
#include <chrono>
#include <iostream>

void duration_to_end_of_year()
```

```
{
    std::chrono::time_point now = std::chrono::system_clock::now();
    constexpr auto year = 2022;                                          ◁──── Hardcodes a
    auto new_years_eve = std::chrono::year_month_day(                           year for now
        std::chrono::year(year),
        std::chrono::month(12),
        std::chrono::day(31)
    );                                                                   ◁──── Converts to
    auto event = std::chrono::sys_days(new_years_eve);   ◁───                   a time point
    std::chrono::duration dur = event - now;             ◁──── Finds the
    std::cout << dur << " until event\n";        ◁──           difference
}                                                   │
                                                    │
int main()                        Finds operator ───┘
{                                 << for duration
    duration_to_end_of_year();
}
```

If you have an older compiler that does not support `operator<<` for durations yet, you can use the `count` method to send a value to `cout` in the last line of the function:

```
std::cout << dur.count() << " until event\n";
```

Alternatively, you can clone Howard Hinnant's date library (https://github.com/HowardHinnant/date) somewhere sensible:

```
git clone https://github.com/HowardHinnant/date.git
```

Include `"date/date.h"` from the library and add

```
using date::operator<<;
```

when you need to use the stream insertion operator. When you build your code, don't forget to use the `-I` switch to point to the `date/include` directory.

The exact output will depend on when we run listing 4.2, but we get a number and some units. Using Visual Studio 2022 gave

```
69579189669221[1/10000000]s until event
```

The number is in fractions of a second, indicated by `[1/10000000]s` in the output. Using the Compiler Explorer and either GCC 12.2 (https://godbolt.org/z/8Gj345e3d) or Clang 15.0 (https://godbolt.org/z/9zGvqfhPs), we get

```
-1508892372000803ns until event
```

It would be nice to decide the granularity for ourselves and use the actual year, rather than hardcoding 2022. We will take a deeper dive into durations in the next section to achieve this.

Let's take a moment to remind ourselves precisely what we have used so far. If we try the code on C++ Insights, mentioned in the first chapter (https://cppinsights.io/s/7a85b40e), we can see the full types spelled out. Your compiler may use slightly different types and values, but the insight gives an idea of how much is happening in the code. The insight for the two lines

```
auto event = std::chrono::sys_days(new_years_eve);
std::chrono::duration dur = event - now;
```

near the end of the function in listing 4.2 is as follows.

Listing 4.3   C++ Insights showing the full types

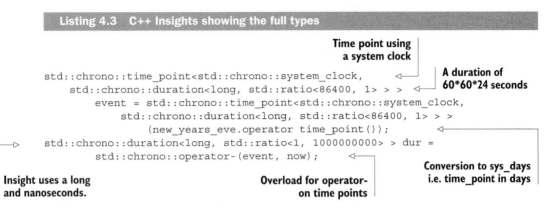

We can see from the C++ Insights output that durations are using ratios, so we need to start with ratios; then we can unpack durations in more detail.

4.2   Understanding durations in detail

We obtained a time interval or `duration` when we subtracted two time points, and we displayed the value. A `duration` counts *ticks*, either as whole numbers or floating-point numbers, in a unit, such as microseconds. A `duration` is therefore defined as a template taking two types, one for each part:

```
template<class Rep,class Period = std::ratio<1> > class duration;
```

The representation, `Rep`, will be a numeric type such as an `integer` or a `float`. The `Period` is a `ratio` telling us how to convert the ticks to seconds. It's worth taking a moment to understand the `ratio` type in more detail; then we will be better prepared to work with various durations.

4.2.1   Ratios

A minute has 60 seconds. We could divide seconds by 60 whenever we need minutes, but littering code with magic numbers is asking for trouble. We might not find every place they are used if we decide we want hours instead. We could write a utility function to do the conversion, or we could rely on something more generic. A ratio of 60:1 would be very useful. Fortunately, C++ provides exactly what we need in the `ratio` header. A `ratio` can be used to represent any rational number, so it needs two numbers: a numerator and a denominator. C++ defines this as a `template` using the two numbers:

```
template<std::intmax_t Num, std::intmax_t Denom = 1> class ratio;
```

The `intmax_t` is the largest signed integer type, which can vary between implementations. Using a `template` allows arithmetic with ratios to happen at compile time.

Notice that the numerator and denominator are both *nontype template parameters*; in this case, numbers rather than types. We could create a ratio of 3:6 using `std::ratio<3, 6>`. If we look at the numerator and denominator

```
std::cout << std::ratio<3, 6>::num << '/' << std::ratio<3, 6>::den << '\n';
```

we find that the ratio has been reduced to the simplest form, 1/2. In fact, the helper method `ratio_equal` tells us the two ratios are equivalent:

```
bool same = std::ratio_equal<std::ratio<3, 6>, std::ratio<1, 2>>::value;
```

The `ratio` header also provides arithmetic functions, such as `ratio_add`, allowing us to perform compile-time arithmetic with fractions such as

```
using fract = std::ratio_add< std::ratio<3, 6>, std::ratio<1, 2>>;
std::cout << fract::num << '/' << fract::den << '\n';
```

which gives 1/1.

The default duration we saw at the start of this section uses a ratio of 1:1, `Period = std::ratio<1>`, equating to 1 second per tick. The `chrono` header provides various periods, from nanoseconds to years, each based on definitions in the `ratio` header. A nanosecond is 1/1,000,000,000 seconds. Counting how many zeros there are in such a number is error prone. Fortunately, the `ratio` header defines `std::nano` for us as

```
std::ratio<1, 1000000000>
```

We can use this instead of creating our own constant. The `ratio` header also defines milli-, kilo-, and other International System of Units (SI) ratios.

In listing 4.3, we saw C++ Insights using a duration with a `long` for the representation and a period of `std::ratio<1, 1000000000>`. The representation and period used for a `system_clock` can vary between compilers, but that does not matter. Whatever is in use, we can ask for seconds between time points or any other duration. We can now change our countdown to provide the duration in whatever units we choose.

4.2.2   *Durations*

Our countdown was in fractions of a second, but we might want to report it in days or minutes instead. So how do we convert between durations? To get a duration in minutes, we employ `std::chrono::minutes`, which uses a ratio of 60:1. Various periods are available. Hours use 3,600:1, milliseconds 1:1,000, and microseconds 1:1,000,000. C++20 introduced days, weeks, months, and years as well. Days and weeks are straightforward enough, but how many days are there in a month or a year? It depends. C++20 uses 365.2425 days for a year and 30.436875 days, exactly 1/12 of a year, for a month. The *civil* calendar models the solar system approximately, and `chrono` models the civil calendar precisely. We could even write our own calendars that can interoperate with `chrono`. Howard Hinnant gives examples including the Julian and Islamic calendars on his GitHub pages (http://mng.bz/A89Q).

We can switch between durations implicitly or explicitly. Assigning a finer-grained interval from a coarser-grained one will not round, so an implicit cast works:

```
std::chrono::milliseconds ms = std::chrono::hours(2);
```

Getting back to the finer-grained milliseconds may involve rounding, so we need to use a named cast:

```
auto two_hours_from_ms = duration_cast<hours>(ms);
```

This example will give us back the original 2 hours. In most cases, going from milliseconds to hours might lose some precision. Two hours is 7,200,000 milliseconds. If we only had 7,199,999 milliseconds, we would be a millisecond under 2 hours, so we would get 1 hour instead of 2. Similarly, 23 hours is nearly a day, but transforming this into a day will round toward zero, so we get 0 hours if we round trip.

Let's try this out. We will add a `using` directive so we no longer need to fully qualify the types and functions in `std::chrono`. However, be wary of doing this thoughtlessly and never do this in a header file. ISOCpp's core guideline SF.7 tells us not to write `using namespace` at global scope in a header file (see http://mng.bz/xjR6). Doing so might bring two names into scope and cause ambiguity. In our case, we have a small function, so we will not introduce naming collisions.

So how many days is 23 hours? We need a `duration_cast` to find out.

Listing 4.4   Using `duration` to move to a coarser representation

```
void durations()
{
    using namespace std::chrono;
    auto nearly_a_day = hours{23};          ⟵  Starts with almost a day
    days a_day = duration_cast<days>(nearly_a_day);     ⟵  Casts to days
    hours round_trip = a_day;                ⟵  Gets 0 hours back
    std::cout << nearly_a_day << " cast to " << a_day
        << " and cast back to " << round_trip << '\n';
}
```

Call `durations` from `main` to see

```
23h cast to 0d and cast back 0h
```

The `operator<<` reports `0d`, meaning 0 days, which is `0h`, or 0 hours. Don't forget you can use the duration's `count` method instead or `using date::operator<<` if you need to. A value in days can be assigned to hours without an explicit cast because we do not drop precision. So given one whole day `a_day{1}`, we can assign

```
hours n_hours = a_day;
```

and check that they are the same:

```
assert(a_day == n_hours);
```

We could use an explicit `duration_cast` instead of the direct assignment, but reserving the use of `duration_cast` for only those conversions that lose precision is a good approach. This makes it easy to find such lossy conversions in our code if we suspect a lossy conversion is the source of an error. Needing to use a `duration_cast` when we might lose precision is a good thing because the cast makes the potential loss explicit, as figure 4.1 shows.

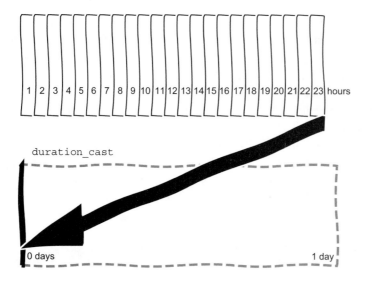

Figure 4.1 Transforming 23 hours to days loses precision, so it needs a `duration_cast`.

We can even write our own `duration`; for example, a century. We need to provide a type for the period. A century has 100 times as many seconds as a year, so we need the ratio 1:100, or `std::hecto`. We can then use `ratio_multiply` from the `ratio` header to get the type we need. The `multiply` function calculates the appropriate numerator and denominator for us, so we can define centuries using a *type alias*, with the keyword `using`:

```
using centuries = std::chrono::duration<long long,
    std::ratio_multiply<std::chrono::years::period, std::hecto>>;
```

The `using` statement works like a generalization of `typedef`, and we will see more details in chapter 8. We can use our century duration just like any of the `chrono` durations; for example, converting centuries to seconds, hours, or days. Seconds and hours can be converted without a cast, but to get days, we need a `duration_cast`. This might be surprising because a century is 100 years, and a year has either 365 or 366 whole days. However, C++ defines a year as 365.2425 days, so one century is 36,524.25, which has a partial day. We therefore need the explicit `duration_cast`.

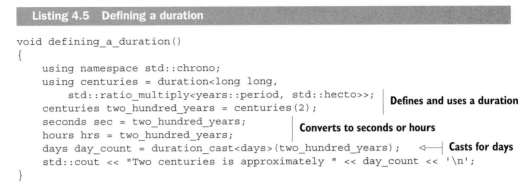

```
void defining_a_duration()
{
    using namespace std::chrono;
    using centuries = duration<long long,
        std::ratio_multiply<years::period, std::hecto>>;
    centuries two_hundred_years = centuries(2);
    seconds sec = two_hundred_years;
    hours hrs = two_hundred_years;
    days day_count = duration_cast<days>(two_hundred_years);
    std::cout << "Two centuries is approximately " << day_count << '\n';
}
```

If we run this code, we see

```
Two centuries is approximately 73048d
```

The predefined convenience durations are sufficient for counting down to an event, but the careful design of this library allows us so much flexibility. In fact, there is even more in the library to make our lives easier. We do not need to spell out `std::chrono::month(12)` in full because the durations and other types support *literal suffixes*. Let's look at the literal suffixes in more detail.

4.2.3 *Literal suffixes and operator / for readable code*

We noted that trying to read numbers with many zeros, such as 1000000000, can be error prone, but adding a digit separator, such as 1,000,000,000, helps. C++ now supports a digit separator, but a comma is an operator, so we use a single quote instead:

```
int readable_nano = 1'000'000'000;
```

This is a small but useful addition to the language. In listing 4.4, we used

```
auto nearly_a_day = hours{23};
```

which is perfectly readable, but `chrono` supports literal suffixes too. By adding `h` for hours, we can also write

```
auto nearly_a_day = 23h;
```

The literal suffix of `'h'` for hours is quite intuitive. Either approach is fine. How does this work? The seemingly magic `'h'` is using the `operator""h` from `chrono`. The operator takes a number and returns the stronger type of hours, implemented along these lines:

```
hours operator""h(long long _Val) {
    return hours(_Val);
}
```

When `23h` is encountered, this function is called, giving us the hours we wanted. We need to be using a suitable namespace for this to work. We have a choice here. We can either use one of the namespaces

- `std::literals,`
- `std::chrono_literals,`
- `std::literals::chrono_literals,`

or, more simply, use `std::chrono`, which makes `chrono_literals` visible via the directive:

```
using namespace std::literals::chrono_literals
```

The `operator""h` is an example of a *user-defined literal*, providing a conversion to hours when we use an `'h'` as a suffix on a number. Other literals are supported, including minutes with `'min'` and seconds with `'s'`. These were introduced in C++11, and C++14 added milli-, micro- and nanoseconds. This gives us two ways to define durations, as shown in table 4.1.

Table 4.1   Two ways to define a specific duration

Duration	Literals example
`hours{12}`	`12h`
`minutes{34}`	`34min`
`seconds{1}`	`1s`
`millisecond{1}`	`1ms`
`microsecond{1}`	`1us`
`nanosecond{1}`	`1ns`

There are no literals to help construct the durations days, months, or years. However, there are literals for a day, month, or year in a calendar. Notice that all the predefined `chrono::duration` types are plural, while the calendar types are singular. They behave differently. We can add months but cannot add January and December. To specify a month, we can spell out the name of the month in full; for example, using the named constant `December`. A conversion from a numeric type would mean arguing over whether to start at `0` or `1`. As it happens, C++20 uses `1` for January, but if we type `January` in full, we don't need to remember where to start. Day, month, and year are *calendrical specifiers*, and they can also be defined in two ways, as shown in table 4.2.

Table 4.2   Two ways to define a specific day, month, or year

Civil calendar	Literals example
`year{2023}`	`2023y`
`month{1}`	`January`
`day{23}`	`23d`

User-defined literals extend the idea of writing `1u` to mean an unsigned or `1.0f` to mean a float. The C++ standard library provides literals for time, which we just saw. We also have `'i'` for complex numbers; for example, `2 + 3i`, or `'s'` for `std::string`. Yes, that is another `operator""s`, which is in the `string_literals` namespace, but it takes a `const char*`, while `chrono`'s seconds literal takes a numeric type, so they are unambiguous. The string literal is useful. If we initialize a variable with `"Hello"`, we are using a `char` array. If we use `"Hello"s` instead, we have an `std::string` directly. We are allowed to define our own literals too by providing an appropriate operator; however, we have to begin our suffix with an underscore to avoid potentially clashing with standard literal operators.

At the beginning of this chapter, in listing 4.1, we created a date explicitly stating the year, month, and day without using these literals:

```
year_month_day(year(2022), month(12), day(31));
```

We could rewrite this as

```
year_month_day{2022y, December, 31d};
```

In fact, we have a further option. Another trick the `chrono` library uses for readable code is overloading the `operator /` to create a year, month, and day. CppReference (http://mng.bz/rjRj) lists about 40 overloads to create a variety of different dates. We want a full year, month, and day, so we can spell out the month in English, use the `'y'` suffix to specify a year, and give the day separated with `'/'`. For example:

```
auto new_years_eve = 2022y / December / 31;
```

The 31st does not need a `'d'` at the end because it must be the day once the year and month have been specified. A `year_month_day` can be constructed in a vast number of ways, but three orders work for a full date:

- Year/month/day
- Month/day/year
- Day/month/year

We will use this shortly to find out how many days until the end of the current year. Before we do that, we will revisit the `time_point` used at the start of the chapter. We know a `time_point` is defined by a `clock` and a `duration`. We saw a few different clocks, and we now know how durations work. Although we have enough knowledge to finish our small countdown project, the documentation for `chrono` uses C++ features that crop up in many places. In particular, requirements are mentioned, and the innocuous-seeming phrase *as if* is used. What do they mean?

4.2.4   *Requirements and concepts*

We started this chapter by finding out the current time using

```
std::chrono::time_point now = std::chrono::system_clock::now();
```

The `time_point` is a class template comprising two types, a `clock` and a `duration`:

```
template<
    class Clock,
    class Duration = typename Clock::duration
> class time_point;
```

When we found the current time, we used a `system_clock`, and the `duration` defaulted to that clock's `duration`.

CppReference (https://en.cppreference.com/w/cpp/chrono/time_point) says `time_point` is implemented *as if* it stores a value of type `duration` indicating the time interval from the start of the `Clock`'s epoch. We haven't seen the word *epoch* yet. If you have used C's `time_t` before, you will be familiar with the idea of counting ticks since the start of a given moment, or epoch, such as the start of January 1970. Other systems start at different instants. For example, Excel for Windows uses the start of January 1900 (http://mng.bz/ddl1). More importantly, notice the phrase *as if*, which crops up frequently in C++. The as if *rule* allows the compiler to reorder instructions or completely remove them under some circumstances, provided the observable behavior of the program will not differ. For a clock, the actual implementation can store whatever it likes, as long as it behaves as if it stores a duration. The compiler can also reorder or remove instructions under other circumstances too. If a program reads an uninitialized variable, the compiler can also do anything because this is undefined behavior, usually shortened to UB. Ovle Maudel wrote a short piece called "Demons may fly out of your nose" a while ago (http://mng.bz/BAjl), referencing the phrase "nasal demons" (from the Usenet group `comp.std.c`) used to mean "unexpected behavior of a C compiler on encountering an undefined construct." No one has ever reported demons flying out of their nose because of undefined behavior, but strange things do happen. Sometimes the as if rule means the compiler can optimize our code, which is a good thing, while sometimes it means we have undefined behavior, which is a bad thing. In either case, notice as if in the documentation.

The `time_point` also uses a `Clock` class, and CppReference says this must meet the *requirements* for `Clock`. Now it is down to us to ensure the clock we use does this; otherwise, we might end up with nasal demons. Some of the operations could work if a "not-quite-clock" is used, so this requirement will be dropped by C++23 (http://mng.bz/lVBR).

The word *requirements* also crops up frequently and forms part of the *concepts* language feature. We saw the separation between containers, such as a `vector` and algorithms, back in chapter 2. The separation is possible through templates. The algorithms are generic and therefore able to be used for different types, operating on a range of elements. Templates allow a form of *duck typing*, a phrase often applied to dynamic languages, but equally applicable when we use templates at compile time in C++. Stack Overflow (http://mng.bz/D95g) gives a splendid example

```
template <typename T> void f(T x) { x.Quack(); }
```

to illustrate the phrase "If it looks like a duck and quacks like a duck, it's a duck," hence the name duck typing. If we try to pass an object without a `Quack` function, we get a compiler error, which may or may not be helpful. If we had a way to specify that the object requires a `Quack` function, along the lines of

```
template <typename T>
T must have a Quack function
void f(T x) { x.Quack(); }
```

the compiler could stop immediately and let us know if the object used had no `Quack` method.

Using a clearer function name than `f`, if we have

```
template<typename T>
void might_be_a_duck(T x) { x.Quack(); }
```

and call it like this

```
might_be_a_duck(42);
```

we will get an error. According to Visual Studio 2022, `"left of '.Quack' must have class/struct/union"`. In this case, it isn't so hard to track down what the problem is, but a requirement, specified by using a `requires` clause, will make the problem clearer. To specify that the `Quack` function must exist, we can write a *concept*, giving a name to our *requirement* and adding it to the function signature.

Listing 4.6   Writing and using a concept

```
template<typename T>
concept Quacks = requires(T t)        ◁─┐ Names our
{                                        │ requirement
    t.Quack();        ◁─┐ Specifies what
};                      │ we require

template<typename T>
requires Quacks<T>       ◁─┐ States T
void must_be_a_duck(T x)   │ must Quack
{
    x.Quack();
}
```

The concept names the idea "`T` must have a `Quack` function" we wanted. When we use it, we do not need to spell out

```
template<typename T> requires Quacks<t>
```

in full. We can be more succinct if we use `auto`:

```
void also_must_be_a_duck(Quacks auto x)
{
    x.Quack();
}
```

In either case, `must_be_a_duck(42)` and `also_must_be_a_duck(42)` still cause an error, but this time, Visual Studio 2022 says

```
no matching overloaded function found, could be 'void must_be_a_duck(T)',
the associated constraints are not satisfied
```

The message is much more helpful. Let's get back to times and countdowns.

C++20 introduced several named requirements in the `concepts` header. To satisfy the clock requirements, the following four types must be defined

- `rep`
- `period`
- `duration`
- `time_point`

and the clock must also support `is_steady` and `now()`. `chrono` provides a *type trait* called `is_clock` to check whether the requirements are met. Traits describe properties of a type, and we will revisit them in chapter 6. The `is_clock` trait has a Boolean member called `value`, which reports if a type satisfies the requirements. If we apply this to an `int`

```
std::chrono::is_clock<int>::value
```

the `value` is false because `int` is not a clock. Although the `time_point` itself does not enforce the requirement, other functions using `time_points` might. When the requirements are used, the compiler can indicate the problem with a message such as `'Clock type required'` exactly where the wrong type is used. The clock requirements can therefore give clearer compiler error messages.

More generally, requirements and concepts help to give better diagnostics when code using templates does not compile. In the last chapter, we used `auto` in listing 3.15 to pass a message provider:

```
void guess_number_with_clues(int number, auto message)
```

We started with an `std::function` but needed something more general. The function tries to call or *invoke* the `message` parameter. If we passed something that is not invocable, we would get an error when the message is used, a distance from where we passed something inappropriate. For example, calling

```
guess_number_with_clues(number, "Help!");
```

from `main` would complain inside the function. Visual Studio 2022 says, `"term does not evaluate to a function taking two arguments"`; the term being "Help!" We can add `invocable` from the `concept` header to the function signature, stating the message should be callable with two `int`s:

```
void guess_number_with_clues(int number,
        std::invocable<int, int> auto message)
```

With this addition, the compiler pinpoints the problem more precisely. Visual Studio 2022 says, "`message : 'guess_number_with_clues'`: `the associated constraints are not satisfied`". Rather than just telling us a term is wrong, it has stated which parameter is wrong and why.

We have only scratched the surface here. Watch out for the word requirements, try out some of the other concepts, and try writing your own. Now that we have a better understanding of clocks and durations, we will improve our countdown to the last day of the year by reporting back the duration in various units.

4.2.5 *How many days until the last day of the year?*

In listing 4.2, we found the current time and used a `year_month_day`, hardcoding each value, including the year, to calculate

```
std::chrono::duration dur = event - now;
```

We printed out the value, but we got a huge number in fractions of a second.

We can now convert this to a duration in days and also use the current year instead of hardcoding 2022. Starting with the current `time_point` from `system_clock`'s `now` method gives us a date and time. We cannot assign this directly to a `year_month_day` because this would lose the time part. We can explicitly truncate the time part by flooring `now` first; then we can create another `year_month_day` object and find out the current year. Pulling this together, we can find out how many days there are until the last day of the year.

> **Listing 4.7 Finding how many days there are until the last day of the year**

```
void countdown()
{
    using namespace std::chrono;
    time_point now = system_clock::now();

    const auto ymd = year_month_day{          Floors now
        floor<days>(now)                      to days
    };

    auto this_year = ymd.year();              Uses the current year
    auto new_years_eve = this_year / December / 31;

    auto event = sys_days(new_years_eve);
    duration dur = event - now;
    std::cout << duration_cast<days>(dur)     Converts
            << " until event \n ";            to days
}

int main()
{
    countdown();
}
```

Running this code tells us how many days there are until the last day of the year:

```
343d until event
```

Calling the stream insertion `operator<<` adds a `'d'` suffix to the number. As we noted earlier, just after listing 4.2, some older compilers do not support the `operator <<`, so we would either need to use the `date` library instead or call `count` and spell out the units ourselves:

```
std::cout << std::chrono::duration_cast<std::chrono::days>(dur).count()
        << " days\n";
```

We have our countdown to the last day of the year, but there is still more to learn. We can now write a different countdown, using the `last` operator from `chrono`, to find the last Friday in a month. Maybe you get paid then, so finding out how many days to payday could be useful.

4.2.6   *Using last to find how long to payday*

December always has 31 days, but we could use `last` instead:

```
auto new_years_eve = 2023y / std::chrono::December / std::chrono::last;
```

This is useful if we want to find the last day of February, which could be the 28th or 29th. We could try to work this out ourselves, but `chrono` does the work for us. `last` was introduced in C++20. It is an instance of a very simple `struct`, known as a *tag type* (http://mng.bz/NVax):

```
struct last_spec
{
    explicit last_spec() = default;
};
inline constexpr last_spec last{};
```

Tag types are used to help pick overloads of functions. Operator slash—`operator/`— has many overloads, including several taking a `last_spec`. For example:

```
constexpr year_month_day_last operator/( const year_month& ym, last_spec);
```

Each `operator/` takes two parameters. We had a year, month, and `last`, so

```
this_year / std::chrono::December / std::chrono::last;
```

is using the operator twice:

```
(this_year / std::chrono::December) / std::chrono::last;
```

First, we combine the year and month to get a `year_month`, and that value is used with the `last` struct to create a `year_month_day_last`. We can use C++ Insights again to hint at what's hiding under the hood when we use

```
auto new_years_eve = 2023y / std::chrono::December / std::chrono::last;
```

The insight generated is

```
std::chrono::year_month_day_last new_years_eve =
 operator/
     (operator/(std::operator""y(2023ULL), std::chrono::December),
     std::chrono::last_spec(std::chrono::last));
```

(See https://cppinsights.io/s/84b34f6d.)
The two `operator/` calls are made obvious,
and they give us a `year_month_day_last`
type. C++ Insights has a link to the Compiler
Explorer, which will show us more (https://
godbolt.org/z/qroM6xoT1). In figure 4.2,
we can see that the value of the day has not
been calculated.

```
main:
        push    rbp
        mov     rbp, rsp
        mov     WORD PTR [rbp-4], 2023
        mov     BYTE PTR [rbp-2], 12
        mov     eax, 0
        pop     rbp
        ret
```

**Figure 4.2   Output for GCC 12.2 on the
Compiler Explorer**

We can see instructions on the left and
operands on the right. The actual instruc-
tions vary between dialects. In figure 4.2, move, spelled `mov`, moves data between a
register and memory, so `mov rbp, rsp` moves what was pushed to `rbp` to `rsp`. `eax` is
another register, used for returned values. `push` pushes operands onto the stack. `pop`
pops them. The instruction `ret` returns from a function. Jason Turner's C++ Weekly
episode 34 introduces reading assembly language, if you want more details (see
https://www.youtube.com/watch?v=my39Gpt6bvY). You don't need to be able to read
assembly code to see that we have a 2023 and a 12, but no 31. The value 31 is not
required when `year_month_day_last` is created. Until we try to find out the day or
stream this out, we do not care. The `chrono` library makes a huge effort to be as efficient as possible.

Having looked briefly under the hood for a few more details on how to create a
date, we will now use `last` a bit more for practice. The `last` `struct` will tell us the
date of the last day of February, as we noted:

```
auto end_of_feb = 2023y / std::chrono::February / std::chrono::last;
```

The 28th or 29th is not calculated unless used. We can use `last` in other ways too.
Chrono also provides a `weekday_last`, which can be used in conjunction with a
`weekday_indexed`. We can use these directly or use the `operator[]` (http://mng.bz/
E96D) to find the first Monday of the year or the last Friday of a month. To find the
last Friday, or indeed any specific day of a month, we say

```
auto last_friday_in_year = this_year / December / Friday[last];
```

If we stream this out, we get

```
2023/Dec/Fri[last]
```

Again, the `last` is used to pick an appropriate overload and does no calculations. We
still need to say the month because `last` applies to days or weekdays. We could also say

KA 843 1770

Friday[1] to find the first Friday. A `weekday_indexed` takes a value in the range [1, 5] to mean the first, second, third, fourth, or fifth weekday of some month, so it is 1 rather than 0 based.

Let's write another countdown. Suppose you get paid on the last Friday of the month. How many days until payday? We have all the parts we need. Armed with the current time and the last Friday of the current month, we can use `sys_days` like we did before to make a date and then find the duration.

Listing 4.8   Days until payday

```
void pay_day()
{
    using namespace std::chrono;

    time_point now = system_clock::now();
    const auto ymd = year_month_day{        Current year,
        floor<days>(now)                    month, day
    };

    auto pay_day = ymd.year() / ymd.month() / Friday[last];    Last Friday of the
    auto event = sys_days(pay_day);                            current month
    duration dur = event - now;
    std::cout << duration_cast<days>(dur)      Subtract to find the
        << " until pay_day \n";                days until payday.
}

int main()
{
    pay_day();
}
```

Five days to go at the time of writing, and possibly a few hours, but we rounded down by using `duration_cast`. We have two countdowns and have covered a lot of ground. We haven't written any tests, though. Let's pause to think about how to test code using times and dates.

4.2.7   Writing testable code

We could stop here, as we have the countdown we set out to make and more. However, this code writes the output straight to the screen, which makes it hard to test. It also uses the current date and time directly, which often causes problems in tests. We can do better. Once we have improved the code, we will call it in a loop to watch time ticking down to the end of the year.

If we return the duration, the calling code can do what it wants with the value, and this makes testing the code easier. If we also pass in the value of `now`, we can vary the time for tests. Calling the current time inside a function makes it notoriously hard to test. At the extreme, I watched someone write a test that they claimed would take 24 hours to run because they wanted to check the difference between results over a day in a financial calculation. I suggested passing in the required times, rather than calling `now` and waiting for a day. You probably have similar stories too.

Our testable countdown will return the duration. In addition, if we mark the function as `constexpr`, we can use a static assert in some tests. Let's use `last` instead of 31 this time for practice. Apart from sending in the current date–time, the code is similar to the code in listing 4.7, but more flexible.

> ### Listing 4.9   A testable countdown

```
constexpr                                    ◁──┤ Possible at compile time
std::chrono::system_clock::duration
      countdown(std::chrono::system_clock::time_point start)   ◁──┐ Passes in a
{                                                                  │ time point
    using namespace std::chrono;

    auto days_only = floor<days>(start);

    const auto ymd = year_month_day{days_only};

    auto this_year = ymd.year();
    auto new_years_eve = this_year / December / last;

    auto event = sys_days(new_years_eve);
    return event - start;           ◁──┐ Returns a
}                                        │ duration

int main()
{
    std::cout << countdown(std::chrono::system_clock::now())
              << " until event \n";
}
```

We can now test our function more easily and even use `static_assert` to provoke compile time errors like we have done before.

> ### Listing 4.10   Checking the countdown function

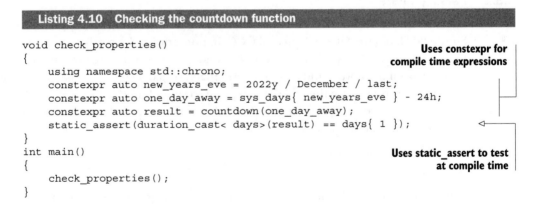

```
void check_properties()                         Uses constexpr for
{                                          compile time expressions
    using namespace std::chrono;
    constexpr auto new_years_eve = 2022y / December / last;
    constexpr auto one_day_away = sys_days{ new_years_eve } - 24h;
    constexpr auto result = countdown(one_day_away);
    static_assert(duration_cast< days>(result) == days{ 1 });   ◁──┐
}
int main()                                    Uses static_assert to test
{                                                      at compile time
    check_properties();
}
```

We have covered several central C++ ideas so far. We can sit back and watch some time tick by if we call our countdown on a loop and show seconds instead of days. If we include the `thread` header, we can `sleep` for a while between each call, using the chrono literals to specify how long for (e.g., `5000ms`). That's quite nice, don't you think? Try it out!

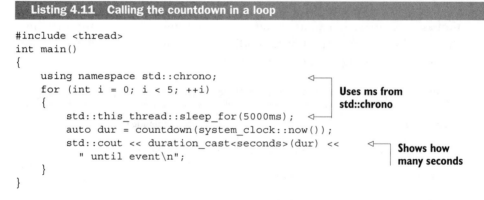

Listing 4.11   Calling the countdown in a loop

```
#include <thread>
int main()
{
    using namespace std::chrono;              ⟵ Uses ms from
    for (int i = 0; i < 5; ++i)                 std::chrono
    {
        std::this_thread::sleep_for(5000ms);  ⟵
        auto dur = countdown(system_clock::now());
        std::cout << duration_cast<seconds>(dur) <<   ⟵ Shows how
          " until event\n";                              many seconds
    }
}
```

If we run this, we see seconds until the end of the year tick down for a while:

```
4343635s until event
4343630s until event
4343625s until event
4343620s until event
4343615s until event
```

We hardcoded New Year's Eve, initially with a fixed year, and then learned how to generalize to the current year. We also saw how to find how long it is until the last Friday of a month. We haven't read in a date yet, though.

4.3   Input, output, and formatting

If we input an event date, we can make our countdown more general. How do we read a date from a stream?

4.3.1   Parsing a date

We can use the parse method from chrono to read a date. This is supported in Visual Studio 2022, but the latest Clang and GCC do not support the method, so you will need to use the date library mentioned at the end of section 4.1. Again, include "date/date.h" from the library and change std::chrono::parse to date::parse in what follows. Don't forget to use the -I switch to point to your cloned date/include directory.

We can choose the format required; for example, %Y-%m-%d for a hyphen-separated four-digit year, month, and day:

```
std::chrono::year_month_day date;
std::cin >> std::chrono::parse("%Y-%m-%d", date);
```

If the format entered does not match the expected format, the stream is in error, which we can check for.

We could also use the from_stream method, which takes the stream as a parameter, like this:

```
std::chrono::from_stream(std::cin, "%Y-%m-%d", date);
```

There are several overloads for `parse` and `from_stream` to cover times, including `sys_time`, and the year, a month, a day, and so on. In essence, each overload of `parse` maps to a corresponding `from_stream`, so you can use whichever suits you.

We can add a function using the `parse` method to allow a user to enter an event date and report back how long until this happens. The input might be invalid, so we need a way to deal with that situation. In listing 3.4, we wrote a function called `read_number`, taking an `std::istream` and returning an `std::optional<int>` to handle invalid input. We can use a similar pattern here, clearing invalid input if something goes wrong. While we have literals fresh in our mind, we will use the `operator""s` to make the format an `std::string`. We do not *need* to do this because a format specifier of `"%Y-%m-%d"` works, but it's worth knowing how to make a string directly. This operator lives in the `std::string_literals` namespace in the `string` header, so we need to include this header. We also need to include the `optional` header so we can write the following function to read a date.

Listing 4.12 Reading a date

```
#include <optional>
#include <string>
std::optional<std::chrono::year_month_day> read_date(std::istream& in)
{
    using namespace std::string_literals;       | Uses ""s to
    auto format_str = "%Y-%m-%d"s;              | create a string
    std::chrono::year_month_day date;
    if (in >> std::chrono::parse(format_str, date))    ◁─┐ Is the input
    {                                                    | valid?
        return date;        ◁─┐ Returns a
    }                         | valid date
    in.clear();               ◁─┤ Clears invalid input
    std::cout << "Invalid format. Expected " <<
            format_str  << '\n';
    return {};               ◁─┐ Returns optional
}                              | with no value
```

In listing 4.9, we used a hardcoded event date in the `countdown` function, so we need a new function that takes the date a user provides. If you are using the `date` library instead of `chrono`, switch the `using` namespace in the next listing to

```
using namespace date;
```

instead. Pass in the chosen date as a second parameter.

Listing 4.13 Countdown to any event

```
constexpr std::chrono::system_clock::duration
countdown_to(std::chrono::system_clock::time_point now,
    std::chrono::year_month_day date)
```

```
{
    using namespace std::chrono;
    auto event = sys_days(date);
    return event - now;
}
```

By reading in a date, we can make a general-purpose countdown. We should think about how we want to display the output because this gives us another opportunity to use format.

4.3.2 *Formatting time points and durations*

We can call the countdown from listing 4.13 from main once we have read in the chosen event date. If we get input into a string, we don't need to mop up any invalid characters, as they have been read into the string. Because we get an optional value back, we check that this is okay before calling our countdown. If we want the output in days, we need to cast the duration to days.

Listing 4.14   A general-purpose countdown

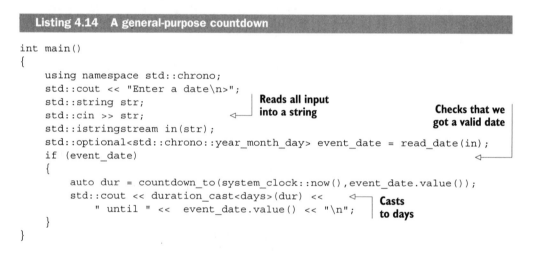

```
int main()
{
    using namespace std::chrono;
    std::cout << "Enter a date\n";
    std::string str;                                        Reads all input
    std::cin >> str;                                        into a string
    std::istringstream in(str);                                                        Checks that we
    std::optional<std::chrono::year_month_day> event_date = read_date(in);             got a valid date
    if (event_date)
    {
        auto dur = countdown_to(system_clock::now(),event_date.value());
        std::cout << duration_cast<days>(dur) <<        Casts
            " until " <<  event_date.value() << "\n";    to days
    }
}
```

Of course, we could use any other time period. Furthermore, we can use std::format instead of a duration or time_point. This gives us a choice about how to report the duration, as well as how to display the date. If we want the duration in seconds, we use :%S, and for a four-digit year, followed by a month, then a day, we can either use :%Y-%m-%d or the shortcut :%F:

```
std::cout << std::format("{:%S} until {:%F}\n", dur, date);
```

Several format strings are available for durations and time points (see http://mng.bz/84gW). If you can't find what you need, you can drop back to the duration casts we initially used or pull out parts of the date you need from a time point. The chrono library is powerful and flexible, and there is usually more than one way to do what you need.

We have a countdown; in fact, we have a few countdowns. Now, it's all very well reporting how many seconds until an event; however, if daylight savings happens between now and then, our output will be incorrect. The system clock works in coordinated universal time (UTC), so we need to use a time zone to take local time into account.

4.4 *Time zones*

British Summer Time (BST) began at 2 a.m. on March 27 in 2022. If we call our general `countdown_to` method to find out how many hours there are between 3 a.m. on 27th and the next day

```
auto got = countdown_to(sys_days{ 2022y / March / 27 } + 3h,
                             { 2022y / March / 28 });
auto got_hours_bst = duration_cast<hours>(got);
```

we get 21 hours, 3 hours less than a full 24-hour day. On the face of it, this is fine; however, our countdown is taking the current time in UTC. In BST, it would be 4 a.m., and so there would only be 20 hours left. C++20 introduced time zones, but they are not widely supported. Visual Studio 2022 and GCC 13.2.0 do support them, but at the time of writing, Clang does not as yet. If you cloned the date library earlier, you need to use the `tz.cpp` file from the library to use the time zones. We have only used features in the header file so far, but the time zones need this source file too. Rainer Grimm's website has instructions for compiling and using the library (http://mng.bz/ 9Qe0), as do Howard Hinnant's GitHub pages (http://mng.bz/K9XE). You also need to use namespace `date` instead of `chrono`.

We can convert a system time to a `zoned_time` using a time zone and calling `get_local_time`. We can choose a time zone by name and pair that with a time point to make a zoned time:

```
zoned_time("Europe/London", when).get_local_time();
```

The names come from the Internet Assigned Numbers Authority (IANA) time zone (tz) database (https://www.iana.org/time-zones). If the location does not exist, we get an exception. Alternatively, we can use `current_zone()` to get the local time for the current time zone. If we stick with a function taking a system time and event date, and returning a duration like we had in listing 4.13, we need to convert the event to a `zoned_time` and find the difference in `sys_time`. Arithmetic with `local_time` ignores time shifts. For example, if we have a meeting at 9 a.m. local time every day, then adding one day in `local_time` gives 9 a.m. local the next day, even if there is an intervening UTC offset shift. We want to know the physical difference in time, so we use `sys_time`. The return type has the precision of the difference between the `event` and now, which is `system_clock::duration:`.

Listing 4.15 Countdown in local time

```
std::chrono::system_clock::duration
countdown_in_local_time(std::chrono::system_clock::time_point now,
    std::chrono::year_month_day date)
```

```
{
    using namespace std::chrono;
    auto sys_event = zoned_time(current_zone(),
                    local_days{ date }).get_sys_time();
    return sys_event - now;
}
```

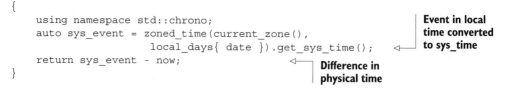

Event in local time converted to sys_time

Difference in physical time

This countdown takes daylight savings into account.

We have only scratched the surface of chrono. Howard Hinnant has written a list of examples (http://mng.bz/0lnW) if you need to work out how to do something not covered here.

We practiced reading input and using format for output. We also used the literal suffix. One thing we have not done yet is written our own class, so we will do that in the next chapter, creating a deck of playing cards to make another game.

Summary

- There are various clocks, each supporting a now method that returns a time_point.
- The system clock is not steady, so it might go backward if the system time is changed.
- Use a year_month_day to access year, month, or date fields and turn it into a time_point using sys_days.
- Durations are defined by a numeric type and a ratio, telling us which units they are in. An std::ratio<1> means seconds, while std::ratio<60> means minutes.
- Durations can be implicitly converted if the conversion will not lose precision; otherwise, we must use a duration_cast.
- We can define our own durations.
- chrono provides literal suffixes, such as operator""s for seconds.
- We can use operator/ to form a year_month_day using the literals to create dates, such as 2022y / December / last.
- A time point consists of a clock and a duration.
- Requirements can be used for templates to help provide clearer diagnostic messages when template code fails to compile.
- A concept is a named set of requirements.
- We can write dates and durations to streams using operator<<. Durations append the literal for their units; for example, 'd' for days.
- Use parse or from_stream to read a date or time.
- The format library also supports time_point and duration.
- System times can be converted to local zones using current_zone() or a named time zone and take daylight savings into account.

5

Creating and using objects and arrays

In this chapter, we will create a deck of cards and write a higher-or-lower card game for guessing whether the next card from a deck is higher or lower. We will create a class for a card and store a deck of cards in an `array`. We need to consider how to define comparison operators for our cards, as well as how to write constructors and other member functions. We'll need to use a random shuffle too. We will then extend the game to include jokers and learn how to use `std::variant`. By the end of the chapter, we will have a working card game and be ready to do more with classes.

5.1   *Creating a deck of playing cards*

We will start by defining a card class. We can declare a card using either the keyword `class` or `struct`. If we use a `struct`, everything is public by default, which is a simple starting point. A card has a suit and a value. There are four suits and 13 possible values per suit: 1, or ace; 2 up to 10; and three court cards. We will also need to display and compare cards, as well as a way to create a whole deck. We will start with the cards themselves.

Up to now, we have put all our code in a `main.cpp` file. For this chapter, we will make a header file, called `playing_cards.h`, and include it in our `main.cpp`. As we add functions, most of them will go into a `playing_cards.cpp` source file. Let's take a moment to remind ourselves of the basics of using source and header files. When we use header files, we always need an *include guard*. This stops a header file from being included more than once in the same source file, which can lead to problems, including violation of the *one definition rule*. Without the guard, including the same header twice, which can easily happen indirectly if one header includes another, means enums, structures, and so on will be defined twice, which is not allowed. This is nothing new. CppReference provides more details on this topic (http://mng.bz/z0Rg). Some people still use macros for include or header guards, picking a unique name.

Listing 5.1   Macro-style include guards

```
#ifndef PLAYING_CARDS_HEADER
#define PLAYING_CARDS_HEADER
...
#endif
```

However, the `pragma` directive `once` is now widely supported. If this directive does not work on your compiler, it's fine to use the macro version. Let's create a namespace for our cards, keeping structures and functions in the `namespace` scope.

Listing 5.2   `playing_cards` header file

```
#pragma once            ⟵─┤ Include guard

namespace cards         ⟵─┐ Namespace for
{                          │ subsequent declarations
}
```

Finally, we include this header in `main.cpp`, using quotation marks, `""`, rather than angle brackets, `<>`, which indicate it is ours rather than a library header. The specifics of where the search for an included header file is conducted are implementation defined, but the quoted version searches where the angled-bracket version would if its initial search fails. People often use angled brackets for standard library headers and quotation marks for their own headers. Our main function doesn't do much yet, but we now have places to put our code.

Listing 5.3   Including the header file

```
#include "playing_cards.h"    ◁──┐  Includes
                                  │  our header
int main()
{
}
```

We are now ready to create some playing cards for our game.

5.1.1 Defining a card type using a scoped enum for the suit

We know we need a suit and a value for each playing card. We can use integers for the value initially, and although we could use an integer for the suit too, using an enum is clearer. C++11 introduced *scoped enumerations*, which look very similar to the old unscoped enum but have the word class, or, equivalently, struct, between the enum keyword and the name. Add an enum to the playing_cards.h file, with one *enumerator* per suit, inside the namespace.

Listing 5.4   Scope enum for suits

```
#pragma once    ◁──┤ Include guard

namespace cards    ◁──┤ Namespace
{
    enum class Suit {    ◁──┐  Notice the
        Hearts,              │  word class.
        Diamonds,
        Clubs,
        Spades
    };
}
```

The small addition of the word class makes a big difference. Without it, we have an old-style enum and could use Hearts or any of the other values, or enumerators, without qualification. This means we can compare values from different enums by mistake. If two different enums are used to indicate whether a function succeeds, they might both designate success with OK and a failure with one of many values. It then becomes possible to check whether a result is OK, conflating the two different enums. To use our suit, we need to say Suit::Hearts, making potential unintended comparisons impossible.

There is no implicit conversion from the values of a scoped enumerator to integral types, which was possible with the old enums. We need to explicitly use a cast if we want to use the value as a number. Scoped enums are safer.

We begin with a struct to hold value and suit for an initial card type inside the namespace in the header file.

Listing 5.5   A card structure

```
struct Card
{
    int value;
    Suit suit;
};
```

We can then create a card with a value and a suit in `main`, provided we include our header and use the `cards` namespace. We will use *aggregate initialization*, which looks remarkably like the uniform initialization using an initializer list. We used this in chapter 2 to make the first row of Pascal's triangle: `std::vector<int> data{1}`. Aggregate initialization is different, though. The initializer list is a list of values of the same type, but our aggregate initialization uses a list of different types. Our `Card` struct has an `int` data member, followed by a `Suit`, so we provide these in that order to instantiate a `Card`.

Listing 5.6   Using the `Card` struct

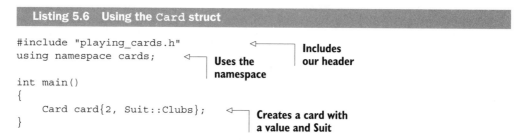

```
#include "playing_cards.h"          Includes
using namespace cards;              our header
                       Uses the
                       namespace
int main()
{
    Card card{2, Suit::Clubs};      Creates a card with
}                                   a value and Suit
```

We can just specify the value, `Card card{2}`, and the suit will be default initialized to the first `enum` value. However, we cannot say `Card card{Suit::Clubs}`. We can leave out initializers toward the end but not at the start.

Had we not used a scoped `enum` for the suit, we would be using two `int`s to make a card and would have to remember which was which. Using `card{2, Suit::Clubs}` is much clearer and less error prone than `card{2, 3}`. As it stands, though, we could use 0 or 14 for the face value of a card. We learned about the whole value idiom in the last chapter when we used a `year_month_day`. We can employ the same idea now by making a type for the card's value and also ensuring only values from 1 to 13 are used. In addition to validating the value used, we will see how to use the type to display the cards easily later on.

5.1.2   *Defining a card type using a strong type for the face value*

The face value needs to take an `int` and store it, providing a getter function, so code can use the value if needed. In the last chapter, we considered the whole-value idiom to create lightweight types to ensure parameters are passed correctly. If we make a `FaceValue` class with an `explicit` constructor, we can't pass an `int` where a function requires a face value. For example, if we have a function with signature

```
void do_something_with_face_value(const cards::FaceValue & value);
```

we cannot call it with an `int`. Instead, we need to create a face value:

```
do_something_with_face_value(cards::FaceValue{ 5 });
```

An `int` cannot be implicitly converted to our new type because the constructor is explicit.

We will throw an exception if the value used is invalid. An `std::invalid_argument` exception from the `stdexcept` header makes sense.

Listing 5.7   A type for a face value

```
#include <stdexcept>
namespace cards
{
    class FaceValue
    {
    public:
        explicit FaceValue(int value) : value_(value)          ◁──┐ Explicit
        {                                                          │ constructor
            if (value_ < 1 || value_ > 13)
            {
                throw std::invalid_argument(
                        "Face value invalid"
                    );           ◁──┐ Validates
            }                       │ the value
        }
        int value() const
        {
            return value_;
        }
    private:
        int value_;
    };
    ...
}
```

We can then change the type in the `Card` definition from `int  value` to `FaceValue` value. To create a card like we did in listing 5.6, we have to explicitly make a FaceValue, `Card card{ FaceValue(2), Suit::Clubs}`, rather than being able to say `Card card{2, Suit::Clubs}`. We will have to make a tiny bit more effort when we construct a card, but we will get a suit and a valid value for a card if we construct one properly. Before we start using the `FaceValue`, we should think slightly more about how we make cards. Things can still go wrong. Let's revisit our card type, ensuring we only make useful playing cards.

5.1.3   Constructors and default values

Before we use our `FaceValue`, consider our `Card` type defined in listing 5.5. Our struct has two members, an `int` value and a `Suit`. We can create a card without a value or suit:

```
Card dangerous_card;
```

However, the two member fields will not be initialized. If we try to read those fields, we have undefined behavior. In Visual Studio 2022, I happen to get a value of -858993460 and a suit of -858993460 as well in the Debug build. In a release build, I might get different garbage values. The compiler can do as it pleases with such code, so you are likely to get different behavior with another compiler. If we use brace initialization

```
Card less_dangerous_card{};
```

the members are default initialized. We have seen brace or uniform initialization before, and remembering to initialize variables is a good habit to get into. We could try to be very careful not to use the uninitialized values, but it's safer to ensure we cannot create dangerous playing cards in the first place. We can adopt a variety of approaches to avoid the uninitialized member variables.

The simplest approach is to use default values to initialize the value and suit. Since C++11, we can use *default member initializers*, giving a default value directly to any members we want to initialize. An integer default initializes to 0, and an enum to the first value.

Listing 5.8   A card structure

```
struct Card
{
    int value{};        Initializes members
    Suit suit{};        with defaults
};
```

Our previously dangerous card now has values, which we can safely read, giving us a 0 of hearts: a very unlikely playing card but with no undefined behavior. If we now use the FaceValue instead, we can't make a card with a value of 0, so we need to choose an acceptable value, say, 1.

Listing 5.9   A card structure

```
struct Card
{                                Initializes FaceValue
    FaceValue value{1};     ←──  with a viable default
    Suit suit{};
};
```

We could use this definition for our game, but let's consider an alternative approach first because we still have potential problems. A struct's members are public by default, which means we can use them directly. We can therefore easily change their values, which might not be a good idea. We can either flag them as private or use the word class instead of struct because the members of a class are private by default then. In either case, we need a way to set the values; otherwise, every card will have the same value. We can add a public constructor, taking a value and a suit, and store them.

If we need these values from outside the `class` or `struct`, we will need to add getters as well. These should be flagged as `const`, as they do not change the `Card` member values. This allows them to be called by a card variable, regardless of whether or not it is `const`. We can either change the name of the original structure or remove it and make a new, improved type in the header file in the namespace.

Listing 5.10   A card class

```
class Card
{
public:
    Card(FaceValue value, Suit suit):        Constructor taking
                                             value and suit
        value_(value),
        suit_(suit)          Stores the value and suit
    {
    }
    FaceValue value() const { return value_; }
    Suit suit() const { return suit_; }          Getters, flagged as const
private:
    FaceValue value_;
    Suit suit_;          Private members
};
```

We can no longer default construct a card. Having written our own constructor taking parameters, we no longer get a default constructor generated for us. The dangerous card we created before is now impossible. Trying

```
Card impossible_card;
```

will not compile. This should also be familiar if you have used C++ before.

We need to default construct cards when we use an `std::array` to build a deck of cards. C++11 introduced a way to *default* default constructors. If we add

```
Card() = default;
```

to the class in listing 5.10, our `impossible_card` then becomes possible. The compiler defines a default constructor, even though we wrote another constructor. We should still add default member initializers for the value and suit like we did before so the default constructor initializes these.

Listing 5.11   A default constructible card

```
class Card
{
public:
    Card() = default;          Default
                               constructor
    Card(FaceValue value, Suit suit):
        value_(value),
        suit_(suit)
    {
```

```
    }
    FaceValue value() const { return value_; }
    Suit suit() const { return suit_; }
private:
    FaceValue value_{1};
    Suit suit_{};                        Member initializers
};
```

We can also mark a constructor as deleted with = delete. This will stop the constructor from being generated. We can do this for any special member function, such as copy or move constructors, assignment operators, or the destructor. Prior to C++11, we often made the functions we wanted to hide private to avoid them being used. Being able to say a function is deleted is much simpler and makes our intentions clear. We will look at the special member functions in more detail in the next chapter. For now, we have a robust card type. We need a way to display a card; then we can move on to create a deck of cards and write our game.

5.1.4   *Displaying playing cards*

To display a card, we want to be able to write

```
std::cout << card << '\n';
```

Therefore, we need to provide a stream insertion operator for our Card type. We wrote a stream insertion operator in listing 2.5. We need an overload taking a reference to an std::ostream as the first parameter and a constant reference to a Card as the second:

```
std::ostream& operator<<(std::ostream & os, const Card & card);
```

We return a reference to the stream so calls can be chained together:

```
std::cout << card << ', ' another_card << '\n';
```

The std::ostream lives in the iostream header, so we include that and add the declaration of our operator to our header file in the namespace.

Listing 5.12   Declaring operator<< for a card

```
#pragma once
#include <iostream>          ⊲──┐ Includes the
                                │ header we use
namespace cards
{                                                          Declares our
    ...                                                      function
    std::ostream& operator<<(std::ostream & os, const Card & card);   ⊲──┘
}
```

We have two data members to stream out. The FaceValue member has a getter called value that we can use to stream out the underlying int. A card's value will show as a number, even if it's an ace or court card. We'll improve on that later. The suit is a scoped `enum`, which we can also stream out as an `int` for now. By default, scoped enums use `int`s for the enumerators, so we can cast the suit to an `int`, using `static_cast`, and stream that out too. Our header file promised a function in a namespace, so we define the function inside `namespace cards` in the source file called `playing_cards.cpp`.

Listing 5.13 Defining `operator << ` for a card

```cpp
#include "playing_cards.h"        ◁──┐   Includes
                                       │   our header
                                                              Defines
namespace cards   ◁──┐   Adds codes inside                   the function
{                    │   a namespace
    std::ostream& operator<<(std::ostream& os, const Card& card)    ◁──────┘
    {
        os << card.value().value()                        ◁──  Gets the
            << " of " << static_cast<int>(card.suit());  ◁──  FaceValue's value
        return os;
    }                                          Casts the enum
}                                                  to an int
```

If you are building this from a prompt, you need to state both `cpp` files for your build command:

```
clang++ --std=c++20 main.cpp playing_cards.cpp -o ./main.out -Wall
```

Armed with `Card card{FaceValue(2), Suit::Clubs}`, we can now write

```cpp
std::cout << card << '\n';
```

and get `2 of 2`. Clubs is the third element in the `enum`, so using a zero-based index does give us 2 for clubs, but seeing `2 of Clubs` would be nicer.

We could update the stream operator for a card, but we may have situations where we only want to show the face value or suit. We could write a stream operator for each, or we could write a `to_string` method. C++11 added `to_string` methods for numeric types. These functions live in the `string` header.

We can write our own `to_string` overloads, one for a `Suit` and one for a `Face-Value`. The declaration for the `Suit` takes a `Suit` and returns a `string`:

```cpp
std::string to_string(Suit suit);
```

As with the other declarations, it belongs in the header file. We also include the `string` header in our header because we are using an `std::string`. So much for the declaration. How do we define the function? In the last chapter, we noted we can use the `operator ""`s from `std::literals` to make an `std::string`. `"Hearts"s` creates an `std::string`, while `"Hearts"` is a char array. This is not a big deal, but we are returning a string, so let's create a string. The simplest approach possible for our `to_string` function is to use a `switch` statement, pairing up enumerators and suits. We add a default to silence potential warnings about a code path without a return statement.

Listing 5.14   Turning an enum value into a string

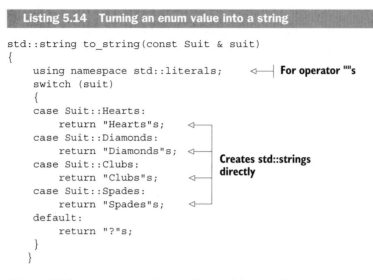

```
std::string to_string(const Suit & suit)
{
    using namespace std::literals;        ⊲─┤ For operator ""s
    switch (suit)
    {
    case Suit::Hearts:
        return "Hearts"s;        ⊲─┐
    case Suit::Diamonds:
        return "Diamonds"s;      ⊲─┤
    case Suit::Clubs:                     Creates std::strings
        return "Clubs"s;         ⊲─┤     directly
    case Suit::Spades:
        return "Spades"s;        ⊲─┘
    default:
        return "?"s;
    }
}
```

We could throw an exception at the end rather than returning a question mark. There are options, but this simple approach is good enough.

> **NOTE** Java and C# enums support a `ToString` method, but C++ does not. If C++ had reflection, we could convert an enum value to a string. However, C++ does not support reflection yet, but there is a technical specification (called TS for short; see https://www.iso.org/deliverables-all.html) for compile time, or static, reflection (http://mng.bz/G9n8). Potential C++ features sometimes have example implementations, and some compilers also offer experimental headers, for example, `<experimental/reflect>` (see http://mng.bz/YRMQ). There is more than one reflection proposal (http://mng.bz/OPjO), so time will tell which approach C++ ends up taking.

We can now get 2 of Clubs when we display the card we created. However, court cards and aces will be displayed as numbers as it stands. Because we created a `FaceValue` type, we can write another `to_string` overload, with special cases for court cards and an ace. Any other value will use the `std::to_string` method for ints. As usual, we declare the function in the header and define it inside our namespace in the playing cards source file.

Listing 5.15   Converting card value to a string

```
std::string to_string(const FaceValue & value)
{
    using namespace std::literals;        ⊲─┤ For operator ""s
    switch (value.value())
    {
    case 1:
        return "Ace"s;           ⊲─┐
    case 11:                             Creates std::strings
        return "Jack"s;          ⊲─┘    directly
    case 12:
```

```
        return "Queen"s;      ◁──┐  Creates std::strings
    case 13:                     │  directly
        return "King"s;       ◁──┘
    default:
        return std::to_string(value.value());  ◁──┐  2 to 9
    }                                              │  as strings
}
```

We can now update our stream insertion operator to use our overloaded `to_string` functions

Listing 5.16   Showing ace, jack, queen, king, or number

```
std::ostream& operator<<(std::ostream& os, const Card& card)
{
    os << to_string(card.value())
        << " of " << to_string(card.suit());   │  Uses our new functions
    return os;
}
```

If we stream out a special value card

```
std::cout << Card{ FaceValue(1), Suit::Hearts } << '\n';
```

we see `Ace of Hearts`. We can make individual cards, so now we need to make a deck of cards.

5.1.5   Using an array to make a deck of cards

We previously used a `vector` when we wanted a collection of elements. The `vector` is great when we have an unknown number of elements, but we know we need 52 cards for a full deck. C++11 introduced the array type (https://en.cppreference.com/w/cpp/container/array) for a fixed-size array. It lives in the `array` header and is defined with a type and a size:

```
template<class T, std::size_t N> struct array;
```

The `vector` took the type of elements, `T`, but `array` also needs a compile time size, `N`. A vector can resize dynamically, but the array size is fixed at compile time to the chosen size. The array has a very small overhead for housekeeping and can be placed on the stack rather than the heap. This is illustrated in figure 5.1.

Our deck of cards can therefore be declared as

```
std::array<Card, 52> deck;
```

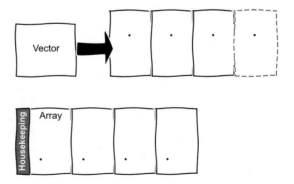

Figure 5.1   A vector has more overhead, places elements on the heap, and can change size dynamically, while an array has a smaller overhead and fixed size.

AL 858 2396

We could use a C-style array, `Card deck[52]`, instead, but the `std::array` keeps us safer because we always know the size of the array. In both cases, we get 52 default constructed cards. With a `vector`, we would `push_back` or `emplace` any new cards we needed, and the `vector` would grow. We can initialize some or all of the cards using aggregate initialization. Thus

```
std::array<Card, 52> deck{Card{FaceValue(2), Suit::Hearts}};
```

puts a 2 of hearts at the start and uses the default constructor for the remaining 51 cards. We can access specific elements like we would in a `vector` or a C-style array, using `operator[]`, so `deck[0]` is the first card. If we need to pass our `array` to a function taking a pointer to the array type (e.g., in a C library function), we can call the `data` member function to obtain a pointer to the underlying data.

Let's write a function to create a deck of cards. We need to include the `array` header, declare the function in our header, and then define it in the source file. We need 13 values for each of the four suits. Unfortunately, we cannot simply iterate over the `Suit` enumeration. Nothing forces the values to be contiguous, even though they are in our case. Using `operator++` might therefore use an invalid enum value in the general case. What we can do instead is put the values into an `initializer_list`. We used brace initialization in chapter 2 when we discussed the uniform initialization syntax. By making an initializer list of the suits

```
{Suit::Hearts, Suit::Diamonds, Suit::Clubs, Suit::Spades}
```

we have an array-like object we can use in a loop. We need to cycle through the 13 face values for each suit. Starting with an iterator at the beginning of the `array`, we can set its contents using `*card` and move to the next card using `++card` each time around the loop.

Listing 5.17   Building a deck of cards

```
std::array<Card, 52> create_deck()
{
    std::array<Card, 52> deck;
    auto card = deck.begin();          ⟵┐  Iterator starting
    for (auto suit :                        with the first card                    Initializer list
        {Suit::Hearts, Suit::Diamonds, Suit::Clubs, Suit::Spades})    ⟵   of suits
    {
        for (int value = 1; value <= 13; value++)    ⟵┤  Cycles round values
        {
            *card = Card{ FaceValue(value), suit };  ⟵┤  Sets the card's values
            ++card;           ⟵┐  Moves to
        }                         next card
    }
    return deck;
}
```

We could use what we have so far to make a card game, but we noted the encouragement to avoid raw loops and prefer algorithms in chapter 2. We can refactor the function in listing 5.17 to create a deck of cards using algorithms instead. We haven't seen any tests in this chapter, but the GitHub code includes a `check_properties` function, similar to the test functions we wrote in previous chapters. Think about what we should test before we refactor the code. Do we get an exception for a card with face value 0? Do we really have 52 distinct cards?

5.1.6 *Using generate to fill the array*

The `algorithm` header includes a method called `generate`, which assigns successive values generated by a function object to a range [`first, last`). C++20 introduced newer versions, including overloads that apply to ranges, so we can use the `std::array<Card, 52> deck` directly, without finding `begin` and `end` ourselves. We can use a lambda as the function object to generate the values:

```
std::ranges::generate(deck, []() { return Card{value, suit}; });
```

We want to cycle through values from 1 to 13, with one of each value per suit. We noted there is no `operator++` for an enum, since that might use an invalid enum value; therefore, we used an initializer list in listing 5.17 to loop over each enumerator. Let's consider an alternative and learn a little more about scoped enums. In our case, the enum values are contiguous, and in fact, when we get to the last suit, we could start back at the beginning, allowing us to use an array of 104 cards to get two decks of cards if we wanted. We can cast the enum value to an `int` using `static_cast` because we noted that a scoped enum has an underlying type, which will be an `int` by default. We declared our `enum` like this

```
enum class Suit
```

in listing 5.4. We can also specify a type if we want to; for example:

```
enum class Suit: short
```

This might save a bit of space if we do not need an integer, and we can even use a `char` if we have very few values. Alternatively, we could use a `long long` if we needed a very long list of enumerators. Rather than casting to `int`, we can use `underlying_type` to decide what to cast to in the general case. We can then pick the next suit and go back to the start when we reach the end.

Listing 5.18 Incrementing our enum

```
Suit& operator++(Suit & suit)                                       Underlying
{                                                                   enum type
    using IntType = typename std::underlying_type<Suit>::type;   ⟵
    if (suit == Suit::Spades)
        suit = Suit::Hearts;        ⟵  Back to first suit           Increments
    else                                                            using a cast
        suit = static_cast<Suit>(static_cast<IntType>(suit) + 1);  ⟵
    return suit;
}
```

This code is relying on contiguous enumerator values, and changing the order of the enumerators would break the code. However, it's worth being aware of the `underlying_type` of a scoped enum.

As with all the code for our cards, we put the function in the playing card source file and declare it in the header file. We can now generate the values needed for our `array`. Whether we use the ranges version of `generate` or the `begin`/`end` version, we need to include the `algorithm` header. We start with a card value of one, incrementing for each card generated. If the value is greater than 13, we drop back to one and increment the suit. All of this happens in a lambda, so we capture the value and suit by reference, using `[&value, &suit]`. The `generate` function calls the lambda once per item in the deck, assigning the generated card to each element.

Listing 5.19   Generating the deck of cards

```cpp
#include <algorithm>
std::array<Card, 52> create_deck()
{
    std::array<Card, 52> deck;
    int value = 1;
    Suit suit = Suit::Hearts;          // Starts with ace of hearts
    std::ranges::generate(deck, [&value, &suit]() {    // Captures by ref
        if (value > 13)
        {
            value = 1;                 // Resets value and
            ++suit;                    // increments suit
        }
        return Card{FaceValue(value++), suit};   // Lambda returns a Card and increments value
    });
    return deck;
}
```

We have a full deck of playing cards, so we are nearly ready to build our game. First, we need to be able to compare two cards to decide if one is higher or lower than the other.

5.1.7   Comparison operators and defaults

There are six possible comparisons for a type:

- *Equal* (`==`)
- *Not equal* (`!=`)
- *Less than* (`<`)
- *Greater than* (`>`)
- *Less than or equal* (`<=`)
- *Greater than or equal* (`>=`)

C++ has allowed us to write our own comparison operators for a long time. For example, we can implement a less-than operator inline in the class definition.

Listing 5.20 Less-than operator for a `Card`

```
bool operator<(const Card& other) const
{
    return value < other.value.value() && suit < other.suit;
}
```

We can then compare two cards:

```
Card{FaceValue(2), Hearts} < Card{FaceValue(3), Hearts}
```

Whether we want to include the suit in the comparison might be a discussion point because some card games treat one suit as more valuable than another. More importantly, we would expect greater than or equal (`operator >=`) to return the opposite. However

```
Card{FaceValue(2), Hearts} >= Card{FaceValue(3), Hearts}
```

doesn't compile. If we write a less-than operator, the other comparisons are not generated for us. We could write all the comparison operators ourselves, but this is tedious and error prone. C++20 introduced `operator<=>`, sometimes called the *spaceship operator* because it looks somewhat like a spaceship, to make our lives easier. The spaceship operator gives one of three possible values and is therefore also known as a *three-way comparison operator*:

- $x <=> y < 0$ if $x < y$
- $x <=> y > 0$ if $x > y$
- $x <=> y == 0$ if x is equal y

The return type is an *order category type*. The full details are involved, but for an integral type, such as an `int` or our `Suit` enum, we get an `std::strong_ordering` back, defined in the `compare` header (see http://mng.bz/p1D0). We can use the keyword `auto`, rather than looking up which specific return type we need to use. This result can in turn be transformed automatically into one of the six two-way comparison operators. Now, we could implement the spaceship operator ourselves, but we can also mark it with the keyword `default`. If we do this, the compiler generates all the comparisons for us. The default comparison operators will use the fields in the order defined in the class, so both the value and the suit are compared. The fields, therefore, need to be comparable, so we also need a spaceship operator in our `FaceValue`. The default version will then be able to compare the values of two `FaceValues`, using the `value_` member, which is exactly what we require.

We need to add the `compare` header first, which works out the return type and synthesizes the comparison operators for us. We then add a single line to both our `FaceValue` and `Card` definitions and, finally, have what we need.

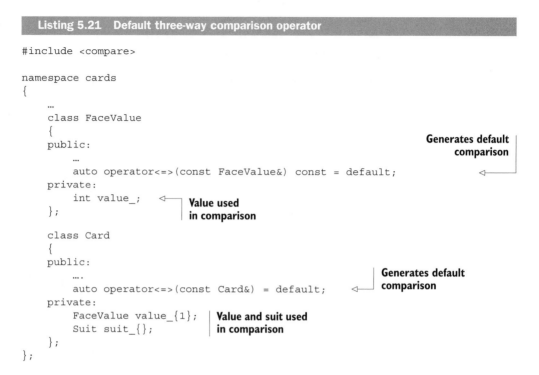

Listing 5.21   Default three-way comparison operator

```
#include <compare>

namespace cards
{
    ...
    class FaceValue
    {
    public:
        ...
        auto operator<=>(const FaceValue&) const = default;    ← Generates default
    private:                                                     comparison
        int value_;    ← Value used
    };                   in comparison

    class Card
    {
    public:
        ....
        auto operator<=>(const Card&) = default;    ← Generates default
    private:                                          comparison
        FaceValue value_{1};    Value and suit used
        Suit suit_{};           in comparison
    };
};
```

That took very little effort to add six comparison operators to both of our types. As we used 1 for an ace, this defaulted operator means aces are the lowest card. We could write our own comparison instead, or use the values 2 to 14, making 14 the ace and therefore the card with the highest value. Feel free to do that instead for extra practice. Armed with a deck of cards and a way to compare cards, we can now create a card game of higher or lower.

5.2   *Higher-or-lower card game*

When we create our deck of cards, they run in order, so we can work out what comes next. Randomizing the order would make the game more interesting, so we need a way to shuffle the cards.

5.2.1   *Shuffling the deck*

We've used random numbers before; however, we now want a random shuffle, rather than a sequence of random numbers. The `algorithm` header has the method we need. If we look at CppReference (http://mng.bz/eEjZ), we see `random_shuffle` and `shuffle` methods. Each of the `random_shuffle` versions has been deprecated or removed. One version used C's `rand` function, which is likely to be deprecated at some point. We have seen how much better the C++ random number generators are. Using `rand` can depend on the global state, which causes problems for multithreaded code. Some naïve implementations of `random_shuffle` also used `rand() % i` for an index `i` to swap elements. Whenever we use a modulus for a random number, we are in danger of skewing a distribution. Stephan Lavavej gave a talk back in 2013 titled "rand() Considered Harmful" (see http://mng.bz/g7Dn), explaining why we should avoid using `rand` in conjunction with `%`. If we wanted to simulate a dice roll, using `rand() % 6` would not give us a uniform distribution because `MAX_INT` is not a multiple of six. Lower dice rolls will therefore be slightly more likely. Try it.

Avoiding the deprecated shuffles leaves us with `std::shuffle`. This requires items to shuffle and a random number generator. We can either pass `begin` and `end` to `std::shuffle` or use the range variant, `std::ranges::shuffle`, on our deck of cards directly. We will use `random_device` to seed an `mt19937` generator, like we have done before. We need to include the `algorithm` and `random` headers for `shuffle` and a random generator, respectively. We need to pass the deck by reference so we can change it.

Listing 5.22 Shuffling the cards

```
#include <algorithm>
#include <random>
void shuffle_deck(std::array<Card, 52> & deck)          ◁──┐ Passes deck
{                                                             by reference
    std::random_device rd;                        ┌── Seeds the random
    std::mt19937 gen{ rd() };         ◁───────────┘   number generator
    std::ranges::shuffle(deck, gen);         ◁──┐ Shuffles
}                                                 the deck
```

For a card game that requires several shuffles, it would be sensible to have a class with a shuffle method, setting up the generator in the constructor. Nonetheless, the simple approach in listing 5.22 is sufficient for our higher-or-lower card game. We now have a way to shuffle a deck of cards, so we can build our game.

5.2.2 Building the game

We will show the first card in the deck and ask the player whether the next card will be higher or lower, and we will continue until we run out of cards or the player is wrong. We can use a single character, `'h'` for higher or `'l'` for lower, so the player doesn't need to type much:

```
char c;
std::cin >> c;
```

We compare the current card and the next card, relying on the automatically generated `operator<` and `operator>` given by default from the three-way comparison in listing 5.21 to see whether the guess is correct.

Listing 5.23 Checking whether the guess is correct

```
bool is_guess_correct(char guess, const Card & current, const Card & next)
{
    return (guess == 'h' && next > current)
```

```
                    || (guess == 'l' && next < current);
}
```

The game starts with the first card in the deck. We can find the first card in the array in various ways, but it might be nice to keep track of how many guesses are correct and report this when the game is over. We can use this count to index into the array, as we would with a C-style array, and the index will tell us how far we are through the deck. We'll run through all the cards in the deck but stop if an incorrect guess is made. Pulling this together gives us our higher-or-lower card game function.

Listing 5.24 Higher-or-lower card game

```
void higher_lower()
{
    auto deck = create_deck();
    shuffle_deck(deck);

    size_t index = 0;
    while (index + 1 < deck.size())          ◁──┐ Loops around
    {                                             remaining 51 cards
        std::cout << deck[index]             ◁──┤ Shows current card
            << ": Next card higher (h) or lower (l)?\n>";
        char c;
        std::cin >> c;
        bool ok = guess_correct(c, deck[index], deck[index + 1]);  ◁──┐ Checks
        if (!ok)                                                        the guess
        {
            std::cout << "Next card was " << deck[index + 1] << '\n';
            break;           ◁──┐ Drops out of
        }                         loop if wrong
        ++index;
    }
    std::cout << "You got " << index << " correct\n";   ◁──┐ Shows how many
}                                                            are correct
```

Higher or lower annotates the `std::cin >> c;` line.

Again, we'll define this in the playing card source file and declare it in our header file. We then call it from `main`.

Listing 5.25 Our game

```
#include "playing_cards.h"
int main()
{
    cards::higher_lower();
}
```

Don't forget, aces are the lowest value, and the suits have an order too. It is difficult to get more than a handful correct. A typical game might play out like this:

```
9 of Spades: Next card higher (h) or lower (l)?
>l
```

```
4 of Hearts: Next card higher (h) or lower (l)?
>h
Next card was Ace of Hearts
You got 1 correct
```

We have a working card game. We created a simple structure and used it in an array. We let C++ do most of the work for us, generating the comparison we needed to decide if a card was higher or lower. We could stop here, but some card games use jokers as well. A joker does not have a suit or value, so how can we add jokers to our deck of cards?

5.2.3   *Using std::variant to support cards or jokers*

The simplest way to define a joker is as an empty struct.

Listing 5.26   A joker

```
struct Joker
{
};
```

That is all we need.

We know how to make a deck of 52 playing cards:

```
std::array<Card, 52> cards = create_deck();
```

How do we add two jokers? We can't add jokers to this deck because they are a different type. We could make a common base type and use pointers for dynamic polymorphism, but that seems over the top. A much simpler approach would be an array of one of two types: cards or jokers. The std::variant, introduced in C++17, makes this possible. It lives in the variant header and behaves like a union, but it is safer. C's union type has a sequence of possible members.

Listing 5.27   A union

```
union CardOrJoker
{
    Card card;
    Joker joker;
};
```

The union is big enough to hold the largest type used. To access a Card from this union, you use the card member, and for a Joker, use the joker member, but you need to track which type is in use. In contrast, a variant knows which type it currently holds, so the variant is often described as a *type-safe union*.

We declare a variant by stating which types it can hold:

```
std::variant<Card, Joker>
```

The `variant` is a class template defined as a *variadic template*. We will look at these in more detail in the last chapter, but for now, notice the three dots in the definition:

```
template <class... Types>
class variant;
```

The dots are called a *parameter pack*, allowing us to use zero or more template arguments. This allows us to define a variant with the two types we need. We used `std::optional` in chapter 3 to handle input, which only needed one type. Declaring an `optional` without assigning a value

```
std::optional<Card> card;
```

has no value. If we use this card in a Boolean context, it will evaluate to false, so we could make an `optional` work, but the code might be hard to follow. We'd need to remember that `if(!card)` meant we had a joker. How do we use a `variant`, then?

A `variant` is initialized to the first of the alternative types, provided that type can be default constructed. If it can't, we get a compile error. Both of our types can be default constructed, so that won't happen here. So using

```
std::variant<Card, Joker> card;
```

gives us a default constructed `Card` because that's the first type. We could also create a `Joker` instead:

```
std::variant<Card, Joker> joker{ Joker{} };
```

In fact, there are various ways to create a variant. We can avoid making a temporary `Joker{}` to construct the variant using the `std::in_place_index` function. For a `Joker`, we want index 1 and do not have any arguments for the joker's constructor, so we'll use `std::in_place_index` with value 1:

```
std::variant<Card, Joker> joker2(std::in_place_index<1>);
```

For a `Card`, we use the zero index and pass the value and suit to the `Card` constructor:

```
std::variant<Card, Joker> two_of_clubs(std::in_place_index<0>,
                            FaceValue(2), Suit::Clubs);
```

For further details, see http://mng.bz/amzY.

We can determine whether we have a joker by checking the variant's type:

```
bool is_joker = std::holds_alternative<Joker>(two_of_clubs);
```

There are various ways to retrieve the values. For example, we can use `get` with an index:

```
Card from_variant = std::get<0>(two_of_clubs);
```

If we try to get a `Joker` instead

```
Joker from_variant = std::get<1>(two_of_clubs);
```

an `std::bad_variant_access` is thrown. Alternatively, we can use `get_if` to avoid the exception. Rather than an index, we can use a type, `std::get<Card>(two_of_clubs)`, which saves having to remember the order of the types. CppReference gives all the details (https://en.cppreference.com/w/cpp/utility/variant), but we now know enough to make a deck of cards with jokers.

We have used `optional` and have met `variant`. There is a third type, called `std::any`, which lives in the `any` header. All three types were introduced in C++17 and offer slightly different alternatives to similar problems. As the name suggests, we can use `any` for almost anything, specifically any copy-constructible type. An `any` variable can be switched to other types as needed:

```
std::any some_card = Joker();
some_card = Card{ 2, Suit::Club };
```

We need to use the `any_cast` method to get the value back. If we have a `Card` rather than a `Joker`, calling

```
std::any_cast<Joker>(some_card);
```

would throw an `std::bad_any_cast`.

We could therefore use `any`; however, using `variant` is clearer because we will either have a `Card` or a `Joker`. We could even employ `optional`, using a variable with no value to indicate a `Joker`, but the intent is clearer when we use a `variant`.

5.2.4 Building the game with an extended deck of cards

Let's make an extended deck. First, we need to add jokers to the deck. We can do this in many ways. We met `array` and noted we can initialize some or all of the elements using aggregate initialization. We can therefore make the first two elements `Jokers` like this:

```
std::array<std::variant<Card, Joker>, 54> deck{ Joker{} , Joker{} };
```

We can also make the usual 52 cards like we have done before:

```
std::array<Card, 52> cards = create_deck();
```

If we copy these 52 cards over, we will have a deck of cards with two jokers. We've used `copy` before in chapter 2. There are several variants of copy, which all live in the `algorithm` header. In chapter 2, we met the `ranges::copy` version. We have two jokers at the start of the deck, so we want to copy cards after the two jokers. Therefore, we need to start copying at `begin + 2`, as shown in figure 5.2.

In code, we write

```
std::ranges::copy(cards, deck.begin() + 2);
```

Figure 5.2 With two jokers at the start of our array, we copy cards to `begin + 2`.

We could use `std::copy` instead, using the `begin` and `end` member functions:

```
std::copy(cards.begin(), cards.end(),deck.begin() + 2);
```

We can even use the `begin` and `end` free functions:

```
std::copy(std::begin(cards), std::end(cards), std::begin(new_deck)+2);
```

Some things, like a C-style array, can be iterated but do not have a `begin` or `end` method, in which case these free functions can be used instead. If we use the free functions when member functions are available, they call the member functions for us, so it won't make any difference for us in this case.

We need to include the `variant` header in our header and declare the function. Using the `ranges` version, we can create an extended deck in the playing card source file.

Listing 5.28   Creating an extended deck

```
std::array<std::variant<Card, Joker>, 54> create_extended_deck()
{
    std::array<std::variant<Card, Joker>, 54> deck{Joker{}, Joker{}};    ◁──    Starts with
    std::array<Card, 52> cards = create_deck();                                  two jokers
    std::ranges::copy(cards, deck.begin() + 2);    ◁──   Copies a normal
    return deck;                                          deck after the
}                                                         two jokers
```

We need to shuffle the extended deck of cards. Our original function worked for an array of 52 cards. We now have an array of variants holding either a `Joker` or a card, so we can declare an overloaded function in our header:

```
void shuffle_deck(std::array<std::variant<Card, Joker>, 54>& deck);
```

We can then define the new function.

Listing 5.29   Shuffling an extended deck

```
void shuffle_deck(std::array<std::variant<Card, Joker>, 54>& deck)
{
    std::random_device rd;
    std::mt19937 gen{ rd() };
    std::ranges::shuffle(deck, gen);
}
```

The only difference between this shuffle and the previous version in listing 5.22 is the type of deck. We could write a function template instead to save the duplication. Try it out!

We need two additions to make our higher-or-lower card game work with the extended deck. First, we need to decide if a guess involving a `Joker` is correct. If we say the guess is correct if either card is a joker, the player in effect gets a free turn. We'll use the `std::holds_alternative<Joker>` function to see whether we have a joker and return `true` in that case. Otherwise, we have two non-jokers, so we can call our original function, using `std::get<Card>` to obtain cards from the variants.

Listing 5.30 Checking whether the guess is correct for an extended deck

```cpp
bool is_guess_correct(char c,
    const std::variant<Card, Joker>& current,
    const std::variant<Card, Joker>& next)
{
    if (std::holds_alternative<Joker>(current) ||
        std::holds_alternative<Joker>(next))          Returns true if either
        return true;                                  card is a joker
    Card current_card = std::get<Card>(current);    Gets cards from
    Card next_card = std::get<Card>(next);          the variants
    return is_guess_correct(c, current_card, next_card);    Otherwise calls the
}                                                           original function
```

We potentially need to display jokers, so we need an overload of the stream insertion operator for our variant. Again, we use `holds_alternative` to see if we have a joker, in which case we send `"JOKER"` to the stream; otherwise, we call our original function.

Listing 5.31 Streaming out cards and jokers

```cpp
std::ostream& operator<<(std::ostream& os, const std::variant<Card, Joker>&
    card)
{
    if (std::holds_alternative<Joker>(card))          A Joker
        os << "JOKER";
    else
        os << std::get<Card>(card);    Streams
    return os;                         the card
}
```

We can now write a new game using an extended deck. The code is identical to our original game from listing 5.24, except for the creation of an extended deck.

Listing 5.32 Higher-or-lower card game with jokers

```cpp
void higher_lower_with_jokers()
{
    auto deck = create_extended_deck();        Creates a deck
    shuffle_deck(deck);                        with jokers

    size_t index = 0;
    while (index + 1 < deck.size())
    {
        std::cout << deck[index]
            << ": Next card higher (h) or lower (l)?\n>";
        char c;
        std::cin >> c;
        bool ok = is_guess_correct(c, deck[index], deck[index + 1]);
```

```
        if (!ok)
        {
            std::cout << "Next card was " << deck[index + 1] << '\n';
            break;
        }
        ++index;
    }
    std::cout << "You got " << index << " correct\n";
}
```

We are relatively unlikely to get a joker, but it could happen. A typical game might look like this:

```
8 of Hearts: Next card higher (h) or lower (l)?
>l
3 of Hearts: Next card higher (h) or lower (l)?
>h
5 of Hearts: Next card higher (h) or lower (l)?
>h
5 of Diamonds: Next card higher (h) or lower (l)?
>h
Next card was Ace of Clubs
You got 3 correct
```

We have built our own type and more. However, we haven't tried object-oriented programming yet. In the next chapter, we will write another class and provide virtual functions to learn more about classes.

Summary

- Headers need an include guard, and the `pragma` directive `once` is now widely supported.
- Use a scoped enum in preference to a C-style enum.
- Certain functions can be flagged as defaulted or deleted.
- The `string` header provides a `to_string` method for numeric values.
- Use `std::array` for a container when the size is known at compile time.
- The three-way comparison (`operator <=>`) was introduced in C++20 and can be marked as `default`, generating comparisons for us.
- Use `std::shuffle` to shuffle a collection, passing an appropriately seeded random number generator.
- Use `std::variant` if an object is one of a limited number of unrelated types.
- Use `std::any` if you need one of any possible copy-constructible types.
- Many containers have `begin` and `end` member functions, but these are available as free functions too for more general use.

Smart pointers and polymorphism

6

This chapter covers

- Using inheritance for dynamic polymorphism
- Special member functions
- Type traits
- Using smart pointers
- Random number distributions

In this chapter, we will work with classes again, but this time using inheritance. We will create various `"Blob"` classes. Our blobs will be able to move forward and backward. If we get our blobs in a line at the bottom of a virtual paper bag, we can set them off racing and see which blob escapes the paper bag first. Separately from practicing with classes, we can then claim and furthermore prove that we can code our way out of a paper bag, a skill all programmers should aim for.

We will start with a simple class hierarchy and create a blob that takes a step at a time. We will consider which special member functions we need when we use inheritance and use type traits to interrogate various member functions. We will use random numbers again, using various distributions to decide how big a step a blob takes. The randomness will make the race more exciting. By storing a blob in a *smart pointer*, we can keep various types of blobs in a `vector`. Their behavior will vary depending on the type of blob, giving us *dynamic polymorphism*. They can then race, and we can sit back, watch, and congratulate ourselves on coding our way out of a paper bag.

6.1   A class hierarchy

We will represent a blob with an asterisk, *, and leave a trail of asterisks to show the path taken. We can indicate the sides of the bag with a | character and the bottom with a – character. All blobs will start at the bottom of a bag and then move a step or so at a time. We might see something like this:

```
  *
|  *       *  |
|  *    *  *  |
|  *  *  *  *  |
 -----------
```

To race blobs out of a paper bag, we need to define a `Blob` type. We could give each blob an x and y coordinate, but we will not vary x, so need only track y. If we store blobs in a `vector`, we can use the vector's index to indicate the x coordinate. For our first race, we will have one type of blob that always moves forward by the same amount. Later, we can add a second type of `Blob` that takes a random step to add some variety.

6.1.1   An abstract base class

We'll create a base class for our blobs and make derived classes later. We know each blob needs to take a step, so we need a `step` function. We will also want to know the total number of steps taken so we can display the right number of asterisks. The `step` function changes the instance, increasing the total number of steps, but the `total_steps` function does not change the instance, so the latter can be marked `const`. Therefore, we need two member functions but keep them abstract, indicated by `= 0` after the declaration. Derived classes can implement their own versions of these functions, giving us the polymorphism we need. Both of the abstract functions need to be marked `virtual`. Virtual methods are implemented via a table of virtual function pointers called a *v-table*. When we call a virtual method via a pointer or reference, the v-table is used to look up which overridden virtual function to invoke. Virtual methods, therefore, allow us to create different derived classes with different `step` functions. The *abstract base class* (ABC) can live in a header file, called `Race.h`, inside a namespace called `Race`. The class doesn't need much code.

Listing 6.1   A first attempt at a base class

```
namespace Race
{
    class Blob
```

```
    {
    public:                          ──┐ Abstract function
        virtual void step() = 0;       ─┘ to take a step
        virtual int total_steps() const = 0;   ◁──┐ Abstract function
    };                                             │ returning total steps
}
```

We can't create an instance of this `Blob` because it has abstract functions. If we write some derived classes, implementing both abstract functions, we can make various blobs and race them. However, we haven't declared a destructor for our base class. In fact, we haven't added any of the special member functions:

- *A default constructor*—`X()`
- *A copy constructor*—`X(const X&)`
- *A copy assignment*—`operator = (const X&)`
- *A move constructor*—`X(X&&)`
- *A move assignment*—`operator = (X&&)`
- *A destructor*—`~X()`

This means all six functions are defaulted because we haven't defined any of them. Writing no code and therefore accepting the six defaults is often called the *rule of zero*. This is perfect for many situations. The core guidelines even tell us to avoid defining defaults if possible (http://mng.bz/M9Km); after all, less code usually means fewer bugs. Sometimes we do need to write some code, though. If we are managing memory or handles to resources, we need to ensure the right thing happens; otherwise, we could get memory leaks. We are not managing memory or handles in our class, but we need *polymorphism*, and therefore, we do have a problem. Consider what happens when we have a derived class.

Our `Blob` has default implementations of all six special member functions, including a destructor. Any derived class will call a base class' destructor automatically. This has always been the case in C++. We need derived classes, filling in the implementation of the two abstract functions, so we can race blobs. If we use pointers or references to various types of blobs, we can call the virtual methods, and the override for the derived class will be used, allowing different `step` implementations. We can define a *derived* class and assign a derived instance to a pointer to the *base* class:

```
Blob * blob = new DerivedBlob();
```

We can call

```
blob->step();
```

The step taken will depend on the type of blob because the `step` function is *virtual*. However, when we are done, if we call

```
delete blob;
```

only the `Blob`'s destructor gets called, not the `DerivedBlob`'s. That's asking for trouble. If we delete polymorphically without a virtual destructor, we have undefined behavior. We need each destructor to be called. If we made a `DerivedBlob` pointer instead

```
DerivedBlob * blob = new DerivedBlob();
```

both destructors would be called. This time, `blob` is a `DerivedBlob`, so the `Derived-Blob`'s destructor is called, followed by the base class' destructor. The defaulted destructor is not virtual, so it is not in the v-table, as illustrated in figure 6.1.

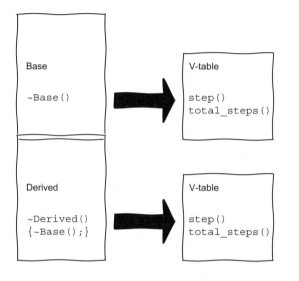

Figure 6.1   **Virtual functions in the v-table, but not the destructor: a `Base` pointer calls the `Base` destructor, and a `Derived` pointer calls the `Derived` destructor, but a `Base` pointer to the `Derived` class does the wrong thing.**

We want to be able to use a pointer to the base `Blob` class so we can have various derived classes to make an interesting race. In fact, we won't use raw pointers; we'll find out how to be smarter. Either way, we need one small change to fix the problem. If we flag the destructor as `virtual`, it goes in the v-table, and the right destructors are called for a `Base` pointer. While we are making this change, we can mark the copy constructor and assignment as deleted because we don't need to copy blobs, and we'll add a default constructor because a base class needs an appropriate constructor.

Listing 6.2   A better base class

```cpp
#pragma once

namespace Race
{
    class Blob
    {
    public:
        virtual ~Blob() = default;          Virtual default destructor
        Blob() = default;          Default constructor
```

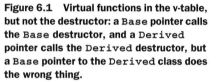

```
        Blob(Blob const&) = delete;              Deletes copies that
        Blob& operator=(Blob const&) = delete;   are not needed

        virtual void step() = 0;
        virtual int total_steps() const = 0;
    };
}
```

We can now safely make a concrete class deriving from `Blob`.

6.1.2 A concrete class

Let's make a new type of `Blob` that will take two steps forward whenever it moves. This new type can derive publicly from `Blob`, so the base class' public methods remain public, and the protected members remain protected, but any private members in the base class are inaccessible to the derived class. For a reminder of how public, protected, and private access modifiers behave, see CppReference (https://en.cppreference.com/w/cpp/language/access). We have three public methods, so these remain public, and we have nothing else to consider.

We need to implement the abstract functions to make a concrete class. We can define these inline in the class because they both need only a single line of code. For larger functions, we would use a separate source file and put the definitions there.

To implement the functions, we *override* them by writing a function with the exact same signature. The base class's member functions must be virtual; otherwise, we are *hiding* rather than overriding a function. This has always been the case in C++. If you've forgotten the details, see Item 33: Avoid hiding inherited names in Scott Meyers' book *Effective C++* (Addison-Wesley Professional, 2005; 3rd edition). C++11 introduced the `override` specifier, which we can add to the end of the declaration of a member function to make clear we are overriding a function. This means the compiler can tell us if we fail to write the signature correctly. For example, it's very easy to forget the word `const` and end up with two different functions. We can also use the keyword `final` if we don't want any further derived classes to override the virtual method.

Both the `step` and `total_steps` functions use the number of steps so far. The former will add to the total steps, and the latter will report the total steps. Our new type of blob will take two steps at a time, so it needs to increase the total number of steps by two. We can remember the number of steps taken so far in an `int` called `y`, indicating the `y` coordinate of a blob. Nothing else should use the variable, so we make it private. Our stepper class goes in the `Race` header file inside the namespace, implementing the two virtual functions inline.

Listing 6.3 A blob taking constant-sized steps

```
class StepperBlob : public Blob
{
    int y = 0;       ◁──┐ Private int to keep
public:                 │ track of steps
```

```
    void step() override            ◄──┐ Two steps
    {                                   │ forward
        y += 2;
    }
    int total_steps() const override ◄──┐ Total number
    {                                    │ of steps so far
        return y;
    }
};
```

We can now create a stepper blob:

```
Race::StepperBlob blob;
```

In fact, we can add a `check_properties` function like we have done before and use `asserts` to check what our code does. If we put this in `main.cpp`, we can check that a step moves us forward by two.

Listing 6.4 Checking that steps move a blob forward

```
#include <cassert>
#include "Race.h"

void check_properties()
{
    Race::StepperBlob blob;
    blob.step();
    assert(blob.total_steps() == 2);
}

int main()
{
    check_properties();
}
```

We can now build a race. We only have one type of concrete blob, so we know in advance there will be no winners or losers, but it gives us a simple warm-up race. We need to decide how to represent the blobs and how to draw the bag.

6.1.3 Warming up for a race

We can put a few `StepperBlobs` in a virtual paper bag and let them walk up the screen. We will use the abstract base class later when we introduce a new type of blob. For this section, we will concentrate on representing the `StepperBlobs` in the race. If we used a proper graphics library, we could build a magnificent display; however, we have lots more to learn about C++. The SFML (Simple and Fast Multimedia Library; see https://www.sfml-dev.org/index.php) is relatively easy to get up and running if you want to give it a try. We'll stick with using the console here.

First of all, we need a paper bag. We decided to represent the paper bag using | and – for the edges and a trail of *s for a blob.

```
       *
|  *        *  |
|  *     *  *  |
|  *  *  *  *  |
 -  -  -  -  -  -
```

We'll make the bag three rows high and build up the display using strings for each
row. Each row starts with either a `'|'` and a space, or two spaces if we are above the
bag, and then two spaces, or `" *"`, per blob, and a final `'|'`. The final row consists of
`'-'` characters for the bottom of the bag.

Let's write a drawing function, taking the `vector` of `StepperBlobs`, so we can draw
the blobs along with the paper bag. We can put four such blobs in a vector

```cpp
std::vector<Race::StepperBlob> blobs(4);
```

and pass this to the function, allowing us to vary the number of blobs. We could use an
`std::array` instead if we wanted, but `std::vector` means we could vary the number
at run time if we wanted to. As we sweep through each row, we can check the current `y`
coordinate against each blob's total steps. If the `y` position is higher than a blob, we
show two spaces; otherwise, we use a space and then an `*`. We made the `steps` function constant because it doesn't change a blob, so we can pass a `const` reference to a
`vector` to the drawing function. We'll put the new function in a `Race.cpp` file, remembering to add the declaration to the header file. We need the `iostream` and `string`
headers too.

Listing 6.5   Drawing each blob's current position

```cpp
#include <iostream>
#include <string>

#include "Race.h"

void Race::draw_blobs(const
    std::vector<Race::StepperBlob> & blobs)
{
    const int bag_height = 3;
    const int race_height = 8;
    for (int y = race_height; y >= 0; --y)
    {
        std::string output =
            y >= bag_height ? "  " : "| ";        ⟵──┘ Left side
                                                       of bag
        for (const auto& blob : blobs)
        {
            if (blob.total_steps() >= y)
            {                                       Blob leaving
                output += "* ";          ⟵──┘      a trail
            }
            else
            {                                      No blob
                output += "  ";          ⟵──┘      here
```

```
                }
            }
            output += y >= bag_height ? ' ' : '|';      ◁──┐ Right side
            std::cout << output << '\n';                    │ of bag
        }
        const int edges = 3;
        std::cout <<
            std::string(blobs.size() * 2 + edges, '-')
            << '\n';         ◁──┐ Bottom
}                                │ of bag
```

We want the blobs to step, so we need another function, move_blobs. Because the blobs change state when they step, we pass our vector by non-const reference. Again, we will use StepperBlob here and build up to using different types of Blob in the next section. We need to add the signature to the header and include the vector header too.

Listing 6.6   Declarations in the header file

```
#include <vector>

namespace Race
{                    ┐ Blob and stepper
...          ◁────┘ like before

    void move_blobs(std::vector<Race::StepperBlob>& blobs);     ◁──┐
    void draw_blobs(                                                │ Function
        const std::vector<Race::StepperBlob>& blobs               │ signatures
    );                                                         ◁──┘
}
```

We then define the function in the Race.cpp file. We can use a range-based for loop to let each blob take a step.

Listing 6.7   Moving all the blobs

```
void Race::move_blobs(
    std::vector<Race::StepperBlob> & blobs    │ Pass by
)                                      ◁──────┘ reference
{
    for (auto& blob : blobs)    ◁──┐ Reference to
    {                                │ each blob
        blob.step();     ◁──┐ Makes
    }                        │ blob step
}
```

If we call these functions in a loop, we'll have a race. We can clear the screen and sleep for a little while between updates. We've used the thread's sleep_for previously in our countdown in listing 4.11, so pausing is straightforward. If we include the thread header, we can pause using chrono literals, such as 1000ms:

```
using namespace std::chrono;
std::this_thread::sleep_for(1000ms);
```

Now, there is no platform-independent way to clear a screen in C++. Sometimes C++ is used for embedded devices without screens, so that makes sense. However, using specific control characters usually works on Linux, Windows, or macOS:

```
std::cout << "\x1B[2J\x1B[H";
```

The \x1B introduces a control character, [2J clears the screen, and [H moves the cursor to the top left. If it doesn't work on your setup, just print a new line character '\n' instead, and you'll get each frame shown down the screen. Again, we add the signature

```
void race(std::vector<Race::StepperBlob>& blobs);
```

to the header file and put the implementation in the source file. The race calls our draw_blobs and move_blobs functions for a while, pausing and clearing the screen between each call.

Listing 6.8   A somewhat predictable race

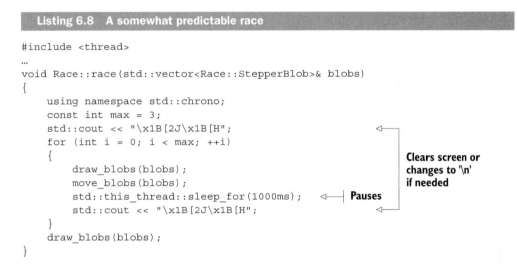

```
#include <thread>
…
void Race::race(std::vector<Race::StepperBlob>& blobs)
{
    using namespace std::chrono;
    const int max = 3;
    std::cout << "\x1B[2J\x1B[H";                          ⊲──┐
    for (int i = 0; i < max; ++i)                            │
    {                                                        │  Clears screen or
        draw_blobs(blobs);                                   │  changes to '\n'
        move_blobs(blobs);                                   │  if needed
        std::this_thread::sleep_for(1000ms);   ⊲─┤ Pauses    │
        std::cout << "\x1B[2J\x1B[H";                      ⊲──┘
    }
    draw_blobs(blobs);
}
```

We need to call this from main with a vector of blobs. Don't forget to include the Race.cpp in your build.

Listing 6.9   A warm-up race

```
#include "Race.h"
int main()
{
    check_properties();
    std::vector<Race::StepperBlob> blobs(4);
    Race::race(blobs);
}
```

When we run this, the blobs move in lockstep, so they all escape together.

```
                          |       |        | * * * * |        | * * * * |      * * * *
                          |       |        | * * * * |        | * * * * |      * * * *
                          |       |        | * * * * |        * * * *          * * * *
                          | * * * |                           * * * *          * * * *
                          -------          | * * * * |        | * * * * |      | * * * * |
                                           | * * * * |        | * * * * |      | * * * * |
                                           | * * * * |        | * * * * |      | * * * * |
                                           -------            -------          -------
```

It is not much of a race but is a simple demonstration of how to code our way out of a paper bag. We're almost ready to make different types of blobs. Before we do, let's think a bit more about the six special member functions that classes might have. Pausing to check which functions are present and absent will help cement the six special functions in our minds.

6.1.4 *Using type traits to check for special member functions*

Before C++11, we had the *rule of three*: defining a destructor, a copy constructor, or a copy assignment operator for a class almost certainly requires all three to be defined. If any one of these functions needed to do something special, like clone a resource, the others would need to do something appropriate too. Since C++11, we must consider move construction and move assignment too, leading to what is known as the *rule of five*. In fact, we noted that a class can have six possible special member functions. The compiler will generate all six operations if we do not define any of them. We added a virtual destructor to the base class to allow polymorphic use. So do we know which of the other functions are still implicitly defined for us? Do we care? Maybe. If the moves are not available for a type, an optimization opportunity may be missed. Remember, we considered two versions of push_back for a vector in chapter 2:

```
constexpr void push_back( const T& value );
constexpr void push_back( T&& value );
```

The first version makes a copy of the value at the end of the vector, while the second version avoids the copy by moving the value. If the type cannot be moved, the first version will be used.

Our Blob class is abstract, so we can't make one and try to copy or move it. How do we test such a class? At the very least, we need the base class to be virtually destructible and not able to be constructed. We can try to find out which functions a Blob has if we use *type traits*. They live in the type_traits header, introduced in C++11. The traits make various operations discoverable via template structs, which take a type and populate a Boolean member called value, telling us whether the operation or trait is supported (see http://mng.bz/yZDE). We can query

```
std::is_constructible<Blob>::value
```

and discover the Blob is not constructible. Rather than spelling out `value`, we can use `_v` instead:

```
std::is_constructible_v<Blob>
```

Various helper templates ending with `_v` equating to the `value` member were introduced in C++17. In either case, we provide the type we are concerned about to the template and receive a Boolean. Reassuringly, `Blob` is not constructible.

In fact, the `is_constructible` trait can check for various ways to construct an object. CppReference (see http://mng.bz/XqyM) shows us the declaration

```
template<class T, class... Args >
struct is_constructible;
```

We met the three dots or *parameter pack* in the last chapter when we used `std::variant`. We can try other types to see if we can make a `Blob` from them. For example, we can verify that a `Blob` cannot be constructed with an `int` by checking whether

```
std::is_constructible_v<Blob, int>
```

is false. We can also use `is_default_constructible_v` to specifically check for a default constructor.

Type traits cover more than construction. We briefly met concepts in chapter 4 and considered using `invocable` from the `concepts` header to ensure a template parameter was invocable or callable. The `type_traits` header has an `is_invocable` trait to discover if the concept applies to a type. We can check a variety of other traits too. Have a look through the `type_traits` header. Traits operate on a type at compile time, so they are part of the *metaprogramming* library, along with the `ratio` header we met in chapter 4, as well as integer sequences, which we haven't looked at yet.

Let's see if we can check which of the six member functions our base class has and ensure the destructor is virtual as well. The traits are `constexpr`, so we can use `static_assert` in the `check_properties` function we made in listing 6.4.

Listing 6.10 Type traits to check for special member functions

```
#include <type_traits>
void check_properties()
{
    ...              <----| Previous checks
    static_assert(
        !std::is_default_constructible_v<Race::Blob>
    );                                              <----
    static_assert(
        std::is_destructible_v<Race::Blob>                  Checks six
    );                                              <----   member
    static_assert(                                          functions
        !std::is_copy_constructible_v<Race::Blob>
    );                                              <----
    static_assert(
```

```
        !std::is_copy_assignable_v<Race::Blob>
    );
    static_assert(
        !std::is_move_constructible_v<Race::Blob>       ┐ Checks six
    );                                                  ┤ member
    static_assert(                                      │ functions
        !std::is_move_assignable_v<Race::Blob>
    );                                                  ┘
    static_assert(
        std::has_virtual_destructor_v<Race::Blob>
    );          ←┐ Checks destructor
}                │ is virtual
```

Some values are true, and some are false. We can't construct a blob at all, even via copies or moves, because `Blob` is an abstract class with pure virtual member functions, but we do have a virtual destructor. However, the move construction and move assignment checks might be misleading. The `is_move_constructible` trait tells us if a type can be constructed from an rvalue reference. Our blob isn't constructible, so it can't be move constructed at all. The move-constructible trait is *not checking for the presence of a move constructor*; rather, it is checking to see if a type can be constructed from an rvalue of the same type. The `is_move_assignable` tells us if a type can be assigned from an rvalue, and that can mean a function taking a `const` lvalue, because a `const` lvalue reference can bind to rvalues. The trait is *not checking for the presence of a move assignment operator*. Do we have the move special functions?

In fact, adding our own destructor blocks implicit moves (see http://mng.bz/ QR6e). The type traits are telling us if we can assign from a temporary, or rvalue, but we are likely to get copies rather than moves. Because we disabled copies, we can't move or copy a blob. Failing to provide a move constructor and move assignment operator is not an error, but we are missing an optimization opportunity, as we noted when we considered the two versions of `push_back` for a `vector`. In Item 17 of *Effective Modern C++* (O'Reilly Media, Incorporated, 2014), Scott Meyers points out that moves are requests. If a type is not move enabled, any `"moves"` are actually copies. Furthermore, he tells us that *C++ does not generate move operations for a class with a user-declared destructor*. The simplest solution is to declare the move special functions using `=default`. When we do this, the `copy` functions will be disabled! We deleted them because we don't need them. We can declare them if we think we need them. This is often referred to as the *rule of five*. Either stick with the rule of zero, accepting the defaults, or declare or delete all five of the special members along with the constructors according to your needs.

Now, if we delete a single special member function, the move-assignment and all the other special member functions are implicitly deleted. Peter Sommerlad suggests deleting the move assignment if a destructor is defined. He calls this pattern *DesDeMovA: Destructor => Delete Move Assignment* (for an overview, see http://mng.bz/ 46Eg). Disabling copies of polymorphic classes can be sensible. We'll examine this along with other design considerations at the end of the chapter. Keep in mind that adding a `destructor` or other special-member function may disable others, so you may need to explicitly add a function if you need it. The `type_traits` can be used to check which functions you have.

This is a big topic. Howard Hinnant talks about it in "Everything You Ever Wanted to Know About Move Semantics," if you want to learn more (ee https://www.youtube.com/watch?v=vLinb2fgkHk). He has also said, "I don't follow a 'rule of 5.' After all, there are 6 special members." (See http://howardhinnant.github.io/classdecl .html.) This article provides a neat table showing which of the special members are default or blocked when we define one of the other functions. He suggests being explicit about what you do and do not want in your class.

Our `Blob` class from listing 6.2 works well enough for our race. We made one concrete class derived from the `Blob`. We even had a warm-up race. Let's make another type of blob so we can have a proper race.

6.2 Writing and using derived classes in a vector

Let's make another stepper that takes a varying number of steps each time, using random numbers. The `StepperBlob` always takes two steps. Creating a new type of `Blob` taking two steps on average but possibly fewer or more seems like a suitable racing opponent. Either is likely to win. We can use a uniform distribution to generate a whole number of steps from 0 to 4 using

```
std::uniform_int_distribution distribution{0, 4};
```

We need a seeded engine, which we've seen before. We can use `random_device` for the seed

```
std::random_device rd;
std::default_random_engine engine{ rd() };
```

and pass the engine to the distribution to get a number:

```
int step = distribution(engine);
```

Without the seed, the engine will use a default value and give the same sequence each time we run the code. The `default_random_engine` is usually a Mersenne Twister, the `mt19937`. This class has two constructors we can use to seed the engine. We've used the version taking a single number. The second version takes a seed sequence, `seed_seq`:

```
std::random_device rd;
std::seed_seq seeder{rd()};
std::default_random_engine engine{ seeder };
```

In theory, the `seed_seq` can give a greater variety of outcomes each time we run the program, and it does allow us to provide a few seeds in a sequence. If the seeds themselves are all random too, we get even more variety. Either approach is fine for when we only need tens, hundreds, or thousands of random outcomes, and the simplest approach using a single number is fine for the simple games we have written. If we ever need millions or billions of different possible sequences of numbers, we'll need to put in more thought. There is a proposal to extend C++11's random number generators (see https://wg21.link/P1932), which gives further details on the limits of the current engines. C++11's random library is completely fine for the games we are making in this book. Problems will only arise if you want to run huge Monte-Carlo simulations or need cryptographic random numbers.

6.2.1 *A blob moving randomly*

We could build a new class, containing a `uniform_int_distribution` and a generator, giving us a new type of blob. We would use these in the `step` function, adding the random number obtained to the current steps:

```
y += distribution(generator);
```

If we wanted to use each of the distributions in C++, we would end up writing 20 different classes. That feels repetitive.

The distributions do not have a common base class, but they all have an `operator()` taking a generator, which they use to create the next random number fitting the distribution. We can therefore write a class template taking a generator and distribution as types. We need a generator and a distribution member of the type specified in the template. We'll pass both into a constructor, which means we can pass anything, including some mocked generators for testing, provided they have the operator we need for the `step` function.

The new class, `RandomBlob`, needs to derive publicly from `Blob`, like the `StepperBlob` did. The `total_steps` function still returns the total number of steps *y*. The `step` function uses the generator and distribution to obtain a random step. Some of the distributions return a double or float rather than an integer, so we can use a `static_cast` to obtain an integer.

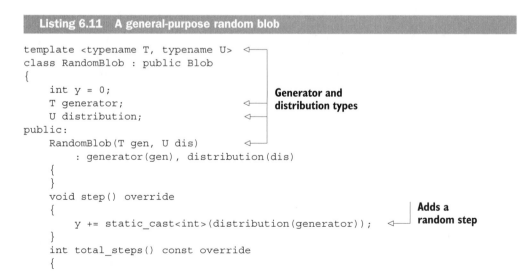

Listing 6.11 A general-purpose random blob

```
template <typename T, typename U>          ◁┐
class RandomBlob : public Blob
{
    int y = 0;                              Generator and
    T generator;                      ◁     distribution types
    U distribution;                   ◁
public:
    RandomBlob(T gen, U dis)          ◁┘
        : generator(gen), distribution(dis)
    {
    }
    void step() override
    {                                                              Adds a
        y += static_cast<int>(distribution(generator));    ◁──┘    random step
    }
    int total_steps() const override
    {
```

```
        return y;
    }
};
```

We make a `RandomBlob` using an engine and distribution. We can use a uniform distribution taking between zero and four steps:

```
std::random_device rd;
Race::RandomBlob rnd_blob{
    std::default_random_engine{ rd() },
    std::uniform_int_distribution{ 0, 4 }
};
```

We can change the distribution parameter to get a blob that behaves differently. We can use a normal distribution, with mean 2.0 and a standard deviation of 1.0, indicating how likely numbers are to deviate from the mean. Bigger means more extreme values are likely:

```
Race::RandomBlob another_rnd_blob{
    std::default_random_engine{ rd() },
    std::normal_distribution{2.0, 1.0}
};
```

The parameters `2.0` and `1.0` mean something very different for this distribution. They no longer tell us the minimum and maximum values. Each distribution has different parameters specific to the underlying distribution function.

C++11's `random` library supports various distributions (see https://en.cppreference.com/w/cpp/header/random):

- *Uniform ints and reals*—Suitable for picking a number in a range with equal likelihood.
- *Bernoulli and related binomial distributions*—Useful for modeling the number of successes or failures.
- *Poisson distribution*—Modeling how many times an event might happen in a period of time; for example, how many buses might turn up in the next few minutes.
- *Normal related distributions*—Producing real (rather than integer) values. This group has six distributions: normal, lognormal, Chi-squared, Cauchy, Fisher, and student. These can be used for a huge variety of models, but the normal is commonly used for people's heights and other situations where most values tend to be nearer the mean, or average, but extreme values are possible.
- *Sampling distributions*—Similar to the uniform distributions but allow us to make specific values or ranges of values more likely by providing a weighting.

In each case, the distribution uses a *probability function* to smear out numbers provided by the engine to give the required properties of the distribution. For a uniform distribution, each number must be equally likely. For a normal distribution, values near the mean are more likely than extreme values. Lots of interesting mathematics are lurking behind this, but generating a plot of probability functions used gives us an idea of how many steps are likely. CppReference gives the function used for each distribution. Comparing the `uniform_int_distribution` and `normal_distribution` we considered, we get plots as shown in figure 6.2.

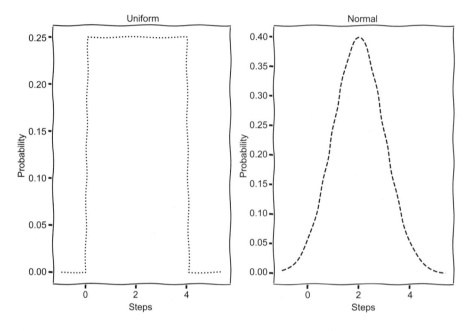

Figure 6.2   Random uniform steps on [0, 4] and normally distributed steps with mean 2.0 and standard deviation of 1.0

On average, we expect two steps from either of these distributions. The normal distribution might take many more or even go backwards, while the uniform steps are never negative. We can use any other distributions we want. We can even use a fake for testing. The template-head we used

```
template <typename T, typename U>
```

has no constraints at all, so the `T` and `U` can be anything. We learn about requirements and concepts in chapter 4, noting we can constrain parameters with concepts, such as invocable

```
void guess_number_with_clues(int number,
        std::invocable<int, int> auto message)
```

to ensure only a function taking two integers is passed as the message parameter to our number-guessing game. Our `RandomBlob` needs an `invocable` generator taking no parameters, written as `std::invocable<>`. The named requirement lives in the concepts header, so if we include the header, we can swap the `typename` keyword to the constraint

```
template <std::invocable<> T, typename U>
class RandomBlob : public Blob
```

to be more specific and get better error messages if we use an unsuitable type. In fact, CppReference gives named requirements for random numbers (see https://en .cppreference.com/w/cpp/named_req), including a `RandomNumberEngine` and a `RandomNumberDistribution`. These named requirements would allow us to be more precise; however, only some of the requirements listed were formalized in the C++20 concepts library. Constraining the generator to be `invocable` is good enough for our simple game.

Another important thing we can do is add tests for our code, using a lambda for the generator and engine, with very little effort. Returning 0 instead of a random number often helps to find bugs since the mathematics with zeros is often easy to do in our heads. We can make a "generator" that always returns 0 and call it in a "distribution" lambda to pass that 0 back.

Listing 6.12   Testing with random generators and distributions

```
void check_properties()
{
    Race::RandomBlob random_blob(          Generates 0
        [] () { return 0; },               every time       Passes on
        [] (auto gen) { return gen(); });                   the 0
    random_blob.step();                         Takes a random step
    assert(random_blob.total_steps() == 0);              0 total steps
}
```

We can make all kinds of different random blobs now. The warm-up race used a `vector` of `StepperBlobs`. We could make a `vector` of `RandomBlobs`, but how can we make the stepper and random blobs compete? They are different types, but they do share a common base type. We could put raw pointers in a `vector`:

```
std::vector<Blob*>
```

Our virtual methods support the polymorphism we need for a race, provided we use a pointer or reference to a `Blob`. Ensuring references don't go out of scope when we still need them is hard work, so pointers are better. However, we would have to delete the blob pointers by hand when we were done or if anything threw an exception. C++11 introduced *smart pointers* to address these challenges, which make our life easier.

6.2.2   *Smart pointers*

The destructors we've written don't do anything. They don't need to. However, one place where C++ shines is by allowing us to do the setup in the constructor and tidying up in the destructor. This is known as *resource acquisition is initialization* (RAII). The STL

UB 509 5281

frequently uses RAII. For example, we know a `vector` creates objects for us on the heap. When the `vector` goes out of scope, the allocated objects are deleted. We don't have to remember to tidy up, because the `vector` is an RAII class. If we put raw pointers in a `vector`, though, the pointers will be cleaned up, rather than what they point to.

Smart pointers are another RAII class, managing raw pointers. We can put smart pointers in a `vector`. When the vector goes out of scope, each contained element's destructor is called. In turn, the smart pointer's destructor clears up the raw pointer. Smart pointers come in different types, but all allow us to write code as presented in the following listing.

Listing 6.13 Using smart pointers in a `vector`

```
void very_smart()
{
    std::vector<SmartPointer<Blob>> blobs;
    blobs.emplace_back(make_smart_pointer<StepperBlob>());
}
```

Puts some blobs in a vector

End of scope, so vector calls smart pointers' destructors

The `memory` header lists four smart pointers:

- `unique_ptr`
- `shared_ptr`
- `weak_ptr`
- `auto_ptr`

The last smart pointer has unusual copy semantics (see https://en.cppreference.com/w/cpp/memory/auto_ptr). A copy would steal the pointer, meaning these smart pointers could not be used in vectors or other containers. If a `vector` resizes, the elements need to be copied or moved, so something with unusual copy semantics causes problems. The `auto_ptr` was deprecated in C++11 and removed in C++17. The remaining three types are much easier to use.

A `unique_ptr` manages a raw pointer. The `unique_ptr` owns the underlying pointer, so copying is disabled, but moving is allowed. After all, if something is unique, you shouldn't be able to make copies of it. In contrast, a `shared_ptr` also manages a raw pointer, but several `shared_ptr` can own the same object. The owned object is destroyed, and its memory is deallocated when all the `shared_ptr` owning the underlying object go out of scope or are reset to point to something else. Shared pointers, therefore, have a shared count, held in what's referred to as a *control block*. We can specify what happens when the unique or shared pointers go out of scope, but they both call `delete` by default. This information is also stored in the control block. Now, the sharing means you might end up with a circular dependency and a potential resource leak, so there is a `weak_ptr` as well. The `weak_ptr` is like a `shared_ptr` but acts more like a passive observer, monitoring the control block. The watched `shared_ptr` can delete the underlying resource, so the `weak_ptr` needs to check to see if the underlying resource has been deleted before trying to use the underlying pointer. See https://www.modernescpp.com/index.php/std-weak-ptr for further details. The relationship among these three types of smart pointers is shown in figure 6.3.

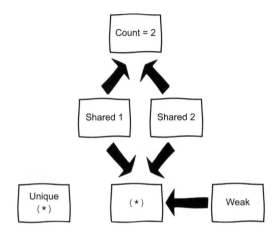

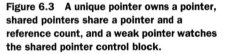

Figure 6.3 A unique pointer owns a pointer, shared pointers share a pointer and a reference count, and a weak pointer watches the shared pointer control block.

These three types of pointers cover a variety of use cases; however, the `unique_ptr` is sufficient for our needs. Nothing needs to share or observe the underlying raw pointer. Furthermore, Herb Sutter suggested using a `unique_ptr` by default (see http://mng.bz/n1D8). The `shared_ptr` is more complicated because it needs the control block, which makes it more heavyweight. Switching to a `shared_ptr` from a `unique_ptr` is straightforward, so starting with a `unique_ptr` makes sense.

We, therefore, need to create a `vector` of `std::unique_ptr<Blob>`. We can then populate the `vector` with any classes deriving from the base class and make them race. We can make a `unique_ptr` in a couple of ways, either by using `new` explicitly

```
std::unique_ptr<Blob> blob(new StepperBlob);
```

or by using the `make_unique` method:

```
std::unique_ptr<Blob> blob = std::make_unique<StepperBlob>();
```

The latter approach is better. First, Herb Sutter's post tells us to avoid using `new`. Using `new` means we may have to handle raw pointers directly, which requires a lot of care. When we pass the `new` `StepperBlob` to the smart pointer, memory is allocated, and the constructor is called. If the constructor were to throw an exception, the `unique_ptr` itself wouldn't be constructed, so its destructor wouldn't get called, and the `StepperBlob` memory would leak. If the allocation and construction happens inside the `make_unique` call, everything is dealt with for us. There is a `make_shared` function for similar reasons.

6.2.3   *Race!*

We are now able to make a vector of various types of blobs and set them racing. We need a new race function, taking an `std::vector<std::unique_ptr<Blob>>`, and new `move_blobs` and `draw_blobs` functions also taking a `vector` of smart pointers. The declaration goes in the header, inside the namespace, and we need to include the `memory` header for the `unique_ptr`.

Listing 6.14   Adding overloaded methods to the header

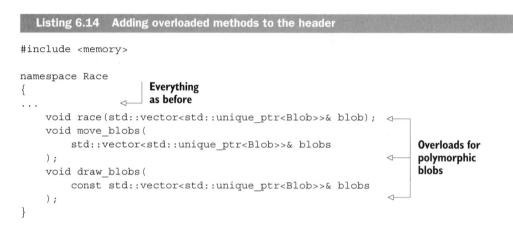

```
#include <memory>

namespace Race
{
...                              Everything
                                 as before
    void race(std::vector<std::unique_ptr<Blob>>& blob);
    void move_blobs(
        std::vector<std::unique_ptr<Blob>>& blobs        Overloads for
    );                                                   polymorphic
    void draw_blobs(                                     blobs
        const std::vector<std::unique_ptr<Blob>>& blobs
    );
}
```

We now need to define the functions. The race function is identical to listing 6.8, apart from the type of the `blobs` parameter. In listing 6.8, we had a `vector` of `StepperBlobs`. Now we can have various blobs in the `vector`.

Listing 6.15   A less predictable race

```
void Race::race(std::vector<std::unique_ptr<Blob>>& blobs)
{
    using namespace std::chrono;
    const int max = 3;
    std::cout << "\x1B[2J\x1B[H";
    for (int i = 0; i < max; ++i)
    {
        draw_blobs(blobs);
        move_blobs(blobs);
        std::this_thread::sleep_for(1000ms);
        std::cout << "\x1B[2J\x1B[H";
    }
    draw_blobs(blobs);
}
```

We need to implement the move and draw functions too. When we moved the blobs in listing 6.7, we called

```
blob.step();
```

for each blob. Now the blobs are unique pointers to blobs, so we need to use the `operator->` to call a member function on the underlying pointer. Apart from that, the function is very similar.

Listing 6.16 Moving all the blobs

```
void Race::move_blobs(std::vector<std::unique_ptr<Race::Blob>>& blobs)
{
    for (auto& blob : blobs)
    {
        blob->step();          ◁──────  -> to call an underlying
    }                                    pointer's method
}
```

Finally, we need to implement the overloaded `draw_blobs` method. Again, this is very like the previous draw method in listing 6.5, but we use `operator->` to find a blob's current steps.

Listing 6.17 Drawing each blob's current position

```
void Race::draw_blobs(const std::vector<std::unique_ptr<Race::Blob>>& blobs)
{
    const int bag_height = 3;
    for (int y = 8; y >= 0; --y)
    {
        std::string output = y > 2 ? "   " : "| ";
        for (const auto& blob : blobs)
        {
            if (blob->total_steps() >= y)     ◁──────  -> to call an underlying
                output += "* ";                          pointer's method
            else
                output += "  ";
        }
        output += y >= bag_height ? ' ' : '|';
        std::cout << output << '\n';
    }
    std::cout << std::string(blobs.size() * 2 + 3, '-') << '\n';
}
```

Armed with the new methods, we can finally have a proper race. We need some blobs, and some steppers racing some random blobs would be good. Since the steppers move two steps at a time, using a uniform distribution of integers between 0 and 4 gives random blobs averaging two steps overall. We realized that gives both types a fair chance. We can make a `unique_ptr` to a `StepperBlob` and then a `unique_ptr` to a `RandomBlob` in a loop, so run half the number requested, adding two Blobs each time. Each `RandomBlob` needs an engine and a distribution. The engine needs seeding, so we'll use `random_device` as usual. Finally, we'll make the distribution range from 0 to 4, using `uniform_int_distribution{0, 4}`.

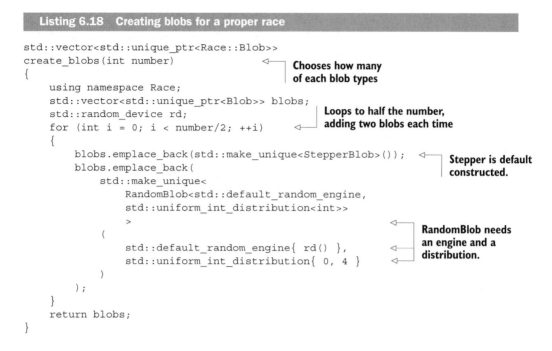

> **Listing 6.18   Creating blobs for a proper race**

```
std::vector<std::unique_ptr<Race::Blob>>
create_blobs(int number)                    ◁── Chooses how many
{                                                of each blob types
    using namespace Race;
    std::vector<std::unique_ptr<Blob>> blobs;
    std::random_device rd;                      Loops to half the number,
    for (int i = 0; i < number/2; ++i)      ◁── adding two blobs each time
    {
        blobs.emplace_back(std::make_unique<StepperBlob>());   ◁── Stepper is default
        blobs.emplace_back(                                        constructed.
            std::make_unique<
                RandomBlob<std::default_random_engine,
                std::uniform_int_distribution<int>>
                >                                              ◁── RandomBlob needs
            (                                                      an engine and a
                std::default_random_engine{ rd() },           ◁── distribution.
                std::uniform_int_distribution{ 0, 4 }         ◁──
            )
        );
    }
    return blobs;
}
```

We can now create our blobs in `main` and race them. Let's try four of each kind of blob, giving us eight to race.

> **Listing 6.19   A proper race**

```
int main()
{
    auto blobs = create_blobs(8);
    Race::race(blobs);
}
```

The random blobs might win, but the steppers can beat them. To start with, the blobs are in the bottom of the bag, raring to go.

```
|                   |
|                   |
| * * * * * * * *   |
---------------------
```

They move, and some random blobs may take the lead.

```
                *
        *     *     *
| * * * * * * * *   |
| * * * * * * * *   |
| * * * * * * * *   |
---------------------
```

The steppers might catch up a bit at the next move.

```
    *         *
  * * * * * * * *
  * * * * * * * *
| * * * * * * * * |
| * * * * * * * * |
| * * * * * * * * |
-------------------
```

And finally, some random blobs win, but one is left behind on this run.

```
    *            *
    *        *   *
  * * *    * * * *
  * * * * * * * *
  * * * * * * * *
  * * * * * * * *
| * * * * * * * * |
| * * * * * * * * |
| * * * * * * * * |
-------------------
```

A second run can give a different outcome. We have raced our way out of a paper bag. Don't forget, we considered other distributions too. Try this out with a normal distribution, and see if any go backward.

6.2.4 *Some design considerations*

We disabled moves and copies on our base class. If we had left the copies, we could make a new derived type:

```
class DerivedStepper : public StepperBlob { };
```

Admittedly, the derived type doesn't do much, but maybe we need it to do something else for the virtual member functions. Nothing is stopping us from writing a function using a `StepperBlob`:

```
void bogus(StepperBlob blob)
{
// ...
}
```

Inside this function, we have a `StepperBlob`, even if we call it with the derived type:

```
bogus(DerivedStepper());
```

Inside the `bogus` function, the blob is a `StepperBlob` because we passed it by value, and it was copied. This is known as *slicing*. We've sliced the derived class down to the `StepperBlob` class, and the wrong virtual functions get called. The core guidelines (http://mng.bz/orDj) suggest making the copy and move operations deleted using `=delete` to avoid slicing (http://mng.bz/6nr5). The DesDeMovA approach would have the same effect. If all these operations go, we can add a clone method if we need to enable copying. Alternatively, just marking the copies as deleted in the base `Blob` class means the call to the `bogus` function with the derived class no longer compiles. Fortunately, we did this in our base class. We could even stop a derived class from being written using the keyword `final` that we met earlier. We can mark functions as `override` or `final`, but we can also mark a whole class `final`:

```
class StepperBlob final : public Blob
```

A `final` class cannot be used as a base class, so the derived class itself does not compile.

Object-oriented programming (OOP) can get very complicated. When we show the race, all we really need are the total steps so far per blob. Using an `std::vector <int>` to collect the steps would work. We could accumulate the total steps for each blob without any need for OOP. We could have done that at the outset but would then have missed the opportunity to learn a lot of C++. In fact, remember when we tested the `RandomStepper` in listing 6.12? We took 0 steps using

```
Race::RandomBlob random_blob(
    [] () { return 0; },
    [] (auto gen) { return gen(); });
```

The `StepperBlob` takes 2 steps, so we could use a fake generator returning 2 instead of 0

```
Race::RandomBlob random_blob(
    [] () { return 2; },
    [] (auto gen) { return gen(); });
```

to make a blob taking 2 steps. Again, we wouldn't need OOP. Templates give us compile-time or *static polymorphism*. OOP has its place, but C++ allows us to work in a variety of paradigms.

We've used `vector` several times now and considered an `array` as an alternative when we know how many items we need at compile time. We haven't built anything needing a lookup table yet. In the next chapter, we will use some associative containers to make dictionaries.

Summary

- Always declare a virtual destructor in a `base` class and mark pure virtual functions with `=0`.
- The rule of zero means the six special member functions are provided if we do not declare any of them. If only a constructor is declared, the remaining five special member functions are provided.
- Add the keyword `override` to an overridden method to ensure you have the signature correct, and use the keyword `final` to stop further overrides.
- Use `type_traits` to find traits for a type; for example, `std::is_constructible_v`.

- Adding a destructor blocks the compiler from implicitly supplying the move special member functions.
- The rule of five means any class requiring move semantics needs to declare all five special member functions, possibly along with constructors, if there is a user-declared destructor, copy constructor, or copy assignment operator.
- Using an `std::seed_seq` can generate a greater variety of random numbers, but just using `std::random_device` is often good enough for simple games.
- Use smart pointers rather than raw pointers, and prefer the simpler `unique_ptr` by default.
- Use the `operator->` of a smart pointer to call a member function on the referenced object.

7

Associative containers and files

This chapter covers

- Filling and using associative containers
- Pairs and tuples
- Reading from files
- Random samples

We have used vectors several times now but haven't used an associative container yet. An associative container holds key–value pairs, giving us a lookup table or dictionary. In this chapter, we will use dictionaries to create a game of answer smash. We'll provide two clues, each a definition of a word. The end of the first word will overlap with the start of the next word, giving the answer. For example, a *vector* is a "sequential container supporting dynamic resizing," and a *torch* could be defined as a "lit stick carried in one's hand," so smashing together the words vector and torch gives the answer *vectorch*.

We'll start by storing a dictionary in an `std::map` defined in the `map` header, which existed before C++11, and then consider other types of associative containers too. We will use the newer `std::unordered_map` in the next chapter, so using `std::map` in this chapter will be a useful revision, and we will learn about an std::pair and the more general std::tuple on the way. We will start with hardcoded dictionaries and read data from a file afterward using a random sample to create variety when we play the game.

7.1 Hardcoded answer smash

We'll begin by hardcoding the words and definitions. We can put these directly into a dictionary or map. A map allows us to store *values* against *keys*. If a key already exists, we can replace the existing entry, but we cannot have two entries with the same key. Now, a language dictionary can have multiple definitions for the same word, so we will need a data structure allowing more than one value per key when we use a proper dictionary. We will start with one definition per word, but the map header also provides a multimap, which does support multiple entries, so we can have several definitions later. Let's start with the old-school std::map using one value per key.

7.1.1 Creating and using an std::map

As with all containers, the map is a class template, so we need to state the type of key and value. Both will be strings, so we need a map of strings to strings:

```
std::map<std::string, std::string> dictionary;
```

We can use operator[] to both query and insert key–value pairs. To add or overwrite an entry, we say

```
dictionary["assume"] = "take for granted, take to be the case";
```

We then have one item in the dictionary, with the key "assume" and value "take for granted, take to be the case". We can look up a string using the same operator; for example:

```
std::string new_value = dictionary["fictional"];
```

When we do this, the new_value is a defaulted string, as "fictional" was not in the dictionary. After the call to operator[], the new key "fictional" and defaulted string value end up in the dictionary, which might not be our intention. Let's make a map and prove this to ourselves.

We'll create a map of string keys to string values and stream the contents to std::cout, so we need to include the map, string, and iostream headers. When we streamed out a vector, we used a range-based for loop along the lines of

```
for(auto item: my_vector)
```

We can do the same with a map, and we will use a const reference to avoid copies. Each map item comprises two strings bundled together as an std::pair, which has a first and second method to access each element. We'll look at this in a bit more detail shortly. For now, we can try to query a map for a nonexistent element and see what happens.

Listing 7.1   Creating and displaying a map

```
#include <iostream>
#include <map>
#include <string>

void warm_up()
{
    std::map<std::string, std::string> dictionary;          Declares
                                                            dictionary
    dictionary["assume"] = "take for granted, take to be the case";   Adds an
                                                                      item
    std::string new_value = dictionary["fictional"];
                                                    Queries
    for (const auto & item : dictionary)            nonexistent item
    {
        std::cout << item.first << " : " << item.second << '\n';   Displays
    }                                                              pairs
}

int main()
{
    warm_up();
}
```

const auto & to avoid copies (annotation pointing to `for (const auto & item : dictionary)`)

When we run this code, we can see the query for `"fictional"` has added an empty string to the dictionary:

```
assume : take for granted, take to be the case
fictional :
```

This behavior is unintuitive and can cause problems. We have deliberately used a `const` reference to containers when we pass them as parameters to functions. We want references, so we do not copy the entire container, but we often only want to query rather than change the elements, so flag the parameter as `const`. If we try to do the same with a `map`

```
void unexpected(const std::map<std::string, std::string> & lookup)
{
    auto value = lookup["cheese"];
}
```

we get a compile error, telling us there is no `operator[]` taking a `const` map. Instead, we can call the `at` method, which is a `const` member function:

```
auto value = lookup.at("cheese");
```

If the key does not exist, an `std::out_of_range` exception is thrown. Using this alternative method allows us to pass a `map` by `const` reference, which will come in handy.

The `operator[]` will also replace an existing entry because a `map` only has one value per key. If we say

```
dictionary["fictional"] = "made up";
```

the fictional entry then has the value `"made up"`. We can avoid overwriting existing entries if we use the `insert` method instead. There are various overloads of `insert` (see http://mng.bz/5oEq), but the simplest version returns two things, an iterator and a `bool`, also bundled as an `std::pair`. When we try to insert a new item, we can pass an initializer list for the key and value:

```
auto result = dictionary.insert({ "insert", "place inside" });
```

The `result`'s second item is true because the new entry was added. The first item holds an iterator to the newly added item. If we try to overwrite an existing item

```
auto next_result = dictionary.insert({ "fictional", "not factual" });
```

the `next_result`'s second item is false, and the first item holds an iterator to the existing item, which allows us to see the existing value.

We can now make a dictionary, which is a useful start. Before building our answer smash game, let's pause to consider the `std::pair`, which has cropped up several times now, in a bit more detail.

7.1.2   *Pairs, tuples, and structured bindings*

The `std::pair` lives in the `utility` header and is defined by a class `template`, based on two types:

```
template<typename T1, typename T2> struct pair;
```

We've used the member variables `first` and `second` already. The `utility` header also provides a helper function, called `make_pair`, which creates the pair we want and also deduces the type for us. If we say

```
auto two_words = std::make_pair("Hello,", "world!");
```

we get a pair of `const char *`s. We could use the string literal `operator` `""s` to obtain a pair of `std::string`s instead:

```
using namespace std::string_literals;
auto two_words = std::make_pair("Hello,"s, "world!"s);
```

Rather than using `auto`, we can say `std::pair` and use an initializer list:

```
std::pair two_words{"Hello,"s, "world!"s};
```

We don't need to spell out the type of the pair of items, as CTAD deduces an `std::string` for each item. The types do not need to be identical, so we can have a pair of two different types if we want. For example

```
std::pair two_numbers{1, 1.23};
```

is `std::pair` holding an `int` and a `double`.

Now, a pair holds two elements, but C++11 introduced a generalization called a `tuple`, which can hold any number of items. Nobody agrees on how to pronounce tuple, so choose one of "two-pel," "tupp-ell," or "chewple." The `tuple` lives in the `tuple` header and is defined using the parameter pack (three dots) we have met before:

```
template<typename... Types> class tuple;
```

There's a `make_tuple` function to create a tuple, so we can make a tuple holding three strings like this:

```
auto three_words = std::make_tuple("Hello "s, "again, "s, "World!"s);
```

However, we can equally say

```
std::tuple three_words = {"Hello "s, "again, "s, "World!"s};
```

and CTAD will kick in, deducing we have a tuple of three `std::strings`. As with the `std::pair`, we can have various types in a tuple, so

```
std::tuple three_numbers{ 1, 1.23, 4.5f };
```

is an `std::tuple` of `int`, `double`, and `float`.

Now, `std::pair` has `first` and `second` members to access either element, but `std::tuple` might not hold two elements. We used a `variant` in chapter 5 when we had a card or a joker and used `std::get` to access the elements. The `tuple` header has an overload of `std::get` that we can use to retrieve a `tuple` element, stating the index of the item we want. For example, calling

```
auto first = std::get<0>(three_words);
```

will return the first string.

In listing 7.1, we used an `std::pair` when we displayed the dictionary, hiding behind the `auto` in

```
for (const auto & item : dictionary)
```

The `item` is actually a pair of strings, so we needed to call `first` and `second` to display the dictionary entries. We can do something neater. C++17 introduced *structured bindings*, allowing us to bind names to pairs, tuples, and more (see http://mng.bz/g7De). If we want our three numbers

```
std::tuple three_numbers{ 1, 1.23, 4.5f };
```

unpacked into three variables, we could get each element ourselves:

```
int x = std::get<0>(three_numbers);
double y = std::get<1>(three_numbers);
float z = std::get<2>(three_numbers);
```

Structured binding allows us to get all three items in one line:

```
auto [x, y, z] = three_numbers;
```

We have to use `auto`, followed by the variable names we want in the `[]`. In effect, the structured binding is syntactic sugar for the handwritten unpacking, but it makes a copy of a hidden tuple or pair. Using C++ Insights (see https://cppinsights.io/s/0579bdbb) for our three numbers, we see a copy of the `tuple`, with a made-up name `__three_numbers6` and three named variables referring to the three elements:

```
std::tuple<int, double, float> three_numbers =
                std::tuple<int, double, float>{1, 1.23, 4.5F};
std::tuple<int, double, float> __three_numbers6 =
                std::tuple<int, double, float>(three_numbers);
int && x =
    std::get<0UL>(static_cast<std::tuple<int, double, float>
     &&>(__three_numbers6));
double && y =
    std::get<1UL>(static_cast<std::tuple<int, double, float>
     &&>(__three_numbers6));
float && z =
    std::get<2UL>(static_cast<std::tuple<int, double, float>
     &&>(__three_numbers6));
```

We've met the rvalue reference `&&` before in chapter 2. We can avoid the copy if we use references instead:

```
auto &[x, y, z] = three_numbers;
```

The hidden `__three_numbers6` is then a reference, giving us a reference for each number because the `&&` is subject to *reference collapsing*, so it happily binds to references.

We can bind to arrays and even a structure's nonstatic members too. For example, given

```
struct DataObject { int x{ 0 }; double y{ 1.23 }; };
```

we can write

```
DataObject data {};
auto [x, y] = data;
```

In each case, we use `auto` and bind to an existing object. The technical editor for this book, Tim van Deurzen, gave a great lightning talk on structured bindings at Meeting C++ in 2019, if you want to know more (see https://www.youtube.com/watch?v=YC_TMAbHyQU)).

We were considering how we used an `std::pair` when we displayed the `dictionary` in listing 7.1. We can now bind the `dictionary`'s key–value pair to two names, writing

```
for (const auto & [key, value] : dictionary)
```

so we can use the `key` and `value` directly, without having to call `first` and `second` on the pair.

Listing 7.2 Using structure bindings to access `map` items

```
#include <iostream>
#include <map>
#include <string>

void structure_bindings()
{
```

```
std::map<std::string, std::string> dictionary;
dictionary["assume"] = "presume, take for granted";
std::string new_word = dictionary["fictional"];
for (const auto & [key, value] : dictionary)          ⊲──┘  Binds the structure
{                                                             to key and value
    std::cout << key << " : " << value << '\n';       ⊲──    Displays key
}                                                             and value
}
```

Similarly, if we use `insert`, we can use a structured binding to hold the result:

```
auto [it, result] = dictionary.insert({ "insert", "place inside" })
```

We can then use the iterator `it` and the bool `result` directly, rather than using `first` to get the iterator and `second` to get the `result`.

The `pair` and `tuple` can be used in a variety of situations, including returning more than one value from a function, as we saw when we considered the `map`'s `insert` function. The structured binding also allows us to write clearer code when we use the returned values. Armed with the basics of `map` and `pair`, we can now make a simple answer smash game.

7.1.3   *A simple answer smash game*

We will create two dictionaries to play answer smash. One will have C++ keywords and types along with their definitions, so we can revise a bit when we play. The second will have English words and definitions. We can use `operator[]` to make the dictionary of keywords.

Listing 7.3   Using `operator []` to populate a `map`

```
                                                        ┌─  Constructs
                                                        │   dictionary
std::map<std::string, std::string> keywords;     ⊲──────┘
keywords["char"] = "type for character representation which can be"   Fills
    " most efficiently processed on the target system";        ⊲──   dictionary
keywords["class"] = "user defined type with private members by default";
keywords["struct"] = "user defined type with public members by default";
keywords["vector"] = "sequential container supporting dynamic resizing";
keywords["template"] = "family of classes or functions parameterized"
                        " by one or more parameters";
```

To use `operator[]`, we need a mutable rather than `const map`, but once we have set up the dictionaries, we won't need to change them. Now, we noticed we can pass an initializer list for the key and value to `insert` earlier:

```
dictionary.insert({ "insert", "place inside" });
```

Likewise, we can use an initializer list of pairs, or even an initializer list of initializer lists comprising two strings to construct our dictionary.

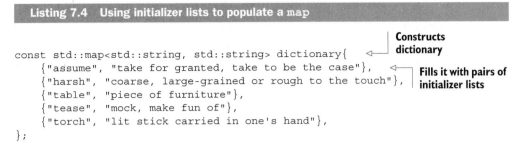

Listing 7.4   Using initializer lists to populate a `map`

```
const std::map<std::string, std::string> dictionary{        Constructs dictionary
    {"assume", "take for granted, take to be the case"},        Fills it with pairs of
    {"harsh", "coarse, large-grained or rough to the touch"},   initializer lists
    {"table", "piece of furniture"},
    {"tease", "mock, make fun of"},
    {"torch", "lit stick carried in one's hand"},
};
```

The second approach means we can mark the dictionary as `const` to ensure we don't accidentally change its contents later.

We can iterate over the keywords, using a structured binding to the key and value by `const` reference to avoid copying the strings:

```
for (const auto & [word, definition] : keywords)
```

For each keyword, we need a word from the dictionary that overlaps so we can smash the keyword and dictionary word together. Given the word `"char"`, we could look for something in the dictionary starting with `"char"`, but the whole word could get swallowed rather than overlapping. That is fine, but it might be more fun to avoid this. Instead, we could try to find something starting with `"har"`. Therefore, we need to start with the substring beginning at the second character, or index `1`, and make a stem or start of the word to look up:

```
size_t offset = 1;
auto stem = word.substr(offset);
```

We can then go through the dictionary looking for words starting with that stem. We need to check if a key's substring starting at index `0` of length `stem.size()` is equal to the stem `"har"`, so we would find `"harsh"` in our dictionary. In the worst case, this does mean we will plod through each key and may not find a word. We'll see a more efficient way to look up keys in a `map` shortly.

If nothing matches the stem `"har"`, we can try again starting at the next letter, so we use `"ar"`. There happens to be a match for `"har"`, so we have a suitable word and don't need to check further. Some words, like `"struct"`, need more searching. We drop the initial `'s'` and search for the stem `"truct"`. However, nothing in the dictionary starts with `"truct"`, so we could then try `"ruct"` and keep trying until we try to match the single letter `"t"`. We need at least one overlapping letter to smash two words together. Some words may have no match at all, so we can indicate this with an empty string. We could return an `optional` instead or even a `tuple` with a Boolean to indicate we cannot find a suitable word, but an empty string works too. Try these different approaches for extra practice.

Writing the search in a separate function means we can test it. We can put the function in a new source file, called `Smash.cpp`, and use a namespace along with a header file, `Smash.h`, to declare the functions we need. The search function takes the word we want to match and a dictionary to search. We need to return a key from the dictionary if we find a word or an empty string otherwise. If we return the offset used too, the calling code can smash together the two words without having to rediscover where the overlap is. As we have seen, a simple way to return two values from a function is via an std::pair, so we can do that here, putting the code in Smash.cpp and declaring the function in the corresponding header.

Listing 7.5   Finding an overlapping word

```cpp
#include <map>
#include <string>
#include <utility>

#include "Smash.h"

std::pair<std::string, int> find_overlapping_word(std::string word,
    const std::map<std::string, std::string>& dictionary)
{
    size_t offset = 1;              ◁──┐  Starts at the second
    while (offset < word.size())        │  letter of the word
    {
        auto stem = word.substr(offset);
        for (const auto & [k, v] : dictionary)       Considers the start
        {                                             of each key
            auto key_stem = k.substr(0, stem.size());
            if (key_stem == stem)
            {                          Finds a match
                return { k, offset };
            }
        }
        ++offset;
    }                    Did not find a match
    return { "", -1 };
}
```

Although we are potentially checking all the keys, the overlap function is good enough for a first attempt at answer smash. We need a function taking the two dictionaries, one of keywords and one of more general words, both with definitions to use as clues. For each keyword, we'll try to find an overlapping word, and if we do find a word, we will display both definitions as clues. If we don't, we get an empty string and offset of -1 back, so we will continue to the next keyword. If we find a suitable word, the correct answer is the start of the keyword concatenated with the second word. We can create the answer using operator+:

```cpp
word.substr(0, offset) + second_word
```

Now, the substring creates a temporary string, and the concatenation then creates another string, so this approach is not very efficient. We do not need to copy the substring. C++17 introduced a string_view in the string_view header, which provides a *view* rather than a *copy* of a string. The std::string_view gives us read-only access to an existing string, which means the existing string needs to remain in scope for the view to be valid. We can take a view of the first part of the first word, avoiding a copy, and use `std::format`, which we saw in chapter 2, to make the answer. We can therefore say

```
std::string answer = std::format("{}{}",
    std::string_view(word).substr(0, offset), second_word);
```

and avoid the temporary copy of the substring. For further details, see http://mng.bz/amzj. Using a `string_view` is often more efficient, but as it is a view of another object, we need to be careful not to use the view after the original string has gone out of scope. We'll stick with `operator+` in this example for simplicity. It's useful to be aware that we are making an extra copy and don't need to, though.

We can use `std::getline` to read the guess. The player can simply press Enter to give up. We can compare the response with the answer to determine whether the guess is correct or not, again putting code in `Smash.cpp` and declaring the function in `Smash.h`.

Listing 7.6   A simple answer smash game

```
#include <iostream>
#include <map>
#include <string>

#include "Smash.h"

void simple_answer_smash(
    const std::map<std::string, std::string> &keywords,
    const std::map<std::string, std::string> &dictionary)
{
    for (const auto & [word, definition] : keywords)       ⟵ For each keyword
    {
        auto [second_word, offset] = find_overlapping_word(word,   Finds an
                                dictionary);               ⟵ overlap
        if (offset == -1)
        {                                                  Checks we have
            std::cout << "Not match for " << word << '\n';  a suitable word
            continue;
        }
        std::string second_definition =                    Uses at for a const map
                dictionary.at(second_word);          ⟵ rather than operator[]
        std::cout << definition << "\nAND\n"
                  << second_definition << '\n';
```
Displays both definitions ⟶
```
        std::string answer =                                Smashes the two
                word.substr(0, offset) + second_word;  ⟵ words together
        std::string response;
        std::getline(std::cin, response);                 Gets the response
        if (response == answer)                       ⟵ Sees whether the
        {                                                 guess is correct
            std::cout << "CORRECT!!!!!!!!!!\n";
        }
        else
```

```
        {
            std::cout << answer << '\n';
        }
        std::cout << word << ' ' << second_word << "\n\n\n";
    }
}
```

We can call this from `main` and play our game.

Listing 7.7   Playing the first version of answer smash

```
#include "Smash.h"          ◁──┐  Includes header declaring
int main()                     │  simple_answer_smash
{
    const std::map<std::string, std::string> keywords{
        {"char", "type for character representation which can be most"
                 "efficiently processed on the target system"},
        {"class", "user defined type with private members by default"},
        {"struct", "user defined type with public members by default"},
        {"vector", "sequential container supporting dynamic resizing"},
        {"template", "used for generic code"},
    };
    const std::map<std::string, std::string> dictionary{
        {"assume", "take for granted, take to be the case"},
        {"harsh", "coarse, large-grained or rough to the touch"},
        {"table", "piece of furniture"},
        {"tease", "mock, make fun of"},
        {"torch", "lit stick carried in one's hand"},
    };
    simple_answer_smash(keywords, dictionary);    ◁──┐  Plays
}                                                     │  the game
```

Sets up keywords → (points to `};` after template)

Sets up dictionary ← (points to `};` after torch)

We thought about the first keyword, `"char"`, and the dictionary word `"harsh"`. For this combination, we see the clue

```
type for character representation which can be most efficiently processed on
    the target system
AND
coarse, large-grained or rough to the touch
```

We can either try a guess or just press Enter and see the answer:

```
charsh
char harsh
```

We have a simple game. If we take a deeper dive into the `map` and other associative containers, we will see how to make the search for an overlap more efficient and learn more C++ too.

7.2   Associative containers

We've used the `std::map` to build a hardcoded game. If we learn about what is going on inside the structure, we will be able to make some slight performance improvements.

With these in hand, we need a related data structure, the `std::multimap`, to allow storage of a proper language dictionary, which lets us have more than one value per key. After all, words sometimes have more than one definition, so when we use a proper dictionary in the final section of this chapter, we may need to store several values for a single key.

7.2.1 The map type in more detail

We know both a `vector` and `array` store their elements contiguously, and we can dynamically resize a `vector` but not the `array`. If we search for an item in a `vector`, we might have to iterate over all the elements before finding what we need, potentially getting to the end without finding the item. If we have n elements in a `vector`, we may need to check all n elements, which is described as `O(n)`, or linear complexity. We've seen that we can dynamically add pairs to a `map`, but we haven't thought about how elements are stored, so we don't know how a search works.

A `map` is designed so we can search for items more quickly. Rather than storing the elements next to each other, the map stores them in a *binary tree*. A binary tree has nodes, storing elements and pointers to other child nodes, like branches in a tree, and has at most two branches at any node; hence the name binary. The nodes are ordered, giving us a *binary search tree*, with smaller elements going to the left and larger elements going to the right. For a `map`, our elements are a key and value, and the key is used to decide whether an item goes to the left or right.

If we put {1:a}, {3:c}, and {5:e} in a `map`, we start with a single node {1:a} and then add {3:c}. As the key 3 is larger than 1, the new element {3:c} goes to the right, as shown in figure 7.1.

When we add the final element {5:e}, two things happen. First, the new node is larger than {3:c}, so it would go below and to the right, but adding a child node here means the tree is unbalanced. In effect, we have a chain of {1:a}, {3:c}, and {5:e} rather than a balanced tree, as we have lots of right branches and no left branches. Pulling {3:c} up to be the top node rebalances the tree, keeping smaller elements on the left and larger elements on the right, giving the layout as shown in figure 7.2.

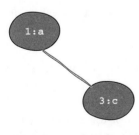

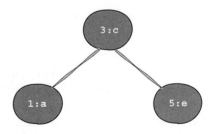

Figure 7.1 `Map` with two nodes: the first node {1:a} at the top and the next larger node {3:c} to the right

Figure 7.2 Three elements in a balanced binary search tree: nodes with smaller keys go on the left and larger keys on the right.

Having put elements in a map, we can now search it. If we want to know if {2:b} is in the map, we start with the top node, {3:c}, and since the key is 2, which is less than 3, we move down to the left node {1:a}. That is not equal to 2 and furthermore is a *leaf* or *terminating node*, so our search is done. We only considered half of the tree. Because the tree is a balanced binary tree, we will either search a left or a right branch, so we have logarithmic complexity, O(log(n)). In fact, search, removal, and insertion operations all have logarithmic complexity. If we double the number of elements, we only need one extra set of comparisons when we search. For the vector, searching is O(n). If we double the number of elements, we might double the number of comparisons when we search. We might get lucky and find an element at the start, but in the worst case, we must check all the items. Figure 7.3 shows the worst case for constant big-O, O(n), and logarithmic, O(log(n)), big-O.

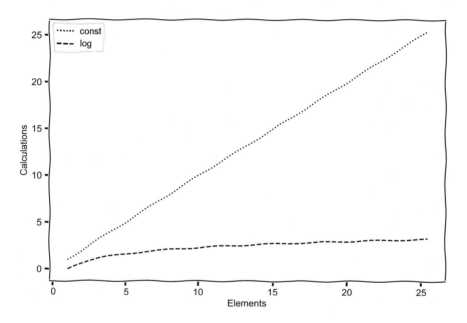

Figure 7.3   Constant time complexity: O(n) grows much faster than logarithmic complexity, O(log(n)), as the number of elements is increased.

The rebalancing keeps searching efficient. C++ maps are usually implemented as red–black trees. The color is extra information on each node, used when insertions or deletions take place. To keep the searches to O(log(n)), the tree needs to be *balanced.* If there are many more nodes down one branch than another, searching through the largest side takes longer. A classic resource for tree data structures and algorithms is Donald Knuth's *The Art of Computer Programming*, Volume 3 (Addison-Wesley Professional, 1998).

If we look at CppReference (see https://en.cppreference.com/w/cpp/container/map), we are told that a map is a *sorted* associative container. C++11 introduced *unordered* containers, which we will look at in the next chapter. We had to specify the key and value types for our maps, but a `map` also takes a comparison type, used to place nodes in the tree. The comparison defaults to `std::less<Key>`. For the `std::string`, we get a default of `std::less<std::string>`, which equates to `operator<` for `std::string`. We can specify other ways to compare. For example, we may want to make all our strings lowercase first. For a user-defined type, we might need to write a comparison operator or define the spaceship operator to use our type in a `map`. If we have a user-defined type, even a simple struct such as

```
struct Stuff { int x; };
```

we get a compile error if we try to use `Stuff` in a map as the key:

```
std::map<Stuff, int> lookup;
lookup[Stuff{ 1 }] = 1;
```

All we need to do is add the spaceship operator to the struct

```
friend auto operator <=> (const Stuff &, const Stuff&)  = default;
```

and we can then use it in the lookup.

The C++ standard often tells us the complexity of operations on a container, helping us make sensible choices when we code. The big-O or complexity is the worst case. For example, a search described as `O(n)` may only look at one element if the first element inspected is a match. At worst, all the elements will be compared. The complexity is a guideline to how many operations might happen, not a guarantee of efficiency. We might still need to benchmark our code to see how fast it is, and a profiler can help us find bottlenecks.

Now, when we built our simple answer smash in listing 7.6, we manually checked the keys, so we potentially compared our stem word against all n keys, giving us `O(n)`. Without profiling, we can improve on this, using other facilities offered by the `std::map`.

7.2.2 *Using lower and upper bound to find a key more efficiently*

The `std::map` has a `lower_bound` and an `upper_bound` function, which help us query the map more effectively. Both functions find the position at which an element would be inserted. The `lower_bound` finds the first element greater than or equal to the queried element, while the `upper_bound` finds the position of an element with a greater value. Nicolai Josuttis' book *The C++ Standard Library, Second Edition* (Addison-Wesley Professional, 2012), is an excellent reference book for further details. The `std::set` and `std::multiset` also support these functions. We haven't used these containers yet. A set allows us to keep a collection of unique values, like a `map` but with keys only, and the multiset allows us to have duplicate keys.

There are free functions, `std::lower_bound` and `std::upper_bound`, as well, which can be used on other containers, provided the elements are ordered by `operator<`. We could therefore use these functions on a sorted `vector`:

```
const std::vector<int> data{ 1, 2, 4, 5, 6, 7 };
auto lower = std::lower_bound(data.begin(), data.end(), 3);
auto upper = std::upper_bound(data.begin(), data.end(), 3);
```

This might be quicker than iterating through the elements trying to find 3. The upper and lower bound both point to the third element, 4, as shown in figure 7.4.

When the lower and upper bound match, the item is not present. If we insert 3 and run the query again, `lower_bound` would then return an iterator to the 3, and `upper_bound` would still return an iterator to the value 4. Because the positions do not match, we have found the value 3. The lower bound is greater than or equal to the element, and the upper bound is always greater than the element, so

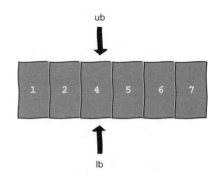

Figure 7.4   The lower bound, `lb`, and upper bound, `ub`, of 3 in a sorted vector

matching bounds mean they are both greater, whereas different bounds mean the lower bound is at the first such element.

We can also find the lower and upper bounds in one call to `equal_range`. This returns an `std::pair` of iterators, so we can use structured bindings again to obtain the lower and upper bounds:

```
auto [lb, ub] = std::equal_range(data.begin(), data.end(), 3);
```

The `std::map`, along with other containers mentioned, has member functions behaving the same way. We sometimes find containers have specialized versions of general functions for performance reasons.

We can rewrite our find overlap function using the `lower_bound` and `upper_bound` member functions, thereby avoiding potentially checking through all the keys. Previously, in listing 7.5, we iterated over all the keys, dropping out of the loop if we found a match to the stem. Now, we can use `equal_range` instead to find the lower and upper bound of the stem, as this function bundles the results of `lower_bound` and `upper_bound` into an `std::pair`. The lower bound finds the insertion point if the word isn't there, so we could be at the end of the dictionary or at a nonmatching word. We need to check that the lower bound isn't at the end of the dictionary before comparing the stem with the first part of the lower bound's key

```
lb->first.substr(0, stem.size())
```

to discover whether we have found a suitable word. Pulling this together gives us the following function.

Listing 7.8   Finding an overlapping word more efficiently

```
std::pair<std::string, int> find_overlapping_word(std::string word,
    const std::map<std::string, std::string>& dictionary)
```

```
{
    size_t offset = 1;
    while (offset < word.size())
    {
        auto stem = word.substr(offset);               No for loop
        auto [lb, ub] = dictionary.equal_range(stem);  any more
        if (lb != dictionary.end() &&
                stem == lb->first.substr(0, stem.size()))  Have we found a
        {                                                   suitable overlap?
            return {lb->first, offset};        Returns word
        }                                      and offset
        ++offset;
    }
    return {"", -1};
}
```

We can use this function in our game instead of the original version we wrote in listing 7.5.

We will only find the first matching word when we call `find_overlapping_word`, which we can improve on. There might be more than one word that overlaps, and furthermore, a proper dictionary might have more than one entry for a word. We can make a random choice when we have more than one suitable word, which will add some variety to our game. We can also use an `std::multimap` to support more than one entry per key. While we are thinking about associative containers, let's learn about multimaps, and then we will be ready to make a new version of our game using a proper dictionary.

7.2.3   *Multimaps*

An `std::multimap` also lives in the `map` header and uses a key and value; for example:

```
std::multimap<std::string, std::string> dictionary;
```

The `multimap` supports multiple values for the same key and behaves like an `std::map` but with a `vector` of values per key.

To insert items, we can use `insert`:

```
dictionary.insert({ key, value });
```
or `emplace`:
```
dictionary.emplace(key, value);
```

As we saw for a `vector` in chapter 2, `insert` needs an element, so we would use `std::pair` for the `multimap` version, while `emplace` constructs the element from the provided arguments. The key–value pairs still live in nodes in a tree, but we can have several to search through, as figure 7.5 shows.

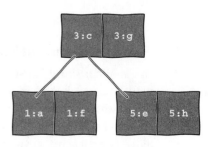

Figure 7.5   A multimap with multiple values for a given key

To retrieve values, we need to cope with potentially having more than one value per key. Furthermore, the `std::multimap` has no `operator[]` or `at` function, so we need to do something else. Fortunately, using `lower_bound` and `upper_bound` or `equal_range` gives us what we need, allowing us to find all values corresponding to a given key. These functions return iterators, letting us use all the values corresponding to a key if there are any.

Let's consider the following example. Using namespace literals, we can make a `multimap` matching figure 7.5:

```
std::multimap<int, std::string> mm{
    {1,"a"s}, {1,"a"s}, {3,"c"s}, {3,"g"s}, {5,"e"s}, {5,"h"s},
};
```

If we search for `mm.equal_range(2)`, we get an iterator to the node with element `3:c` for both the lower and upper bound. This means an element with key 2 would be inserted there. If we search for `mm.equal_range(3)` instead, the lower bound is `3:c`, being the first element not less than the key 3, and the upper bound is `5:e`, being the first element greater than the key 3. We then have a pair of iterators to use to walk over all the elements with key 3.

We need to find a word starting with a stem so we can find the lower bound

```
auto stem = word.substr(offset);
auto lb = dictionary.lower_bound(stem);
```

when the dictionary is a `multimap`. The upper bound we need is any word after the stem. If we copy the stem

```
auto beyond_stem = stem;
```

we can add a character after a `'z'` to get beyond the possible stems of words

```
beyond_stem += ('z' + 1);
```

and use this to find the upper bound:

```
auto ub = dictionary.upper_bound(beyond_stem);
```

We then get the start and end of a range of words if there are matches. We will use the `multimap` to build a better game, randomly choosing a suitable word from this range.

7.3 *File-based answer smash*

We made a simple answer smash game using hardcoded keywords and a tiny dictionary. We can make a more interesting game by loading data from a file. The code provided with this book has two `csv` files in the folder for this chapter. One has a selection of C++ keywords, using definitions based on CppReference (see https://en.cppreference.com/w/cpp/keyword), and the second has various English words based on a subset of Wordnetcode (see http://mng.bz/M9KQ).

7.3.1   *Loading data from a file*

We haven't used files yet, but we have used streams, such as `std::cout` and `std::cin`, and C++ treats files as streams. Files live in the `fstream` header. We can open an input file, `ifstream`, using a filename

```
std::ifstream infile{ filename };
```

and use the stream in a Boolean context to see whether it is open:

```
if (infile)
// all good
```

A file is automatically closed when the variable goes out of scope, so the file streams use *resource acquisition is initialization* (RAII), which we met in the last chapter.

Files can be written in text or binary, so we can specify the mode in the constructor (see http://mng.bz/yZDp). Our dictionary is text, so the default text mode works for us. If we want to write to a file, we use an output file stream, `ofstream`. An output file stream can be text or binary as well, but we might also want to truncate an existing file or append at the end. We can specify open for output and append using bitwise OR (`|`) of the input output stream (`ios`) openmodes `out` and `app`

```
std::ofstream f1("test.txt", std::ios::out | std::ios::app);
```

and so on (see http://mng.bz/Xqy9). To read from a file, we can either use `operator>>` or `std::getline`, which we used with `std::cin` in chapter 3. For the output stream, we would use `operator<<`.

The words in our file are stored in mixed case, but we don't want `Int` and `int` to be treated as different words. We should, therefore, make the keys lowercase so we can compare directly with lowercased input. We need to write something ourselves, so guided by CppReference, we can transform a `string`, making each character lowercase. We can use `transform` from the `algorithm` header and C's `tolower` function from the `cctype` header (see https://shortener.manning.com/QR66). The `tolower` function operates on `int`s, rather than `char`s, so we must be careful. We need to treat each character as an `unsigned char` because the behavior of `std::tolower` is undefined if the argument's value is neither an end of file (EOF) nor representable as an unsigned `char`. We therefore use a lambda taking an `unsigned char` in the transformation.

Listing 7.9   Transforming a string to lowercase

```
#include <algorithm>
#include <cctype>
std::string str_tolower(std::string s) {
    std::transform(s.begin(), s.end(), s.begin(),
      [](unsigned char c) { return std::tolower(c); }
    );
    return s;
}
```

We can now write a function to load a dictionary from a file. Each line will have a word, a comma, and a definition:

```
struct,user defined type with public members by default
```

We can walk through the file one line at a time and try to find the first comma:

```
size_t position = line.find(',');
```

If the `position` is `std::string::npos`, we have an invalid line, which we can log and ignore. Otherwise, we can split the line into a key and value. The key is the substring up to the comma's position

```
std::string key{ line.substr(0, position) };
```

and the definition is the substring starting after the comma's position up to the end of the line:

```
std::string value{ line.substr(position + 1) };
```

If we use an `std::string` for the filename, we can write a function returning a `multimap` to use in our improved game. The `multimap` allows more than one definition per word.

Listing 7.10 Loading a file into a `multimap`

```
#include <fstream>
#include <iostream>
#include <map>
#include <string>

std::multimap<std::string, std::string>
    load_dictionary(const std::string& filename)
{
    std::multimap<std::string, std::string> dictionary;
    std::ifstream infile{ filename };              Creates and opens
    if (infile)                                    a file for reading
    {
        std::string line;                          Reads
        while (std::getline(infile, line))    <─┘ each line
        {
            size_t position = line.find(',');  <─┐
            if (position != std::string::npos)     Splits on
            {                                      the comma
                std::string key{ line.substr(0, position) }; │ Lowercases
                key = str_tolower(key);                      │ the key
                std::string value{ line.substr(position + 1) };
                dictionary.emplace(key, value);   <─┐ Adds key–value
            }                                          pair to multimap
            else
            {
                std::cout << "***Invalid line\n" << line
                        << "\nin " << filename << "***\n\n";
            }
        }
    }
}
```

```
   }
   else
   {
       std::cout << "Failed to open " << filename << '\n';
   }
   return dictionary;
}
```

We can use this function to load the keywords and the dictionary. File paths have back-slashes on some operating systems, so something like `"c:\"` might cause problems in code because the backslash is also used to escape a special character. We can use raw strings, introduced in C++11, indicated with `R()` around a string. If we keep the files in the working directory, we don't need to use a raw string, but it's another new feature that's worth being aware of:

```
const auto dictionary = load_dictionary(R"(dictionary.csv)");
const auto keywords = load_dictionary(R"(keywords.csv)");
```

There is more to raw strings, but we will stick with the `string` filename here. We need to remember that the code needs to be run from a directory containing the files; otherwise, the code won't find the input files.

> **Raw strings and the filesystem type**
>
> We can use various start and stop characters beyond the brackets `'('` and `')'` in raw strings (see http://mng.bz/46ER). We could even use the filesystem path introduced in C++17 (see https://en.cppreference.com/w/cpp/filesystem/path) to represent file paths.

7.3.2 Picking a word randomly using std::sample

Rather than using all the keywords, we can randomly pick a few to play the game. We can also pick one of several overlapping words from the dictionary. C++17 introduced a `sample` function, which allows us to choose some items from a range without replacement. Each item is equally likely. The `std::sample` function lives in the `algorithm` header. It takes a first and last iterator, an output iterator to write the samples to, how many samples to pick, and a random number generator. We can therefore include the `random` header to make a generator

```
std::mt19937 gen{ std::random_device{}() };
```

and find the entries matching the stem of a word. The lower bound matches the stem:

```
auto stem = word.substr(offset);
auto lb = dictionary.lower_bound(stem);
```

The lower bound may or may not match the stem we want. For the upper bound, we want one beyond the stem:

```
auto beyond_stem = stem;
beyond_stem += ('z' + 1);
auto ub = dictionary.upper_bound(beyond_stem);
```

Going beyond the stem ensures we find any word whose first few letters match. If we are looking for "pet", we want to include "petal", and any other words starting with "pet" as well.

If the lower and upper bounds, lb and ub, are equal, we cannot find a suitable word; otherwise, we can sample one item from the range into a vector:

```
std::vector<std::pair<std::string, std::string>> dest;
std::sample(lb, ub, std::back_inserter(dest), 1, gen);
```

Back in chapter 2, we discovered that Pascal's triangle told us how many combinations we can have for tossing a coin or, in this case, selecting an entry from a dictionary. Selecting a single item isn't difficult, but picking more than one is more complicated, so C++ is doing the hard work for us. C++20 introduced a ranges version of the sample algorithm, which we can use to pick a few of the keywords. If we load the keywords using listing 7.10, we can pick 5 using sample:

```
std::vector<std::pair<std::string, std::string>> first_words;
std::ranges::sample(keywords, std::back_inserter(first_words), 5, gen);
```

Now we have all the parts we need to create an answer smash game based on words and definitions in files.

7.3.3 *Answer smash*

First, we need a function to select an overlapping word in a multimap. Because we may get more than one matching word or a matching word with two different definitions, we will select one using the random sample function we just met. If we make a function template, we can send in a sample function, which makes testing easier. We can use a lambda instead to either perform a random sample or always pick the first or last item and so on for testing. Using a template means we should put the function in a header file, so we use our Smash.h header.

In listing 7.8, we found an overlapping word and reported the overlap. We could return the definition as well to save the extra lookup, so we can use a tuple to return the word, definition, and offset using

```
std::tuple<std::string, std::string, int>
```

We'll need several headers: map, string, tuple, and vector. Then we can write our function.

Listing 7.11   Selecting a word from a multimap

```
template <typename T>
std::tuple<std::string, std::string, int>
    select_overlapping_word_from_dictionary(std::string word,
```

```
        const std::multimap<std::string, std::string>& dictionary,
        T select_function)
{
    size_t offset = 1;
    while (offset < word.size())
    {
        auto stem = word.substr(offset);
        auto lb = dictionary.lower_bound(stem);
        auto beyond_stem = stem;
        beyond_stem += ('z' + 1);
        auto ub = dictionary.upper_bound(beyond_stem);
        if (lb != dictionary.end() &&
            lb != ub)
        {
            std::vector<std::pair<std::string, std::string>> dest;
            select_function(lb, ub, std::back_inserter(dest));
            auto found = dest[0].first;
            auto definition = dest[0].second;
            return { found, definition, offset };
        }
        ++offset;
    }
    return {"", "",  - 1};
}
```

Finds suitable words

Checks whether we found suitable words

Picks a dictionary entry

Didn't find a word, so try again

None found

We can test this function. In listing 6.12, we used a fake generator and distribution, but here we use only a single lambda to pick an item. We can always pick the first or last item for testing. The first item is the lower bound

```
auto select_first = [](auto lb, auto ub, auto dest) {
    *dest = *lb;
};
```

and the last item is one before the upper bound:

```
auto select_last = [](auto lb, auto ub, auto dest) {
    *dest = *(--ub);
};
```

We can test our `select_overlapping_word_from_dictionary` function in a `check_properties` function using the `assert` function again.

Listing 7.12 Testing properties

```
#include <cassert>
void check_properties()
{
    auto select_first = [](auto lb, auto ub, auto dest) {
        *dest = *lb;
    };
    auto [no_word, no_definition, no_offset] =
        select_overlapping_word_from_dictionary(
            "class", {}, select_first
        );
```

Uses empty multimap and lambda

```
        assert(no_word == "");
        assert(no_offset == -1);          | No suitable word found
}
```

Finally, we need a new answer smash function taking two multimaps. This is very similar to the hardcoded version with maps we built in listing 7.6, but it now samples one item from the dictionary using a lambda:

```
std::mt19937 gen{ std::random_device{}() };
auto select_one = [&gen](auto lb, auto ub, auto dest) {
    std::sample(lb, ub, dest, 1, gen);
};
```

Five keywords are sampled, and overlapping items from the dictionary are found, giving a `tuple` with a `word`, `definition`, and `offset` to save the extra lookup for the clue.

Listing 7.13   A better answer smash game

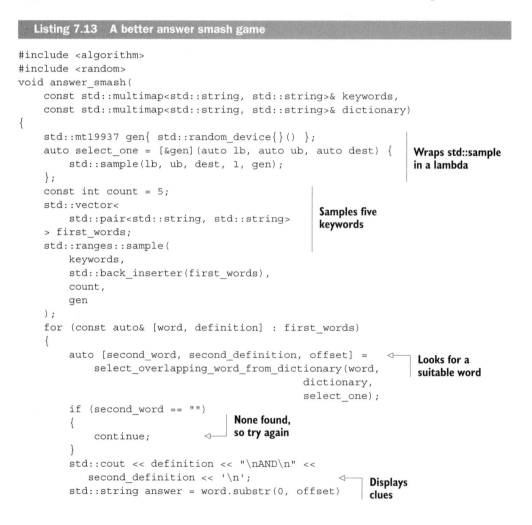

```
#include <algorithm>
#include <random>
void answer_smash(
    const std::multimap<std::string, std::string>& keywords,
    const std::multimap<std::string, std::string>& dictionary)
{
    std::mt19937 gen{ std::random_device{}() };
    auto select_one = [&gen](auto lb, auto ub, auto dest) {     Wraps std::sample
        std::sample(lb, ub, dest, 1, gen);                     in a lambda
    };
    const int count = 5;
    std::vector<
        std::pair<std::string, std::string>                    Samples five
    > first_words;                                             keywords
    std::ranges::sample(
        keywords,
        std::back_inserter(first_words),
        count,
        gen
    );
    for (const auto& [word, definition] : first_words)
    {
        auto [second_word, second_definition, offset] =        Looks for a
            select_overlapping_word_from_dictionary(word,      suitable word
                                     dictionary,
                                     select_one);
        if (second_word == "")
        {                              None found,
            continue;                  so try again
        }
        std::cout << definition << "\nAND\n" <<
            second_definition << '\n';                         Displays
        std::string answer = word.substr(0, offset)            clues
```

```
        + second_word;
    std::string response;                        Checks
    std::getline(std::cin, response);            lowercased
    if (str_tolower(response) == answer)         response
    {
        std::cout << "CORRECT!!!!!!!!!!\n";
    }
    else
    {
        std::cout << answer << '\n';
    }
    std::cout << word << ' ' << second_word << "\n\n\n";
    }
}
```

We can call the game from `main` and see how well we do.

Listing 7.14   A proper answer smash game

```
#include "Smash.h"
int main()
{
    using namespace smashing;
    const auto dictionary = load_dictionary(R"(dictionary.csv)");
    const auto keywords = load_dictionary(R"(keywords.csv)");
    answer_smash(keywords, dictionary);
}
```

Don't forget to include a `Smash.cpp` file in your build, and the code needs to be run from a directory containing the dictionary and keyword files or the path changed in the code.

You should get various clues when you play the game. Some are quite pleasing. For example, the clue

```
is a prvalue expression whose value is the address of the implicit object
    parameter
AND
discipline that interprets past events
```

smashed `"this"` and `"history"` together to give `"thistory"`.

We've built the answer smash game we set out to create and revised using the `std::map` and `std::multimap` along the way. We noted that C++ introduced unordered maps, so we will look at these in more detail in the next chapter.

Summary

- Associative containers are part of the standard template library (STL).
- An `std::pair` holds two values of any type, and we use `first` and `second` to access the values.

- The `std::tuple` is a generalization of an `std::pair`, and we use `std::get` to access values.
- We can use structured bindings to bind pairs, tuples, and more directly into variables.
- The `std::map`'s `operator[]` can be used to query and insert elements, so use the `at` function instead to query if you don't want to add an element by accident.
- An `std::string_view` can be used to avoid copies of strings, but care must be taken over lifetimes.
- The `std::map` search, removal, and insertion operations have logarithmic complexity.
- An `std::map` key must be supported by the `std::less` operator, so we might need to add the spaceship operator to a user defined type to use it as a dictionary key.
- The `std::map`, `std::multimap`, and `std::set` are ordered associative containers, often implemented as red–black trees.
- An `std::multimap` supports non-unique keys.
- Use the lower and upper bound member functions of the ordered associative containers for efficiency.
- Files are streams, so they support `operator<<` and `operator>>`. We can also use `std::getline` to read a whole line from an input file stream.
- The `std::sample` function selects a sample of `k` items from a range without replacement.

Unordered maps and coroutines

8

This chapter covers

- Unordered maps
- Hashes
- Coroutines

In this chapter, we will make a matching-pennies game. The game has two players: us and the computer. We each have a coin and choose heads or tails. If the computer matches our choice, we lose. If the computer's choice differs, we win. We can use a random distribution for the computer's guess, so we don't need much code for the first game.

Once we have the initial matching-pennies game working, we'll see whether the computer can predict our guess by building a mind-reading machine. To be honest, the computer won't really be able to read our minds. Claude E. Shannon wrote a short paper in 1953 called "A Mind-Reading (?) Machine" (see http://mng.bz/vPDp). The question mark in the title is deliberate. The game has been used for thought experiments in game theory and for psychology research. The mind reader needs to keep track of what has previously happened, so we'll use the `std::unordered_map` to track the state. In chapter 7, we used an `std::map`. In this chapter, we'll use an `std::unordered_map` for further practice. As we noted in chapter 7, the `std::map` needs an `operator<` defined for its keys. The `std::unordered_map` requires a `hash` and an equality operator, so we'll learn about `std::hash` too. The computer will use the state to predict our next choice. When we're done, we'll wrap the code in a coroutine for extra practice.

8.1   *Randomly generated matching pennies*

To get started, we will make the computer randomly generate a `0` or `1`, representing heads or tails, using an `std::uniform_int_distribution`. We also need user input. In chapter 3, we read numbers for the number-guessing game, so we need code similar to the function in listing 3.4. That function tried to extract a number from a stream and returned an `std::optional`. In this case, we only want to accept `0` or `1`. Any other input means the player has given up. If we get the whole input as a string, we can compare the input with `"0"` or `"1"` and return an appropriate `optional<int>`. Any input other than `0` or `1` returns an empty `optional` to indicate that the player wants to stop.

Listing 8.1   Reading an `optional` 0 or 1

```cpp
#include <iostream>
#include <optional>
#include <string>
std::optional<int> read_number(std::istream& in)
{
    std::string line;
    std::getline(in, line);
    if (line == "0") {
        return { 0 };        ⟵┤ 0
    }
    else if (line == "1") {
        return { 1 };        ⟵┤ 1
    }
    return {};    ⟵┐ Empty optional to
}                     │ indicate stopping
```

To build our pennies game, we need the computer to pick a random `0` or `1`, so we need a generator and a distribution:

```cpp
std::mt19937 gen{ std::random_device{}() };
std::uniform_int_distribution dist(0, 1);
```

To get the computer choice, we call `dist(gen)`. We compare the player and computer turns to decide who won. If we keep track of how many times the player wins and how many turns are taken, we can report some stats once the play stops. Pulling this together gives us a pennies game.

Listing 8.2   A pennies game

```
#include <random>
void pennies_game()
{
    int player_wins = 0;
    int turns = 0;                                            Track stats
    std::mt19937 gen{ std::random_device{}() };
    std::uniform_int_distribution dist(0, 1);

    std::cout << "Select 0 or 1 at random and press enter.\n";    Computer's
    std::cout << "If the computer predicts your guess it wins.\n";  turn
    while (true)
    {
        const int prediction = dist(gen);

        auto input = read_number(std::cin);          Player's
        if (!input)          Stops if 0 or 1         turn
        {                    is not chosen
            break;
        }
        const int player_choice = input.value();

        ++turns;
        std::cout << "You pressed " << player_choice
                  << ", I guessed " << prediction << '\n';
                                                              Updates stats
        if (player_choice != prediction)
        {
            ++player_wins;
        }
    }
    std::cout << "you win " << player_wins << '\n'
        << "I win " << turns - player_wins << '\n';
}
```

We need to call the `pennies_game` function from a `main` function, and then we can play the game. The computer might win half the time on average. As it stands, this game isn't that interesting. If two human opponents play, they will try to outsmart each other by being unpredictable. If the computer tracks our choices, we have more of a challenge. Let's extend the game by allowing the computer to think, or at least base the prediction on previous moves. Can we manage to behave randomly and outdo the computer?

8.2   Matching pennies using an unordered_map

Shannon tracked the state when a person played against his machine. Rather than tracking both the computer and player's exact choices, he tracked whether a win or loss resulted in a change and whether that change resulted in a subsequent win or loss. For example, the person could lose, choose the same, and then lose again. This gives eight possible states, as shown in table 8.1.

Table 8.1   The eight possible states in the pennies game

Penultimate outcome	Choice	Last outcome
Lose	Same	Lose
Lose	Same	Win
Lose	Change	Lose
Lose	Change	Win
Win	Same	Lose
Win	Same	Win
Win	Change	Lose
Win	Change	Win

For each state, Shannon tracked the last two choices made by the player, noting whether they changed their turn or stuck with the same choice. If the two choices match, they form the prediction. If not, the mind reader makes a random choice. We could track every choice from the start of the game, but using the last two choices works well. Let's think through what happens as we track the choices for each state. We will build up a pair of choices against state and use these to make a prediction if they match.

Imagine we always choose heads, so we never change our minds. Can Shannon's strategy figure out what we are doing? Over time, regardless of whether we win or lose, the choice in the middle of the table will always be Same, so only four rows get populated. Because we always play heads, the two last choices will eventually always be Same, leading to the Outcome column as shown in table 8.2.

Table 8.2   The states and corresponding outcomes if we always choose heads

State			Basis of prediction
Penultimate outcome	Choice	Last outcome	Outcome
Lose	Same	Lose	Same, Same
Lose	Same	Win	Same, Same
Lose	Change	Lose	
Lose	Change	Win	
Win	Same	Lose	Same, Same
Win	Same	Win	Same, Same
Win	Change	Lose	
Win	Change	Win	

Any subsequent turn must correspond to one of the four populated rows because the choice will never change. The machine will find two matching outcomes of Same and predict that the player will choose the same, so it has seemingly read our minds. Were we to change our choice every time instead, the other four rows of the state table would eventually be populated with a pair of Changes, and again, the machine would predict correctly.

It does take a while to populate the state table. Initially, none of the eight states has any entries, so the computer picks at random. Comparing this with the player's choice tells us if the outcome is a win or a lose. We remember this outcome because it gives the first part of the state corresponding to the value for the first column. For the second turn, we still do not have any entries against the eight states to use for a prediction, so again, the computer picks at random, and the player takes a turn. We remembered the penultimate outcome and now know whether the player changed their mind and then won or lost. The extra information on this turn corresponds to the last two columns of the state:

```
{penultimate outcome, choice, last outcome}.
```

Now that we have a full current state, we are ready to add the first of the corresponding choices on the next turn. Again, the computer plays at random, but now we know whether the player sticks with the same choice or changes it. We record this as the first outcome against the previous state and then update the state that is ready for next time. In theory, the state might be the same as before, so on the next turn, we have a full pair for one row; otherwise, we have the start of a pair in another row. Over time, we will start filling in pairs of choices, meaning the computer may have matching outcomes against state and be able to make a prediction. The mind reader checks whether there is a matching pair in the state table for the current state. If so, the prediction is the value in the pair; otherwise, a random choice is made. The player makes their choice too, winning or losing. The state can then be updated, and the latest choice can be stored in the corresponding value.

We noted that always switching or always choosing the same outcome would be detected by the machine. With a less obvious strategy, the eight states tracking the last two moves are too much to keep in our heads, so it's hard to figure out what the machine is up to. The best way to outsmart the mind reader is by tracking the state ourselves so we know what it will predict and do the opposite. The mind reader is not reading the player's mind, but it is difficult to track what it is doing, so it might give the impression of mind-reading or perhaps willfulness. Like many appearances of machine intelligence, what's really going on is pattern matching or some kind of statistical analysis.

Rather than using the last two states, we could keep every choice and use a majority, moving average, or other statistic to make a prediction. Shannon used a pair to keep the circuit he built small and simple but effective. Using the last two choices to make a prediction works surprisingly well, so let's stick with Shannon's original idea.

We can store the eight states in an associative container, using an `std::tuple` for the three-part key and an `std::pair` for the two outcomes. The tuple needs a win or lose, a choice of same or change, and another win or lose. A class enum would be a good way to represent these. We met scoped enumerations in chapter 5 when we made suits for our card game. An enumeration is often clearer than a magic number because we can use a name to indicate the value, and a class enum is strongly typed, so it cannot be implicitly converted to an integer by mistake. The choice and outcome will be unknown initially, so we can use `Shrug` and `Unset` for these values. We only need to add the keyword `class` after `enum` to make scoped enums.

Listing 8.3   Three possible choices and outcomes

```
enum class Choice
{
    Same,
    Change,
    Shrug,
};
enum class Outcome
{
    Lose,
    Win,
    Unset,
};
```

The key for our state will be a tuple of an `Outcome`, a `Choice`, and another `Outcome`, indicating one of the rows from table 8.1, and the value will be a pair of `Choices`, so we need to include the `utility` and `tuple` headers. We could `typedef` the key and value to save typing `std::tuple<Outcome, Choice, Outcome>`, and `std::pair<Choice, Choice>` each time we use them. We can do better than `typedef`. C++11 introduced an *alias declaration*, allowing us to say `using` to introduce an alias for an existing type. We saw this in section 4.2.2 when we defined centuries and said `using centuries`. We can write

```
using state_t = std::tuple<Outcome, Choice, Outcome>;
using last_choices_t = std::pair<Choice, Choice>;
```

The alias declaration can be used for families of templates, so it is more general than a `typedef`, but they are equivalent if we specify all the template parameters. We will have further practice with the using declaration in the next chapter. For now, remember to prefer `using` to `typedef`.

We have a key and value type for our state but need a container. We learned about the `std::map` in the last chapter and could use that again here. However, C++11 introduced *unordered* containers, which we can also use for a lookup table, so let's find out how these containers work.

8.2.1 Unordered containers and std::hash

The `std::map` and `std::multimap`, along with `std::set` and `std::multiset`, are *ordered* associative containers using `std::less` as the default comparison for the ordering. As we learned in the last chapter, the elements are arranged in a balanced binary tree, so searching is `O(log(n))`. The unordered containers use an alternative data structure, called a hash table, which stores elements in slots or buckets. Let's take a moment to learn about hash tables.

A hash table uses a `hash` function to calculate the index of an element, indicating which bucket it belongs to. The index allows us to jump straight to the bucket where an element belongs without having to walk down part of a tree, so searching a hash table might be even quicker than searching an `std::map` or other tree-based structure.

Now, two different elements might give the same `hash` value, known as a *collision*, so we may end up with more than one element in a specific bucket. A search then needs to check each element in the bucket to find a specific element, which slows things down slightly. For a good hash, we won't get many collisions and will usually go straight to a bucket with a single element, but sometimes we might have to check a few elements in a bucket. In the worst case, we might have all our elements in a single bucket, so we would have complexity `O(n)`. However, for a decent `hash` function, we would expect one item per bucket, so the search is `O(1)` on average. In formal terms, we say the big-O or complexity is *amortized constant time*. Sometimes, the standard tells us the worst-case complexity for an operation, but sometimes it tells us the average or amortized time.

Let's visualize a hash table by mapping single characters' keys to integer values. If we use the ASCII value of the lowercase version of the key for the `hash`, lower- and uppercase versions of the same letter will end up in the same bucket. If we add two elements, with keys `'c'` and `'d'`, we do not have a clash, so we have at most one element in a bucket. However, if we then add an element with key `'D'`, we have a clash because elements with key `'d'` and `'D'` go in the same bucket, as shown in figure 8.1.

To search for an element with a key of `'d'`, we need to check both elements in the second table. Now, a collision is not a disaster. We can still find the elements but get better performance with a better `hash` function.

C++11's *unordered* containers are hash tables using `std::hash`, defined in the `functional` header, for the `hash` function. C++ provides specializations of `std::hash` for various types, including numeric types, as well as `std::string` and more (see https://en.cppreference.com/w/cpp/utility/hash). If we want to put a type without a `hash` in an unordered container, we

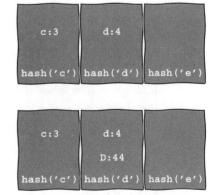

Figure 8.1 Two hash tables, one without a collision and the second with a collision, meaning a bucket contains more than one element

need to provide one. The type must support equality comparison too in case of `hash` collisions.

Let's use an `std::unordered_map` from the `unordered_map` header for our state table. As with an `std::map`, this takes a `key` and a `value` type but also needs a `Hash` and a `KeyEqual` type. These default to `std::hash` and `std::equal_to`, along the lines of

```
template<class Key, class Value,
    class Hash = std::hash<Key>,
    class KeyEqual = std::equal_to<Key>
> class unordered_map;
```

Our key is an `std::tuple`, which supports `std::equal_to`. This was introduced in C++14 and defaults to a function object calling `operator==` on the given type. Comparing tuples works out of the box. Given two tuples

```
std::tuple t1 = {Outcome::Lose, Choice::Shrug, Outcome::Lose};
std::tuple t2 = {Outcome::Lose, Choice::Shrug, Outcome::Lose};
```

we can check for equality:

```
bool match = t1 == t2;
```

This is equivalent to

```
bool match = std::equal_to{}.operator(t1, t2);
```

First, we make an `std::equal_to` instance using `{}`, and then `std::equal_to`'s call operator invokes `operator==` by default. The default `KeyEqual` in the `unordered_map` class template therefore works for our key. However, `std::tuple` does not have a hash implementation, so we need to write our own. We can specialize the `struct`

```
template<class Key>
struct hash;
```

for our tuple. By itself, the `struct` doesn't do much. However, there are several specializations in the `functional` header providing an `operator() const`, taking a `Key`, and returning a `size_t`. Many of the operators are marked `noexcept` because they will not throw an exception. We will implement a specialization for the `state_t`. Cpp-Reference tells us we are allowed to inject a custom specialization of `std::hash` into the standard namespace (see https://en.cppreference.com/w/cpp/utility/hash). We usually add code to our namespaces rather than namespace `std` to avoid clashing with standard code. Defining `std::hash` for a specific type is an exception. This means the `unordered_map` will find the specialization of `std::hash` for our key.

To specialize a template, we state the types we are special-casing. The `hash` only takes one type, `template<class Key>`, so we only have one type to special-case. We drop the `class Key` from the template head, leaving `template<>`, and we specify the type *after* the name in angle brackets, which gives us

```
template<>
struct std::hash<state_t>
```

Our specialization needs an operator taking a key and returning a `size_t`. It needs to be `const`, and we can flag it as `noexcept`:

```
std::size_t operator()(state_t const& k) const noexcept
```

Our tuple has three enums, and the standard library provides specializations of `std::hash` for enumerations. We can write a `hash` function combining the individual elements' hash values to provide the specialization for `std::hash<state_t>`. It would be nice to find a way to combine the hashes so we avoid a collision. Summing the hash values for

```
{Outcome::Lose, Choice::Shrug, Outcome::Win}
```

would map to the same hash as

```
{Outcome::Win, Choice::Shrug, Outcome::Lose}
```

causing a collision. We can do better if we can shift the hashes for each element using `operator<<`. We've used the stream insertion `operator<<` several times. The built-in arithmetic `operator<<` applies to numbers rather than streams, shifting the bits left (see http://mng.bz/n1D5). Shifting the binary number `1`, `1 << 1` gives `10` in binary because the one shifts left. If we then shift that once more, `2 << 1`, we have `100` in binary. By not shifting the first elements, shifting the second element by one and shifting the last element by two, and then summing the three shifted hashes, we happen to avoid clashes for our keys. Our approach is no good in general. The more elements we try to combine, the greater chance of a collision, and the further left we shift, the more likely we are to end up with zeros. However, for our small number of `Outcomes` and `Choices`, this approach does work.

We need to include the `functional` header for `std::hash`. The specialization for our tuple works as follows.

Listing 8.4 Specializing `std::hash` for our state tuple

```
#include <functional>
template<>                                          Specializes std::hash
struct std::hash<state_t>                           for state_t
{
    std::size_t operator()(state_t const& state) const noexcept    ◁── Implements
    {                                                                   operator()
        std::size_t h1 = std::hash<Outcome>{}(std::get<0>(state));  Gets each
        std::size_t h2 = std::hash<Choice>{}(std::get<1>(state));   element's hash
        std::size_t h3 = std::hash<Outcome>{}(std::get<2>(state));
        return h1 + (h2 << 1) + (h3 << 2);    ◁── Shifts
    }                                             and sums
};
```

This will work for our specific-use case. WG21 has discussed hash combination functions (see http://mng.bz/orDZ) and says that implementing a good `hash` function is not trivial. If we needed a more general way to combine fields into a suitable hash, the Boost library has a `hash_combine` method (see http://mng.bz/6nre). Boost is a free peer-reviewed library for C++ that has been around for a very long time. Many new C++ features started life in Boost, including smart pointers and the `optional`, `any`, and `variant` types. The library still includes many features that are not supported in C++ yet but might be adopted one day. It's big but worth having a look at if you've not seen it before.

Armed with a `hash` function, we are ready to keep the state for our mind-reading machine in an `unordered_map`. After including the `unordered_map` header, we can write a function returning the initial state. The eight keys from table 8.1 are represented in our `state_t` tuple. The tuple elements indicate a loss or win, followed by the player's choice of Same or Swap, resulting in a win or lose. The corresponding values are a pair storing how the player chose on the last two occasions the state happened. Initially, there are no player choices to store, so we flag the state as unset, using a pair of `Shrug`s:

```
const auto unset = std::pair<Choice, Choice>{Choice::Shrug,Choice::Shrug};
```

We can initialize the `std::unordered_map` using initializer lists like we did for the `std::map` in the last chapter.

Listing 8.5   An initial state table

```
#include <unordered_map>
std::unordered_map<state_t, last_choices_t> initial_state()
{
    const auto unset = std::pair<Choice, Choice>{Choice::Shrug,
                                                 Choice::Shrug };
    return {
        { {Outcome::Lose, Choice::Same,   Outcome::Lose}, unset },
        { {Outcome::Lose, Choice::Same,   Outcome::Win},  unset },
        { {Outcome::Lose, Choice::Change, Outcome::Lose}, unset },
        { {Outcome::Lose, Choice::Change, Outcome::Win},  unset },
        { {Outcome::Win,  Choice::Same,   Outcome::Lose}, unset },
        { {Outcome::Win,  Choice::Same,   Outcome::Win},  unset },
        { {Outcome::Win,  Choice::Change, Outcome::Lose}, unset },
        { {Outcome::Win,  Choice::Change, Outcome::Win},  unset },
    };
}
```

We tried to ensure we do not get hash collisions. For our eight states, a collision won't noticeably slow the game down, but we can check that each bucket has at most one element. The `std::unordered_map` provides a `bucket_count`, which tells us how many buckets we have in total, and `bucket_size` function, which tells us how many items are in a specific bucket. We can write a `check_properties` function using `assert` to verify that we don't have any clashes.

Listing 8.6   Checking that we have no hash collisions

```
#include <cassert>
void check_properties()
{
    std::unordered_map<
        state_t,
        last_choices_t
    > states = initial_state();

    for (size_t bucket = 0;
            bucket < states.bucket_count();
            bucket++)
    {
        assert(states.bucket_size(bucket) <= 1);
    }
}
```

At most one item per bucket

The test passes, but our handcrafted `hash` function would potentially break if we added more states. Writing a `hash` function can be difficult.

We can now start making predictions as a player makes a choice. Keeping the state separated from the mind-reading game means we can test our code more easily.

8.2.2   *Using an unordered_map to make a prediction*

The mind reader either predicts a player's choice based on the state table or makes a random choice. We'll keep the state table in a class, providing a `getter` function and an `update` function, to use after each turn. We can use a private state table initialized with the `initial_state` function from listing 8.5.

Listing 8.7   Class to track the game's state

```
class State
{
    std::unordered_map<state_t,last_choices_t> state_lookup
                                   = initial_state();

public:
    last_choices_t choices(const state_t& key) const;
    void update(const state_t& key,
                const Choice& turn_changed);
};
```

Private state

Gets choices for a given state

Updates values when a turn is taken

We have eight valid states but need some warmup before we have a valid `state_t` to look up. For example, we will start with no turns and so have state

```
{Outcome::Unset, Choice::Shrug, Outcome::Unset}
```

That state isn't in table 8.1, so we'll make the `choices` function return a pair of `Shrugs` in that case. We try to find a key in the lookup. The `find` method returns the end of the `unordered_map` if the element is not found, so we have an invalid state. If it is found, we return the corresponding value.

Listing 8.8   Find the choices or return two `Shrug`s

```
last_choices_t choices(const state_t& key) const
{
    if (auto it = state_lookup.find(key);          Tries to find
            it!=state_lookup.end())                the key
    {
        return it->second;
    }
    else
    {                                                      In the warmup
        return { Choice::Shrug, Choice::Shrug };   ◁──┘   phase, so Shrug
    }
}
```

To update the state, we also need to be mindful of initial `state_t` not being in our state table. Again, we try to find the key:

```
if (auto it = state_lookup.find(key); it != state_lookup.end())
```

If we have a valid state, we obtain the previous two choices from the iterator:

```
const auto [prev2, prev1] = it->second;
```

We can then update the key with the new pair:

```
last_choices_t value{ prev1, turn_changed };
it->second = value;
```

In effect, updating the state ignores invalid states from the first few turns and only updates valid states.

Listing 8.9   Updating choices for valid keys

```
void update(const state_t& key, const Choice& turn_changed)
{
    if (auto it = state_lookup.find(key);          Checks whether
            it != state_lookup.end())         ◁──┘ key exists
    {
        const auto [prev2, prev1] = it->second;           Forms new
        last_choices_t value{ prev1, turn_changed };   │ pair of choices
        it->second = value;              ◁───┐ Updates
    }                                         │ lookup
}
```

We can use the `last_choices_t` returned by the `choices` to make a prediction, even for an initial invalid state. If the two elements match, we return that value; otherwise, we return `Choice::Shrug` to mean we cannot make a prediction. We returned a pair of `Shrugs` for an invalid state deliberately. Because they match, a `Shrug` is returned for an invalid state, so the mind reader knows to make a random choice.

Listing 8.10 Choice from state

```
Choice prediction_method(const last_choices_t& choices)
{
    if (choices.first == choices.second)
    {                                          Matching, so return
        return choices.first;                  either value
    }
    else
    {                                          Nonmatching, so can't
        return Choice::Shrug;        ◁─┘       make a prediction
    }
}
```

We are now ready to build a mind reader. It will use our `State` class to make a prediction. The mind reader makes a prediction, and the player makes their choice. We then update the state table, ready to make a new prediction.

8.2.3   *The mind reader game*

We can create a `mind reader` class using the `State` class we made in listing 8.7. We need a random flip for some states. We've used random numbers several times now using a generator and distribution. We can make a template class, taking these types so we can fake them in tests. When we tested our random blobs in listing 6.12, we used a lambda that always returned 0 for the generator

```
[] () { return 0; }
```

and can do the same here. For the actual game, we use a proper generator and a distribution returning a 0 or 1:

```
std::mt19937 gen{ std::random_device{}() };
std::uniform_int_distribution dist{ 0, 1 };
```

Using the distribution and generator allows the mind reader to generate a random 0 or 1:

```
int flip() { return dist(gen); }
```

We can use that function to initialize a prediction variable:

```
int prediction = flip();
```

The mind reader's `prediction` will update after the player takes their turn, using the current state, so we need a `state` variable initialized with

```
{Outcome::Unset, Choice::Shrug, Outcome::Unset}
```

We will define the update function shortly. If it returns a `bool`, indicating a flip rather than a prediction, we can track how many guesses the mind reader made as we play the game. Our mind-reading class looks like this.

Listing 8.11   A mind-reading class

```
template <std::invocable<> T, typename U>
class MindReader {
    State state_table;
    T generator;
    U distribution;
    int prediction = flip();              Initially makes a
    state_t state{                        random choice
        Outcome::Unset,
        Choice::Shrug,
        Outcome::Unset
    };                      Stores state and
    int previous_go = -1;   player's turn
    int flip()
    {
        return distribution(generator);
    }
public:
    MindReader(T gen, U dis)
        : generator(gen), distribution(dis)
    {
    }
    int get_prediction() const
    {
        return prediction;
    }
    bool update(int player_choice);
};
```

When a player takes their turn, we update the mind reader, letting it know the player's choice. First, the player's choice either changed or not, so it can be used to update the current state using the function shown in listing 8.9. We work out if the turn changed or not

```
const Choice turn_changed = player_choice == previous_go ?
                        Choice::Same : Choice::Change;
```

and then update the state table accordingly:

```
state_table.update(state, turn_changed);
```

We can then store the current `player_choice` in `previous_go` to be ready for next time.

The current state has now changed, and a new prediction can be made, ready for the next turn. We update the state, shunting the previous win or lose to the front of the tuple and noting whether or not this turn was a change and whether or not it won:

```
state = {std::get<2>(state), turn_changed,
    (player_choice != prediction) ? Outcome::Win : Outcome::Lose};
```

We look that state up in the table, `state_table.choices(state)`, and use the pair to decide a prediction method employing the function from listing 8.10. We get a `Choice` back. For a `Shrug`, we flip the coin. For a `Change`, we want to switch a `0` with a `1` or vice versa so we can use the bitwise `operator^`, with `1`, which calculates `xor` of the choice with `1`, giving the opposite. If the prediction is Same, we know what the player chose this turn, so we update our prediction accordingly. We can do this in a new function in the `MindReader`.

Listing 8.12 Updating the prediction

```
bool update_prediction(int player_choice)
{
    bool guessing = false;
    Choice option = prediction_method(state_table.choices(state));
    switch (option)
    {
    case Choice::Shrug:
        prediction = flip();
        guessing = true;
        break;
    case Choice::Change:
        prediction = player_choice ^ 1;
        break;
    case Choice::Same:
        prediction = player_choice;
        break;
    }
    return guessing;
}
```

The `update` function uses `update_prediction` after updating the state table and current state.

Listing 8.13 The mind reader's `update` method

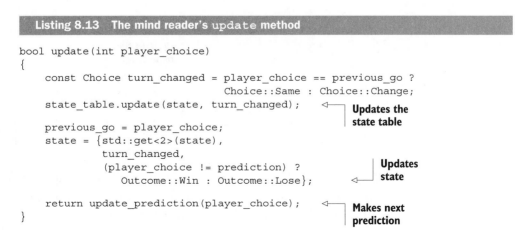

```
bool update(int player_choice)
{
    const Choice turn_changed = player_choice == previous_go ?
                              Choice::Same : Choice::Change;
    state_table.update(state, turn_changed);          ◁──┐ Updates the
                                                         │ state table
    previous_go = player_choice;
    state = {std::get<2>(state),
            turn_changed,
            (player_choice != prediction) ?                  Updates
                Outcome::Win : Outcome::Lose};   ◁──┘        state

    return update_prediction(player_choice);   ◁──┐ Makes next
}                                                 │ prediction
```

The game itself is now very like the pennies game we started with in listing 8.2. Rather than picking a random 0 or 1 in the main game loop, we need to consult the mind reader for a prediction. We will also track how many guesses there are and report that when the player stops.

Listing 8.14 A mind-reading game

```cpp
void mind_reader()
{
    int turns = 0;
    int player_wins = 0;
    int guessing = 0;

    std::mt19937 gen{ std::random_device{}() };
    std::uniform_int_distribution dist{ 0, 1 };
    MindReader mr(gen, dist);

    std::cout << "Select 0 or 1 at random and press enter.\n";
    std::cout << "If the computer predicts your guess it wins\n";
    std::cout << "and it can now read your mind.\n";
    while (true)
    {
        const int prediction = mr.get_prediction();      // Consults the
                                                         // mind reader

        auto input = read_number(std::cin);
        if (!input)
        {
            break;
        }
        const int player_choice = input.value();

        ++turns;
        std::cout << "You pressed " << player_choice
            << ", I guessed " << prediction << '\n';

        if (player_choice != prediction)
        {
            ++player_wins;
        }
        if (mr.update(player_choice))      // Updates the
        {                                  // mind reader
            ++guessing;
        }
    }
    std::cout << "you win " << player_wins << '\n'
        << "machine guessed " << guessing << " times" << '\n'      // Reports
        << "machine won " << (turns - player_wins) << '\n';        // guesses
}
```

Call this from main, and see if you can outsmart the mind reader. If you track the state yourself, you can see what it will predict and win, but without pen and paper, you are likely to forget. It turns out it is very difficult to behave randomly.

We have a mind reader, and we can pack it up in a coroutine to learn about another new C++ feature.

8.3   Coroutines

Coroutines were invented in the 1950s, and Melvin Conway coined the term in 1958. Later, in 1978, Tony Hoare described a type of coroutine called *communicating sequential processes* (CSP) in a paper in *Communications of the ACM* (see https:// dl.acm.org/doi/10.1145/359576.359585) and subsequently wrote a book of the same title in 1985. He developed a concurrent programming language using sequential processes communicating through message passing. His approach avoids some common problems in concurrent code, such as deadlocks. His formal language allowed mathematical proof that such problems would not happen. At a very high level, the processes are functions with inputs and outputs. By wiring together inputs and outputs, several functions can run simultaneously without the need to protect shared memory.

C++20 introduced Coroutines (see http://mng.bz/5oEO). The support is relatively low level, so C++ coroutines often require a fair amount of boilerplate code. We can write a coroutine to yield the player's choice and predictions. This will neither change the game nor harness the full power of asynchronous code, but we'll discover what is required to build a coroutine and revise the rule of zero we learned about in chapter 6. It's worth having an overview of the building blocks needed even if we don't use coroutines' full potential.

Coroutines are powerful and flexible. Suspending and resuming work, possibly on different threads, provides a type of parallelism. Lewis Baker wrote a series of blog posts going into a lot of detail (see http://mng.bz/mjda), and there are a lot of talks and blog posts on the internet about C++ coroutines because they are a big new feature that can be used in a variety of ways. Let's learn the basics.

8.3.1   How to make a coroutine

A coroutine is a function containing one or more of the three keywords: `co_yield`, `co_await`, or `co_return`. *Yield* returns a value and *pauses* the function. The state of the coroutine is packaged up, allowing the suspended execution to continue later. An *await* expression calls an asynchronous operation and *resumes* when that completes. A *return* completes the function. Unlike a normal function, a coroutine's lifetime is not tied to the caller. For example, the resumption can happen on a different thread. We won't use that feature here but instead learn what we require to make a normal function into a coroutine. A coroutine function returns an object providing the required boilerplate, which allows the compiler to generate the coroutine code.

In most cases, we need to write code for the returned object, although C++23 introduced `std::generator` (http://mng.bz/7vmv), which provides a concrete type to return from a simple generator coroutine. CppReference gives sample code to output the letters of the alphabet from a coroutine called `letters`. The `letters` function is a coroutine because it uses `co_yield`. The function returns an `std::generator`, which provides what is required to wire up the initialization of the coroutine and handle the `co_yield`. The function has no `co_return`, which we noted completes a coroutine, so `letters` potentially generates an infinite sequence. We can call it as many times as we like. For example, we can use range's `views` to obtain the first 26 letters via the `take` function. Unfortunately, `std::generator` isn't widely supported yet, but Visual Studio 2022 does provide an `experimental` version in the `experimental/generator` header.

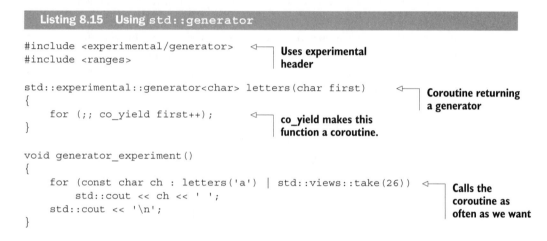

Listing 8.15 Using `std::generator`

```
#include <experimental/generator>        Uses experimental
#include <ranges>                        header

std::experimental::generator<char> letters(char first)    Coroutine returning
{                                                          a generator
    for (;; co_yield first++);           co_yield makes this
}                                        function a coroutine.

void generator_experiment()
{
    for (const char ch : letters('a') | std::views::take(26))    Calls the
        std::cout << ch << ' ';                                  coroutine as
    std::cout << '\n';                                           often as we want
}
```

Over time, we will probably see more concrete return objects for coroutines supported by the standard. For now, we usually have to write the boilerplate code ourselves, unless the `std::generator` is supported by our chosen compiler and works for our use case.

We will write a coroutine that `co_yields` a player's input along with the mind reader's prediction. The calling code will obtain and display the results. A coroutine version of our game is unnecessary, but understanding how to use this new C++ feature will be informative. We will gradually build up the code required for a coroutine. So far, we have discovered that a coroutine

- Is a function containing `co_yield`, `co_await`, or `co_return`
- Returns an object providing the required boilerplate

Listing 8.15 has a `co_yield`, and the generator provides the required boilerplate. To make our game into a coroutine, we will

- Write a function containing `co_yield` and `co_return` (section 8.3.2)
- Return a user defined class called `Task`, although any other name can be used (section 8.3.3)
- Implement a `promise_type`, which must be called that just because the compiler expects it (section 8.3.3)

The `Task` and `promise_type` start, stop, and yield data from the coroutine function, so we will add details:

- Creation and destruction of the `Task` and `promise_type` (section 8.3.4)
- Starting and stopping the coroutine and how to `co_yield` data or `co_return` (section 8.3.5)
- To the `Task` itself, allowing the calling code to resume the coroutine after it has suspended until the game is done (section 8.3.6)

We end with calling code using the `Task`, which gives us a new version of the game.

8.3.2   A coroutine function

In listing 8.14, we wrote a `mind_reader` function, handling user input, obtaining a prediction, and displaying outcomes. We will pull out the user input and predictions to form a coroutine. We need to include the `coroutine` header, and our new function will return an object that provides the boilerplate needed for a coroutine. Let's call it a `Task` and implement it in the next section. We'll start with the coroutine itself.

Like before, we create a `MindReader` object and loop while the user wants to play. Our coroutine will stop using `co_return` if the player gives up. Otherwise, we `co_yield` the player's choice and the mind reader's prediction. Adding `co_return` or `co_yield` to a function and returning a suitable object makes a coroutine.

Listing 8.16   Our first coroutine

```
#include <coroutine>          ┐  Forward-declares the Task we
struct Task;            ◁─────┘  will implement shortly
Task coroutine_game()    ◁────────────────────┐ Coroutine function
{                                              │ returning a suitable object
    std::mt19937 gen{ std::random_device{}() };
    std::uniform_int_distribution dist{ 0, 1 };
    MindReader mr(gen, dist);
    while (true)
    {
        auto input = read_number(std::cin);
        if (!input)
        {                       ┐ Stops if player
            co_return;    ◁─────┘ gives up
        }
        int player_choice = input.value();
        co_yield{ player_choice , mr.get_prediction() };  ◁──┐ Yields player's turn and
        mr.update(player_choice);                             │ reader's prediction
    }
}
```

The compiler uses functions from the returned `Task` to wire up what's needed for the yields and return, as well as making a *coroutine frame*. This packages up the function, allowing it to suspend when it hits a `co_XXX` function. When we yield a choice and a prediction, the coroutine is suspended until resumed. The coroutine then picks up on the next line, with the same state as when it was paused, updating the mind reader. If we debug the coroutine, we will seem to teleport into the middle of the `while` loop when we resume.

The coroutine state is usually dynamically allocated, so it is often described as *stackless*. In effect, a coroutine is a function bundled up as a dynamic object so that it can be paused (*suspended*) and *resumed* until completed. A coroutine can even be resumed on a different thread. The control passes between the caller and the coroutine, as figure 8.2 shows.

We forward-declared a `Task` to return from our coroutine, so let's implement it next.

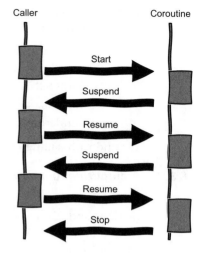

Figure 8.2   A coroutine can be suspended and resumed as needed.

8.3.3   *The coroutine's return object*

A coroutine's return object is often described as a promise or task, but we are free to use any name we like. We'll need to add several functions for our coroutine to work. The requirements vary, depending on each coroutine, but we always see two things. First, a *promise object*, which is used to send results or report exceptions to code outside the coroutine, and second, a coroutine handle, which is used inside the coroutine to resume execution or destroy the coroutine frame when finished.

Let's gradually build up our `Task`. The compiler requires something called `promise_type` inside our `Task`. We can either define a class separately and add a `using` declaration to the task, or we can define a class inline as a nested class in `Task`. We'll use a nested class, so our `Task` returned by the coroutine starts like this.

Listing 8.17   Structure to wire up coroutine

```
#include <coroutine>            Task returned by
struct Task          ◁──┘       listing 8.16
{
    struct promise_type    ◁──┐ Required
    {                          │ structure
    };
};
```

The compiler uses the `Task`, which we returned from the `coroutine_game` in listing 8.16, and its `promise_type` to generate code. We need several more details in the `promise_type` and `Task` to make our `coroutine_game` compile. We could use any name for our return type, although `Task` is a commonly used name; however, we must have an associated class called `promise_type`. The `Task` and `promise_type` allow the coroutine to start, stop, and yield data. Let's fill in the details.

8.3.4   *RAII and the rule of zero*

In listing 8.16, we wrote a coroutine returning the `Task` we just started creating. The code generated by a compiler for a coroutine gets a `Task` from the `promise_type` by calling a `get_return_object` function, something along the lines of this pseudocode:

```
promise_type promise;
auto task = promise.get_return_object();
```

We don't create a `Task` directly. Only the `promise_type` does this in the `get_return_object` function. As it stands, we could add a function to the promise_type:

```
Task get_return_object() {  return Task{}; }
```

However, we can still create `Tasks` anywhere, which aren't of much use to anything other than the compiler. If we give `Task` a private constructor, the `promise_type` can make a task because we made it an inner class, but nothing else can.

In addition, we noted the promise object sends results or reports exceptions to code outside the coroutine, and we use a coroutine handle to resume execution or destroy the coroutine frame when finished. Coroutines provide a `from_promise` method to obtain an `std::coroutine_handle`, so if we store a pointer to the `promise_type` in `Task`

```
promise_type * promise;
```

we can contain a handle when needed with

```
auto handle = std::coroutine_handle<promise_type>::from_promise(*promise);
```

Now, raw pointers are often troublesome. We don't need to delete the pointer because the compiler deals with the coroutine's lifetime for us, but we should call the `destroy` method when we're done. If we add a destructor to `Task`, we can perform the necessary tidy-up using RAII. In the destructor, we could make a handle from the `promise` and call

```
handle.destroy()
```

However, chapter 6 told us that adding our own destructor blocks implicit moves but leaves copy operations available. Copying a `Task` is a potential resource leak. We can either explicitly delete the copies and default the moves or use a smart pointer for the promise pointer. Using a smart pointer means we no longer need a destructor to tidy up for us.

In chapter 6, we met `std::unique_ptr`. We accepted the default `"delete"` there because we had raw pointers we wanted to be deleted. Now we want something different to happen. Smart pointers take a type and a deleter, which defaults to calling `delete`:

```
template<class T, class Deleter = std::default_delete<T>> class unique_ptr
```

Our deleter needs to call `destroy` on a handle obtained `from_promise` with our `promise_type` pointer. We can write a more general function for any promise type using a class template.

Listing 8.18   Custom "deleter"

```
template<typename Promise>
struct coro_deleter                                          Template function
{                                                            for any promise type
    void operator()(Promise* promise) const noexcept
    {
        auto handle =
            std::coroutine_handle<Promise>::from_promise(
                *promise
Gets handle       );
from promise    if (handle)                    Calls destroy if
            handle.destroy();                  there is a handle
    }
};
```

We can then declare a family of templates utilizing the deleter with the `using` statement we met earlier. We use an `std::unique_ptr` of any type, `T`, with a `coro_deleter<T>`:

```
template<typename T>
using promise_ptr = std::unique_ptr<T, coro_deleter<T>>;
```

We can now use a `promise_ptr` in the `Task` and rely on the rule of zero. There are no copies to delete or moves to default because we don't have to define a destructor anymore, as the `std::unique_ptr` will do the tidying up for us.

We can now fill in a few more functions in `Task`. First, we add a private constructor taking a `promise_type` pointer and store that in a `promise_ptr`. We can then add a `get_return_object` function to the `promise_type` returning a `Task`.

Listing 8.19   Structure to wire up coroutine

```
#include <coroutine>
#include <memory>
struct Task
{
    struct promise_type
    {                                         Task only created by
        Task get_return_object()             the promise_type
        {
            return Task(this);
        }
    };
private:
                                              A smart pointer
    promise_ptr<promise_type> promise;        for RAII
    Task(promise_type* p) : promise(p) {}              Private constructor
};
```

We've written enough for a `Task` to be created and a coroutine handle destroyed when we're done. We still need to add a few more functions to deal with what happens between creation and destruction. Let's fill in the details to make the `co_yield` and `co_return` used in listing 8.16 work.

8.3.5 *Filling in the promise_type*

Let's begin with the `promise_type`. The compiler injects code based on functions in this class. We always need to define three functions stating what happens in the following cases:

1 When we first start the coroutine
2 If an exception is thrown
3 When the coroutine stops

Any uncaught exception in the body of the coroutine invokes an `unhandled_exception` method. The simplest implementation does nothing:

```
void unhandled_exception() {}
```

Alternatively, we could log the problem and even call terminate.

We also need methods called `initial_suspend` and `final_suspend` to indicate whether to suspend. As part of coroutines support, C++20 introduced two helper classes, `suspend_always` and `suspend_never`, to suspend or not, respectively. We want our coroutine to get the user input and prediction ready for the calling code, so we use `suspend_never` to indicate it should run initially:

```
std::suspend_never initial_suspend() noexcept { return {}; }
```

Notice the `noexcept` we met in section 8.2.1 when we wrote a `hash` function. Never suspending is sometimes called a hot start, whereas pausing the coroutine initially is a cold start. When we're finished, we always suspend to flag we are done:

```
std::suspend_always final_suspend() noexcept { return {}; }
```

This sets a flag on the coroutine handle so the `Task` can see if the coroutine has finished.

We have dealt with the start and end of the coroutine but have not provided code to handle `co_await`, `co_yield`, or `co_return` yet. Our coroutine in listing 8.16 yields a choice from the player and a prediction:

```
co_yield { player_choice , mr.get_prediction()};
```

The compiler therefore hunts for a `yield_value` method returning a pair of ints in our `promise_type`. If we didn't use `co_yield`, we would not need this method. We can store the `std::pair` of ints in the promise so the `Task` can access them and return them to the code outside the coroutine.

After a yield, we suspend the coroutine and indicate this by returning `suspend_always` from the `yield_value` method:

```
std::suspend_always yield_value(std::pair<int, int> got)
{
    choice_and_prediction = got;
    return {};
}
```

Control then returns to the calling code.

We called co_return when a player gives up, so we need to add another function to the promise_type. The co_return can either be void or followed by an expression to return. Ours is void, so we need a return_void method:

```
void return_void() {}
```

If we wanted to return a value, we would need a return_value function instead. Our complete promise type is as follows.

Listing 8.20   Complete promise type

```
struct promise_type
{
    std::pair<int, int> choice_and_prediction;        ◁─┤ Data

    Task get_return_object()       ◁─┤ Creates a Task
    {
        return Task(this);
    }
    std::suspend_never initial_suspend() noexcept      ◁─┤ Starts up
    {
        return {};
    }
    std::suspend_always final_suspend() noexcept      ◁─┤ Stops
    {
        return {};
    }                                            Exception
    void unhandled_exception() {}    ◁─┘ handling             ┌─ Called by Task's
    std::suspend_always yield_value(std::pair<int, int> got)  ◁─┘ co_yield
    {
        choice_and_prediction = got;
        return {};
    }
                                  ┌─ Called by Task's
    void return_void() { }    ◁─┘ co_return
};
```

We are nearly done. The promise_type now has all the methods needed by the coroutine. The Task returned by the coroutine gives us a place to indicate the data in the promise and will resume the coroutine until it's done. Let's fill in these missing pieces.

8.3.6   *Filling in the Task type*

To return the choice and prediction from the Task, we provide a getter function, obtaining the std::pair of data from the promise_ptr:

```
std::pair<int, int> choice_and_prediction() const
{
    return promise->choice_and_prediction;
}
```

We can check if the coroutine is finished by calling the handle's done method. This flag is set to true when the promise_type's final_suspend method is called and returns a suspend_always. We use the from_promise method to get the handle and then see if we're done:

```
bool done() const
{
    auto handle =
        std::coroutine_handle<promise_type>::from_promise(*promise);
    return handle.done();
}
```

When we used co_yield in listing 8.16, the coroutine paused. The calling code then does what it wants with the player's choice and mind reader's prediction, but it needs a way to resume the coroutine to get the next pair. We resume the coroutine by calling the handle's operator()(). We can add a function to our Task called next, resuming the coroutine:

```
void next()
{
    auto handle =
        std::coroutine_handle<promise_type>::from_promise(*promise);
    handle();
}
```

The calling code can then call next when it's used the previous choice and prediction. Adding these new methods to Task, we have the following.

> **Listing 8.21 The coroutine's Task and promise_type**

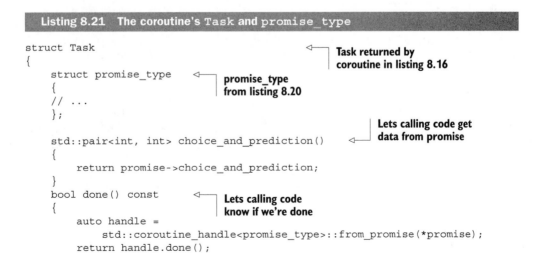

```
struct Task                                          Task returned by
{                                                    coroutine in listing 8.16
    struct promise_type          promise_type
    {                            from listing 8.20
    // ...
    };
                                                     Lets calling code get
    std::pair<int, int> choice_and_prediction()      data from promise
    {
        return promise->choice_and_prediction;
    }
    bool done() const            Lets calling code
    {                            know if we're done
        auto handle =
            std::coroutine_handle<promise_type>::from_promise(*promise);
        return handle.done();
```

```
    }
    void next()                    ⟵┐    Resumes
    {                               │    coroutine
        auto handle =
            std::coroutine_handle<promise_type>::from_promise(*promise);
        return handle ();
    }
private:                                    ┌   Smart pointer
    promise_ptr<promise_type> promise;  ⟵──┘   for RAII
    Task(promise_type* p) : promise(p) {}   ⟵┐   Private constructor
};                                           │   visible by promise_type
```

Our `Task` is now complete, and we can use the coroutine.

8.3.7   A coroutine mind reader

To use our coroutine, we can use code similar to the original game in listing 8.14, but the `MindReader` and user input are now bundled inside the `coroutine_game`. We call the coroutine using

```
Task game = coroutine_game();
```

We use the `Task` to control the coroutine. We loop until `done`, getting the player's choice and prediction at each turn. This pauses the coroutine at the `co_yield`. Our calling code then gets control back and displays the results. By calling `next` on the `Task`, control then returns to the coroutine, and it picks up where it left off. Our calling code looks like this.

Listing 8.22   A coroutine version of a mind reader

```
void coroutine_minder_reader()
{
    int turns = 0;
    int player_wins = 0;

    std::cout << "Select 0 or 1 at random and press enter.\n";
    std::cout << "If the computer predicts your guess it wins\n"
                    "and it can now read your mind.\n";

    Task game = coroutine_game();    ⟵┐   Gets the
                                      │   coroutine
    while (!game.done())          ⟵────────┐   Sees if the
    {                                       │   user stopped        ┌   Gets data
        auto [player_choice, prediction] =                          │   from coroutine
                game.choice_and_prediction();               ⟵──────┘
        ++turns;
        std::cout << "You pressed " << player_choice
                    << ", I guessed " << prediction << '\n';

        if (player_choice != prediction)
        {
            ++player_wins;
        }
```

```
        game.next();                  ◄────────────────────┐  Lets coroutine
    }                                                       │  resume
    std::cout << "you win " << player_wins << '\n'
        << "machine won " << (turns - player_wins) << '\n';
}
```

Using a coroutine makes no difference to our mind reader, but we have used a frequently discussed feature from C++20. We could extend this and write another coroutine to co_await input from std::cin, a function returning a random flip, or even another mind reader.

Coroutines can be used in a variety of places, including asynchronous operations waiting on input or other resources. Andreas Fertig's book *Programming with C++20: Concepts, Coroutines, Ranges, and More* (Fertig Publications, 2021) has a chapter devoted to parsing a byte stream with coroutines. He published an overview in Overload in 2022 (see https://accu.org/journals/overload/30/168/fertig/). Rayner Grimm lists several possible use cases on his blog, including event-driven programming and cooperative multitasking (see http://mng.bz/qjPr). If a coroutine is suspended, another part of the program can then run instead, so coroutines offer a constrained concurrency model.

We've been through many C++ features, and we are nearly done. We have used templates with parameter packs several times now, but we have not looked into how they work. Let's round off our learning with a final chapter exploring templates further.

Summary

- We can alias a declaration with the keyword using, including families of templates.
- C++'s unordered containers use hash tables.
- Hash tables store elements in buckets and use a hash function to locate a bucket.
- An std::unordered_map uses std::hash and std::equal_to for the keys by default.
- We can inject a hash function into namespace std to support a user-defined type in an std::unordered_map.
- A C++ coroutine is a function containing one or more of the following three keywords: co_yield, co_await, or co_return.
- A coroutine can be suspended and resumed.
- The return type of a coroutine is usually a user-defined type, containing functions required to start and stop the coroutine, as well as functions backing co_yield and co_await as needed.
- C++23 introduced an std::generator for use as the return type of a coroutine, providing a potentially infinite sequence, but for other uses, we currently have to write our own promise or task, providing the required boilerplate code.
- We used a *custom deleter* for std::unique_ptr to allow us to use the rule of zero.

NJ 272 2387

Parameter packs and std::visit

This chapter covers
- Practicing with algorithms and execution policies
- Template parameter packs
- The `std::visit` method and `Overload` pattern
- Mutable lambdas
- Extra practice with variants, `std::format`, and ranges

We have used parameter packs (the three dots in a template) several times now, but we have not paused to understand how they work. In the final chapter, we will fill in the dots, as well as practice many things we have learned so far. We will generate triangle numbers and briefly consider some of their properties. Triangle numbers crop up in various places (e.g., counting how many handshakes would happen in a group of people if everyone shakes hands). Because we started with Pascal's triangle, returning to a number sequence feels like a good way to round off.

We'll discover we can create triangle numbers in a couple of lines of code using numeric algorithms, and then we will build a slot machine using the first few triangle numbers. We will build a simple machine first, which only spins the reels. We will then improve the game, allowing holds, nudges, or spins. To implement these options, we will learn about `std::visit` and the `Overload` pattern. We will practice what we have learned in previous chapters, which will help us write more C++ using new features, being confident we can keep up to date with any future changes.

9.1 The triangle numbers

The triangle numbers are 1, 3, 6, 10, and so forth, formed by summing 1, 1 + 2, 1 + 2 + 3, 1 + 2 + 3 + 4, and so forth. If we racked up that many snooker balls, we could make a triangle. Hence the name. To add another row to the five shown in figure 9.1, we use six more snooker balls. A further row would add seven and so on.

We will use the first few triangle numbers in this chapter, so let's make a function called `make_triangle_numbers`. We will take a `count` and return a `vector` of ints. `std::vector` and `std::string` have supported `constexpr` since C++20 (see http:// mng.bz/wjDP), so we can mark the function as `constexpr`, which we first saw in chapter 3 when we

Figure 9.1 Snooker balls racked up, forming a triangle with 15 = 1 + 2 + 3 + 4 + 5 balls

learned how to use `static_assert` for testing. We will be able to perform similar checks here too. Our new function starts with the following signature:

```
constexpr std::vector<int> make_triangle_numbers(int count)
```

Let's add the details. If we start with the numbers 1, 2, 3, and so on, we can then sum these to obtain the triangle numbers. C++11 introduced the `iota` function in the `numeric` header, which fills a container with sequentially increasing values, starting with a chosen value. If we make a vector with space for 20 numbers

```
std::vector<int> numbers(20);
```

we can then call `iota`, starting with the value 1, to create the numbers 1, 2, 3, and so on:

```
std::iota(numbers.begin(),numbers.end(), 1);
```

Alternatively, we can use the ranges version, introduced in C++23:

```
std::ranges::iota(numbers, 1);
```

C++23 isn't widely supported yet, so you might have to wait until your compiler offers the ranges' version. In either case, this fills the `vector` with numbers starting at 1 and increasing by 1 each time. This gives us 1, 2, 3,...20. The `iota` function came from the APL programming language and was proposed before C++11, but it was not included until later. It's a small but useful function.

If we find the partial or cumulative sums of these numbers (1, 1 + 2, etc.), we obtain the triangle numbers. To do this, we can use the function std::partial_sum from the numeric header:

```
std::partial_sum(numbers.begin(),numbers.end(),numbers.begin());
```

We then have the triangle numbers we wanted (1, 3, 6, 10, 15,…210).

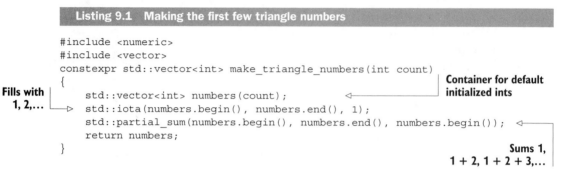

Listing 9.1   Making the first few triangle numbers

```
#include <numeric>
#include <vector>
constexpr std::vector<int> make_triangle_numbers(int count)
{                                                                   Container for default
    std::vector<int> numbers(count);            ◄───────────────   initialized ints
    std::iota(numbers.begin(), numbers.end(), 1);
    std::partial_sum(numbers.begin(), numbers.end(), numbers.begin());  ◄──
    return numbers;
}                                                                   Sums 1,
                                                                    1 + 2, 1 + 2 + 3,…
```

Fills with 1, 2,…

We've used an older C++ function, std::partial_sum, as well as the newer std::iota function from the numeric header. There are many other algorithms we haven't had a chance to use in this book. Have a look through the algorithm and numeric headers, and try one you haven't used before, or even implement one yourself. This is a great way to keep practicing.

9.1.1   *Testing our triangle numbers with algorithms*

We should test our triangle numbers and can use a few more algorithms to do so. We can undo the partial_sum, using adjacent_difference, which gives the difference between adjacent elements in a container. If we make a vector for the differences, we can compare these with the integers from 1 to 20 created by iota, and we can assert that they match.

Listing 9.2   Testing our triangle numbers

```
#include <cassert>
void check_properties()
{
    const int count = 20;
    const auto triangle_numbers = make_triangle_numbers(count);
    std::vector<int> diffs(count);
    std::adjacent_difference(triangle_numbers.begin(),
                             triangle_numbers.end(),       Finds the
                             diffs.begin());          ◄──  differences
    std::vector<int> numbers(count);
    std::iota(numbers.begin(), numbers.end(), 1);     Compares with 1, 2,…
    assert(numbers == diffs);
}
```

Let's spend a little time adding a few more `asserts` to our test function. If we find the `adjacent_difference` a second time, we should obtain a `vector` of `1`s. We can check this using the `all_of` algorithm with a lambda:

```
#include <algorithm>
std::adjacent_difference(diffs.begin(), diffs.end(), diffs.begin());
assert(std::all_of(diffs.begin(), diffs.end(),
                   [](int x) { return x == 1; }));
```

We can count the `1`s to check that we have the number we started with using `std::coun`:

```
assert(std::count(diffs.begin(), diffs.end(), 1) == count);
```

We have a small handful of tests and will add another shortly. Before we do, it's worth filling in a few more dots. Most algorithms have various overloads. For example, `std::count` has three versions (see https://en.cppreference.com/w/cpp/algorithm/count). We used the first version. The second is marked `constexpr`, so it could be used at compile time, and the third uses an *execution policy*, allowing parallel execution of an algorithm.

9.1.2 *Execution policies for algorithms*

C++17 introduced several execution type policies that live in the `execution` header. By default, a `sequenced_policy`, `std::execution::seq`, is used, which causes the algorithm to operate in sequence, one item at a time. We can also use `std::execution::par` or `std::execution::par_unseq` and C++20's `std::execution::unseq`. The latter three allow parallel execution, and the unsequenced policies may cause execution to happen in any order. They indicate the algorithm *can* be parallelized, so it is a *permission* rather than a *requirement*. These policies fall back to a sequential policy if the implementation cannot be parallelized, and even if it can, the code might end up being slower (see Bartlomiej Filipek's blog at http://mng.bz/JdGV). The parallel versions give us a simple way to indicate that work can be fired off to different threads, but they are not guaranteed to speed our code up. They might, but setting up work on new threads can have an overhead.

If we add `std::execution::par` as the first parameter, we use the overload for parallel execution:

```
#include <execution>
assert(std::count(std::execution::par, diffs.begin(), diffs.end(), 1)
                                        == count);
```

Requesting parallel execution is straightforward and may speed up your code. Experiment and measure to see what happens. Threading and parallel execution is a big topic. Anthony Williams's book *C++ Concurrency in Action* (Manning Publications, 2019; see http://mng.bz/PR5n) is an excellent resource, and you can find many of his talks on the internet.

9.1.3   *Mutable lambdas*

Our tests so far are necessary but not sufficient. There is a closed-form formula for the triangle numbers, calculating the nth number directly as

$$\frac{n(n+1)}{2}$$

We can use this relationship to make our tests sufficient, at least for the first few numbers, by checking that each value matches the equation's value.

Listing 9.3   Checking each value

```
for (size_t i=0; i< triangle_numbers.size(); ++i)
{
    const int n = i + 1;
    assert(triangle_numbers[i] == n*(n+1)/2);
}
```

We have seen that we can often use an algorithm instead of a `for` loop, and because we want to check the relationship holds for all of the numbers, `std::all_of` will work. However, when we switch to the algorithm, we no longer have the variable `i` to use in the calculation. We can declare a variable in a lambda's square brackets `[]` and flag the lambda as `mutable`, which allows us to increment the variable. Without the `mutable` keyword, we get a compiler error, telling us a by-copy capture cannot be modified in a nonmutable lambda.

In addition, `mutable` allows the lambda to modify the objects captured by copy and to call non-const member functions of by-copy–captured objects. Using `std::all_of` instead of the `for` loop from listing 9.3 with a mutable lambda gives us the following code.

Listing 9.4   Checking each value with a mutable lambda

```
assert(std::all_of(triangle_numbers.begin(), triangle_numbers.end(),
    [n = 0](int x) mutable          n set to 0 and mutable
    {                               because n is incremented
        ++n;
        return x == n * (n + 1) / 2;
    }
));
```

We have the triangle numbers and some tests. If we pause to look at more properties, we can get a bit more practice with algorithms. We will also discover a useful property making the triangle numbers suitable for use in our slot machine.

9.1.4   *More properties of the triangle numbers*

First, let's consider whether the triangle numbers are odd or even. Then, we will find another pattern we can use for our slot machine. We will also get a bit more practice with algorithms and the `std::map` as we investigate. The first two triangle numbers, 1 and 3, are odd, and then we get two even numbers, 6 and 10. Does this pattern continue? We will find out if we transform our `vector`, flagging odd numbers with a dot (`'.'`) and even numbers with an asterisk (`'*'`).

   We can declare another `vector` to hold the transformation. We've used the `std::transform` algorithm from the `algorithm` header in chapter 7 to make the characters in an `std::string` lowercase. There are various overloads, but each applies a function to an input range and stores the results in an output. The original version took a pair of input iterators, first and last, an output iterator, and a unary function: a function taking one input, like our lambda. C++20 introduced a ranges' version, which takes an input source, rather than a pair of iterators, along with the output iterator and unary function. There is also a version taking two input ranges and a binary function to create the output, as well as a version taking execution policies.

   Let's write a function called `demo_further_properties`. We will use a single character for each number, so we can use a `vector` of `char` to store the results:

```
std::vector<char> odd_or_even
```

We can write a lambda for the transforming function, taking an `int` and returning the appropriate character to indicate the parity of a number:

```
[](int i) { return i%2? '.':'*'; }
```

If `i%2` is nonzero, we have an odd number, so we return `'.'`; otherwise, we return `'*'`. We use this in the transformation, with a `back_inserter` to grow the output as needed:

```
std::vector<char> odd_or_even;
std::ranges::transform(triangle_numbers,
    std::back_inserter(odd_or_even),
    [](int i) { return i%2? '.':'*'; });
```

We could use a range-based `for` loop to display the parity of the numbers, but back in chapter 2, we noted that we can use `std::copy` or the ranges' version to insert the contents of a container into a stream. The first parameter is the container, or its `begin` and `end`, and the second is an `std::ostream_iterator` constructed with a stream (in our case, `std::cout`) and a delimiter (say, a space). We can then stream out the odd or even markers in one line of code once we include the `iostream` header:

```
std::ranges::copy(odd_or_even, std::ostream_iterator<char>(std::cout, " "));
```

Our further properties function looks like this.

Listing 9.5   Checking whether the numbers are odd or even

```
#include <algorithm>
#include <iostream>
#include <iterator>
```

```
void demo_further_properties()
{
    const int count = 20;
    const auto triangle_numbers = make_triangle_numbers(count);
    std::vector<char> odd_or_even;                              ⊲—| Vector for results
    std::ranges::transform(triangle_numbers,
        std::back_inserter(odd_or_even),                            | Lambda to
        [](int i) { return i % 2 ? '.' : '*'; });              ⊲—| check parity
    std::ranges::copy(odd_or_even,
        std::ostream_iterator<char>(std::cout, " "));          ⊲—| Copies to cout
    std::cout << '\n';
}
```

If we call this from `main` and look at the output, we see

```
. . * * . . * * . . * * . . * * . .
```

It appears that we do get two odd numbers followed by two even numbers, over and over. Stack Exchange's math site explains why this happens (see http://mng.bz/1JBj).

We found one neat pattern. To build a slot machine, we want a selection of items to display on some reels. If some items match, the slot machine will pay out. The final digits of the triangle numbers have another pattern. Some digits occur more frequently than others, so we can use the final digits of triangle numbers for our slot machine. The less frequent digits will give a higher pay out. By keeping a tally in an `std::map` and calculating `% 10` rather than `% 2`, we will see how often each digit occurs. We need to map the last digit, which is an `int`, to a count, so after including the `map` header, we can use

```
std::map<int, size_t> last_digits;
```

in our `demo_further_properties` function. We can base the payout of our slot machine on the likelihood of the digits. We'll use a raw loop to find the last digit of each triangle number. We need to look up the number `% 10` using `operator[]` and increment the value we obtain. We learned that `operator[]` will insert a key–value pair into a map if the key does not exist in chapter 7 when we built the answer smash game. The corresponding value is the default for the value's type, in our case, a `size_t` of 0. This is what we need. We create tallies of the last digits as follows:

```
for (int number: triangle_numbers)
{
    ++last_digits[number % 10];
}
```

We can stream out the tallies so we know which digits happen most frequently:

```
for (const auto& [key, value] : last_digits)
{
    std::cout << key << " : " << value << '\n';
}
```

Pulling this into the function gives us the following.

> **Listing 9.6   Adding tallies of digits to further properties**

```
#include <map>

void demo_further_properties()
{
    const int count = 20;
    const auto triangle_numbers = make_triangle_numbers(count);
    // … as before
    std::map<int, size_t> last_digits;          ◁─┐  Uses a map to
    for (int number: triangle_numbers)            │  store tallies
    {
        ++last_digits[number % 10];             ◁─┐  Counts the
    }                                             │  final digits
    std::cout <<
        "Tallies of the final digits of the first 20 triangle numbers\n";
    for (const auto& [key, value] : last_digits)     ┐
    {                                                │  Streams
        std::cout << key << " : " << value << '\n';  │  out results
    }                                                │
}
```

Calling this from `main`, we see

```
0 : 4
1 : 4
3 : 2
5 : 4
6 : 4
8 : 2
```

`8`s and `3`s are unlikely; `0`, `1`, `5`, and `6` are twice as likely. In fact, the final digits repeat the pattern

```
13605186556815063100
```

over and over. If we pick any three triangle numbers, we are unlikely to get three `3`s or `8`s as final digits, so such an outcome could be a jackpot in a game.

Let's build a slot machine using three reels of triangle numbers. We need to make three reels, putting the numbers in random order. We also want to display the reels and make them spin for each turn, deciding whether to pay out.

9.2 A simple slot machine

We need three reels of numbers to spin. We will show the numbers on the current row, along with the numbers on the rows above and below. We can indicate the current row with a `'-'` sign like this:

```
    28  91 153
-   45 120  45-
    36   1   3
```

We will start by spinning the reels on each turn. If two of the final digits match, we pay out, and if all three match, we pay out more. Once we have a working game, we will extend it in section 9.3, awarding a jackpot if we get three 3s or 8s.

9.2.1   *Revision of constexpr and std::format*

Listing 9.1 generates triangle numbers as an `std::vector<int>`. If we utilize the `using` statement we met in the previous chapter, we won't need to spell out `std::vector<int>` each time we refer to the reels:

```
using Reel = std::vector<int>;
```

This can live near the top of the `main.cpp` file. We can now make three reels for our slot machine, with 20 numbers in each in a new function called `make_reels`:

```
constexpr int numbers = 20;
constexpr size_t number_of_reels = 3u;
std::vector<Reel> reels(number_of_reels, make_triangle_numbers(numbers));
```

The numbers should be shuffled for the game. We can use `std::shuffle` directly on a reel:

```
std::shuffle(reel.begin(),
    reel.end(),std::mt19937(std::random_device{}()));
```

However, we know testing code with random behavior can be difficult. If we use a template with an invocable function rather than a random number generator, we can swap out the generator for testing. The invocable function takes two iterators into a vector of `Reel`s, so we use

```
std::invocable<std::vector<Reel>::iterator,
    std::vector<Reel>::iterator>
```

instead of the keyword `typename` in the template head:

```
template<std::invocable<std::vector<Reel>::iterator,
        std::vector<Reel>::iterator> T>
```

We would get away with

```
template<typename T>
```

but using a concept instead of the raw typenames means we are likely to get clearer diagnostics if we don't provide a suitable type for `T`.

We need to include the `concepts` header, and we can flag the function as `constexpr`. Our `make_reels` function looks like this.

Listing 9.7   Seting up `reels`

```
#include <concepts>
template<std::invocable<std::vector<Reel>::iterator,      ◁──┐ Passes in shuffle
        std::vector<Reel>::iterator> T>                       to allow testing
```

```
constexpr std::vector<Reel> make_reels(int numbers,
                                       int number_of_reels,
                                       T shuffle)
{
    std::vector<Reel> reels(number_of_reels,
                            make_triangle_numbers(numbers));

    for (auto& reel : reels)
    {
        shuffle(reel.begin(), reel.end());
    }
    return reels;
}
```

Passes in shuffle to allow testing

Makes the reels

Shuffles the reels

We can call this code in two ways. To use the function in our game, which we will create shortly, we need a seeded generator

```
std::random_device rd;
std::mt19937 gen{ rd() };
```

and capture this generator by reference in a lambda:

```
auto shuffle = [&gen](auto begin, auto end)
               { std::shuffle(begin, end, gen); };
```

We can then call `make_reels` using our lambda:

```
std::vector<Reel> reels = make_reels(numbers, number_of_reels, shuffle);
```

In addition, as the function is `constexpr`, we can use `static_assert` in the `check_properties` function we started in listing 9.2, mocking out the random behavior with a no-op lambda:

```
constexpr auto no_op = [](auto begin, auto end) { };
static_assert(make_reels(1, 1, no_op).size() == 1);
```

This doesn't test much but indicates what's possible.

Armed with three shuffled reels, we need to display the numbers on each. We will show the previous row, the current row, and the next row, indicating the current row with a `'-'`. We used `std::format` back in chapter 2, so let's use it again for practice. If your compiler doesn't support `std::format`, look back to chapter 2 for instructions on using the `fmt` library instead. The numbers will be up to three digits long, so we right align them over three characters, padding with spaces. We put a format specifier after a colon, using `>` for right alignment and `3` for the number of spaces, giving `{:>3}`. We pass in reels, along with the stream, so we can test our code.

> **Listing 9.8   Displaying `reels`**

```
#include <format>
void show_reels(std::ostream& s,
    const std::vector<int>& left,
    const std::vector<int>& middle,
```

```
        const std::vector<int>& right)
{
    s << std::format(" {:>3} {:>3} {:>3}\n",
            left.back(), middle.back(), right.back());     ⟵—|  Previous row
    s << std::format("-{:>3} {:>3} {:>3}-\n",
            left[0], middle[0], right[0]);                  ⟵—|  Current row
    s << std::format(" {:>3} {:>3} {:>3}\n",                        indicated with -
            left[1], middle[1], right[1]);   ⟵—|  Next row
}
```

We've set up the reels and can now display them. To make a game, we need to decide if the current row deserves some kind of payout, and then we need to spin the reels. We also want a way to stop the game. We can use `getline` like we have done before:

```
std::string response;
std::getline(std::cin, response);
```

If the `response` is anything other than Enter being pressed, we will quit. Let's spin the reels first and then build the game.

9.2.2   *Using std::rotate to spin the reels*

The `algorithm` header provides an `std::rotate` function we can use for the spin. This function performs a left rotation on the elements. Given some elements

```
std::vector v{1, 2, 3, 4, 5}
```

we can visualize them as a reel, as shown in figure 9.2.

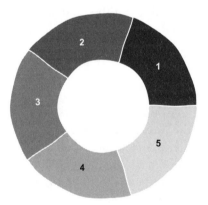

Figure 9.2   Elements arranged on a reel
we can spin or rotate

We can perform a left rotation of the elements by stating a begin, middle (say, the number 4, which is three from begin), and end:

```
std::rotate(v.begin(), v.begin() + 3, v.end());
```

Using `v.begin() + 3` as the middle moves the number 4 to the beginning, and the elements before that move to the end, so we get

```
4, 5, 1, 2, 3
```

as if the reel of numbers has spun. Arranged as a reel, the numbers would have rotated left, as shown in figure 9.3.

Initially, we had 1, 2, 3, 4, and 5. We picked a middle of `begin + 3`, moving 4 to the front. 1 is now at `begin + 2`, so we can rotate again, using the position of the 1

```
std::rotate(v.begin(), v.begin() +
    2, v.end());
```

and the elements end up back where they started.

We want to spin the slot machine reels at random, varying the middle used. The parameters are iterators, so we can add a random number to the

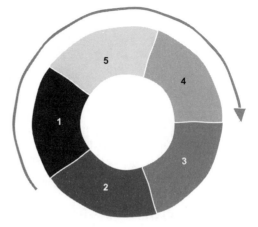

Figure 9.3   Rotating left spins the chosen middle to the beginning.

beginning of a reel to pick which middle to use. We have a random number generator, which we used for the initial shuffle. We now need a distribution too. We want each number on a reel to be possible, but also want the reels to move, so we need to run from the second element to the last element. We can use a distribution of 1 up to and including the size of the reel – 1 to generate an offset to add to `begin`:

```
std::uniform_int_distribution dist(1, numbers - 1);
```

If we allowed 0, the reel would not move. We can then spin all three of the reels:

```
for (auto& reel : reels)
{
    std::rotate(reel.begin(), reel.begin() + dist(gen), reel.end());
}
```

We will use this directly in the simple slot machine function in the next section.

The rotate function has been in C++ for a very long time. If we look at CppReference (http://mng.bz/27E0), we notice a version taking an execution policy, introduced in C++17, and a `constexpr` version, introduced in C++20, along with a link to a ranges' version. We are used to these new features now and will see them frequently when we look up an algorithm. We need one more function to calculate a payout. Then we can create our game.

9.2.3   *The simple slot machine*

To decide on a payout, we need to check whether any of the last digits match. All three matching deserves more than just two matching, while none matching receives nothing, so for now, we will award a payout of 2 for three matches and 1 for two matches.

Listing 9.9   Calculating payout

```
int calculate_payout(int left, int middle, int right)
{
    int payout = 0;
    if (left == middle && middle == right)       ◁——┤ Three matches
    {
        payout = 2;
    }
    else if (left == middle
             || middle == right
             || left == right)        ◁——┤ Two matches
    {
        payout = 1;
    }
    return payout;
}
```

Now, if we want to give higher payouts for 3s or 8s, which are less likely, we are in danger of ending up with a snaky mess of ifs and elses. We will revisit this later when we add more features to our game. For now, we have all the parts we need to make a simple slot machine.

We set up the reels, show the numbers, and award a payout if a line wins. The player can press Enter to continue or anything else to quit. If they continue, we spin the reels and show the numbers again.

Listing 9.10   A simple slot machine

```
#include <iostream>
#include <random>
#include <string>
#include <vector>

void triangle_machine_spins_only()
{
    constexpr int numbers = 20;
    constexpr size_t number_of_reels = 3u;
    std::random_device rd;
    std::mt19937 gen{ rd() };
    auto shuffle = [&gen](auto begin, auto end)
                        { std::shuffle(begin, end, gen); };
    std::vector<Reel> reels = make_reels(numbers,
                                    number_of_reels,
                                    shuffle);        ◁——┤ Setup

    std::uniform_int_distribution dist(1, numbers - 1);   ◁——┐ Random int
    int credit = 1;                  ◁——┐ Tracks              to spin reels
    while (true)                          credit
    {
        show_reels(std::cout, reels[0], reels[1], reels[2]);
        const int payout = calculate_payout(reels[0][0]%10,
                                    reels[1][0]%10,
                                    reels[2][0]%10);
```

```
    --credit;
    credit += payout;
    std::cout << "won " << payout
             << " credit = " << credit << '\n';

    std::string response;
    std::getline(std::cin, response);      Allows player
    if (response != "")                    to quit
    {
        break;
    }
    for (auto& reel : reels)        ◁──┐ Spins
    {                                  │ reels
        std::rotate(reel.begin(),
                    reel.begin() + dist(gen),   ◁──┐ Random int
                    reel.end());                   │ to spin reels
    }
  }
 }
}
```

If we call this from `main`, we can play our game. We probably won't win very often, so watch our credit draining away. A typical output might look like this:

```
  15   1  36
-136  78  91-
   6   3  15
won 0 credit = 0

 210   3  45
- 45   6  66-
  10 153 105
won 1 credit = 0

  36 210 171
-  1 171 153-
  15 190  28
won 1 credit = 0

   3   1 190
-210  78   6-
  45   3 171
won 0 credit = -1

  78  78 171
- 66   3 153-
  21   6  28
won 1 credit = -1
```

The payout is not very fair because two or three matching final digits are not very likely. We can give a fairer payout. If we also allow a reel to be held or nudged by one, we have a greater chance of winning. We can use more new C++ features, including `std::visit`, to achieve this. Let's build a better slot machine.

9.3   *A better slot machine*

We will make two changes. First, we will improve the payout, and then we will allow holds or nudges. Let's deal with the payout first. The payout is based on the last digit of left, middle, and right numbers. We know that 3 or 8 only happen twice out of the first 20 triangle numbers, so each has a 1/10 chance of appearing. Getting three 3s therefore has a probability of $1/10 \times 1/10 \times 1/10 = 1/1000$, as does getting three 8s. The other digits are more likely. Let's also charge two credits per game this time. Without doing a full analysis, let's give 250 credits for three 3s or 8s and 15 for any other three matching digits. Two matching digits are more likely, so let's give 15 credits for two 3s or two 8s and just 1 for the others.

9.3.1   *Parameter packs and fold expressions*

When we calculated the payout before, we didn't use a weighting and noted we were in danger of needing several ifs and elses if we added more conditions. Let's take a different approach. If we find the frequencies of our final digits, we can then pick the most frequent digit to calculate the payout. We are using three reels, so we want a function taking three digits and returning a map from digits to frequencies:

```
#include <map>
std::map<int, size_t> counter = frequencies(left, middle, right);
```

Rather than writing a function taking three numbers, we can do something more general. We've used several classes from the STL taking various numbers of parameters, including a variant. Back in chapter 5, we noted its definition:

```
template <class... Types>
class variant;
```

For a variant, we use a type. We can also use nontype template parameters. For example, we met std::ratio in chapter 4, using ints to form fractions such as std::ratio<3, 6>. We accepted that the three dots or ellipsis in the variant mean a parameter pack, allowing us to state as many types as we want. We can use a parameter pack in a function template, as well as a class, and use nontype template parameter packs too. We can use a function with a nontype template parameter pack to find the frequencies. We will need to unpack the parameters to find the frequencies.

In general, a *variadic template* is a template with at least one parameter pack. These were introduced in C++11 but have become easier to use as the language has evolved. In C++11, we needed to use recursion to unpack the arguments, using one item and then calling the function again with the remaining items. C++17 introduced *fold expression* (see https://en.cppreference.com/w/cpp/language/fold), avoiding the need for recursion.

Let's try an example. We can write a fold expression to sum up one or more items. Afterwards, we will be able to use a variadic template to find the frequencies we want for the improved slot machine payout. We need to pay attention to the parameter pack in three places. First, we say `typename... Ts` to indicate zero or more parameters:

```
template <typename... Ts>
```

It's common to use `Ts` here rather than `T` to draw attention to there being potentially several `Ts`. We are free to use whatever name we want. We can use `class` or `typename`, followed by the ellipsis and then our name `Ts`. Next, the function's parameter is a `tail` of type `Ts....` Notice the ellipsis has switched to appear after the `Ts` now. Finally, in the implementation, we again use three dots in conjunction with `operator+` to find the sum. The return type depends on the parameters, so we can use `auto`, and the compiler works it out for us.

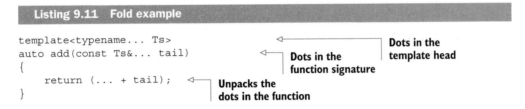

Listing 9.11   Fold example

```
template<typename... Ts>
auto add(const Ts&... tail)
{
    return (... + tail);
}
```

Dots in the
template head

Dots in the
function signature

Unpacks the
dots in the function

The `... +` unpacks the `tail` and is called a fold expression. Such an expression tells the compiler to repeat the operator for each element in a variadic parameter pack. We could use `operator-` instead, or any other operator that applies to the parameters. We can also unpack using

```
return (tail + ...);
```

We can check the value for a few numbers:

```
assert(6==add(1, 2, 3));
```

The arguments 1, 2, and 3 are unpacked by `... + tail` to a left-associative expression:

```
((1 + 2) + 3)
```

If we had the dots on the right instead, we would have the right-associative expression:

```
(1 + (2 + 3))
```

For addition of numbers, the side makes no difference. Subtraction would matter because

```
((1 - 2) - 3) = -1 -3 = -4
```

whereas

```
(1 - (2 - 3)) = 1 - (-1) = 2
```

We can also use a `single` number:

```
assert(1 == add(1));
```

Our function does not compile for no numbers. If we try

```
assert(0 == add());
```

we are told that a *unary fold expression* over + must have a nonempty expansion. A unary fold has the pack and operator, either a right fold

```
tail operator ...
```

or a left fold:

```
... operator tail
```

A unary fold does not work for an empty pack. We can use a binary fold instead, providing an initial value `init` either a right fold, with the initial value on the right

```
tail operator ... operator init
```

or a left fold, with the initial value on the left:

```
init operator ... operator tail
```

We could change the return statement to use a binary fold instead, providing an initial value of `0`:

```
return (0 + ... + tail);
```

We would then need to be able to add the values in the tail to `0`.

Sticking with the unary fold, we can add other types supporting `operator+` as well; for example, some strings:

```
using namespace std::literals;
assert(add("Hello"s, "again"s, "world"s)=="Helloagainworld"s);
```

Be aware that without using a concept to constrain the template, we will get a lot of compiler errors if the type does not have the appropriate `operator+`. Furthermore, we now have three instantiations of `add`, as we have three calls, one using one `int` and one with three `int`s:

```
auto add<int>(int)
auto add<int, int, int>(int, int, int)
```

and one using three strings for the parameter pack:

```
auto add<std::string, std::string, std::string>(std::string, std:: string,
    std:: string)
```

Fold expressions are powerful, and we have only scratched the surface. For further examples, see https://www.foonathan.net/2020/05/fold-tricks/.

9.3.2   *Using a parameter pack to find frequencies*

Back to our game. Let's write a function to find the frequencies of the digits for the payout so we can find which digits appear most often on the current line. We used an `std::map<int, size_t>` to find how often each last digit appeared in the triangle numbers in section 9.1.2. We can do something similar now using another variadic template. Rather than calculating the last digits in the new function, we will write a general-purpose frequencies function. Our game will send in the last digits, like we did when we called our previous `calculate_payout` function in listing 9.9.

We want a function that takes a varying number of numbers. We will only call it with three numbers but can write a general-purpose function for practice. For a variadic template, we noted we put three dots *after* `typename` and then put the dots *before* the parameters in the function signature:

```
template<typename... Ts>
std::map<int, size_t> frequencies(Ts... numbers)
```

We can then call the function with as many numbers as we like, which means we could generalize our machine to have more than three reels if we so wished. Recall that we can also use `auto` rather than the template head:

```
std::map<int, size_t> frequencies(auto... numbers)
```

Before we implement the function, we should ensure the numbers are actually numbers, using a concept. We didn't do that with `add`, so we could concentrate on the dots but noted we might get a lot of compiler errors without a concept. We are making a tally, so we want an integer or something convertible to an integer to tally, and `std::convertible_to<int>` does what we want. We add the requirement before `auto` as follows:

```
#include <concepts>
std::map<int, size_t> frequencies(std::convertible_to<int> auto... numbers)
```

Now we can implement the function. We have some numbers, or at least elements convertible to `int`s using `static_cast<int>`. We used operators with dots to unpack the parameters in the last section. We can also unpack parameters into an initializer list:

```
{ static_cast<int>(numbers)... }
```

We can then use the initializer list in a range based `for` loop to populate a `map` of frequencies.

Listing 9.12 Finding frequencies using a parameter pack

```
#include <map>
std::map<int, size_t> frequencies(std::convertible_to<int> auto... numbers)
{
    std::map<int, size_t> counter{};
    for (int i : { static_cast<int>(numbers)... })     ⟵┐ Unpacks parameters
    {                                                    │ into an initializer list
        counter[i]++;   ⟵┤ Keeps tally
    }
    return counter;
}
```

We can use the frequencies function for different numbers of numbers:

```
auto tally_of_3 = frequencies(1, 3, 5);
auto tally_of_4 = frequencies(1, 3, 5, 999);
```

We obtain a map showing how often each number occurs.

Our slot machine will send in the left, middle, and right digits, like we did when we calculated the payout in listing 9.9. We will write a new function to calculate a fairer payout, which takes the final digit from each reel as before:

```
int calculate_payout(int left, int middle, int right)
```

We can then count how often each digit appears in the current row

```
std::map<int, size_t> counter = frequencies(left, middle, right);
```

and use these counts to decide a payout. We can give a fairer payout based on the likelihood of each outcome rather than our previous approach of 2 for three matches and 1 for two matches.

9.3.3 *A fairer payout*

We have three reels, so a final digit appears one, two, or three times. If we find the digit with the greatest frequency, we can use that to decide a payout. The algorithm header defines `std::max_element`, which finds the greatest element in a range using `operator<` for ordering by default. Our frequencies contain key–value pairs, and we want the element with the largest value. The key is the first element of the pair, and the value is the second, so we use the second element for comparison in a lambda:

```
auto it = std::max_element(counter.begin(), counter.end(),
    [](auto it1, auto it2) { return it1.second < it2.second; });
```

Provided the counter is not empty, we get an iterator to an element and award an appropriate payout. We will now charge 2 credits per go. As we noted, 3s and 8s are less likely. The jackpot is three matching final digits of 3s or 8s, so we award this with 250 credits. Three other matching final digits get 15. Two 3s or 8s can have 10 credits, and any other matching pair gets 1 credit. If the final digit is a 3 or 8, we can use an `std::array` with the right payout at the index corresponding to the frequency:

```
constexpr std::array value = {0, 0, 10, 250};
```

Zero or one gives 0, while two gives a credit of 10, and three gives the jackpot of 250. Similarly, for the more likely digits, we can use

```
constexpr std::array value = {0, 0, 1, 15};
```

to give a payout of 1 or 15.

Listing 9.13 A fairer payout

```
#include <array>
int calculate_payout(int left, int middle, int right)
```

```
{
    std::map<int, size_t> counter = frequencies(left,
                                                middle,
                                                right);
    auto it = std::max_element(counter.begin(),
            counter.end(),
            [](auto it1, auto it2) {
                return it1.second < it2.second;
            });
    if (it != counter.end())
    {
        int digit = it->first;
        size_t count = it->second;
        if (digit == 8 || digit == 3)
        {
            constexpr std::array value = { 0, 0, 10, 250 };
            return value[count];
        }
        else
        {
            constexpr std::array value = { 0, 0, 1, 15 };
            return value[count];
        }
    }
    return 0;
}
```

We now have a much better payout function and have learned even more C++. If we add holds and nudges to the spins, we will have an even better game and can use another new C++ feature.

9.3.4 *Allowing holds, nudges, or spins*

Our initial game only offered spins. We will do one of two things in our improved game. If a player wins, they can either quit or let the reels spin on the next turn. Otherwise, they have three options per reel. In the output for the simple slot machine, the first spin gave

```
  210   3   45
- 45    6   66-
  10  153  105
won 1 credit = 0
```

Had we been allowed to hold the 45, spin the middle reel, and nudge the right reel to move 105 up, we would have two numbers ending in a 5, so we would have won some credit. For example, we might end up with

```
  210 210   66
- 45  171  105-
  10  190   15
```

The middle reel spun, so it could be anything, but we were bound to have 45 on the left and 105 on the right, giving at least two last matching digits.

We can use empty `struct`s to indicate how to move each reel and hold one of these in a `variant`. We have used a `variant` before, so some extra practice is useful. We include the `variant` header and name our `variant` with the `using` directive. It can be one of three empty structs.

Listing 9.14   Allowing more options

```
#include <variant>
struct Hold {};
struct Nudge {};
struct Spin {};
using options = std::variant<Hold, Nudge, Spin>;
```

If the player won last time, they can quit or press Enter to spin all three reels. We can indicate this with a `vector` of `options`:

```
std::vector<options>{Spin{}, Spin{}, Spin{}}
```

We can use `std::getline` like we did in the simple slot machine in listing 9.10 to populate an `std::string`:

```
std::string response;
std::getline(std::cin, response);
```

If the response is Enter, we get an empty string, and the game should then spin all three reels. We can put the parsing in a function. An `optional` is a suitable return type. We can also mark the function as `constexpr`, allowing us to use it in a `static_assert`.

Listing 9.15   Three spins for Enter

```
#include <optional>
#include <string>
#include <vector>
constexpr std::optional<std::vector<options>>
              parse_enter(const std::string& response)
{
    if (response.empty())
    {
        return std::vector<options>{      ◁── Enter pressed,
            Spin{},                            so three spins
            Spin{},                            are returned
            Spin{}};
    }
    else
    {
        return {};      ◁── Something else pressed, so
    }                        empty optional is returned
}
```

We should check whether a player really wants to quit if they type something. We'll ask, giving the opportunity to press Enter to continue playing.

Listing 9.16 Checking for Enter pressed

```
std::optional<std::vector<options>> get_enter()
{
    std::cout << "Enter to play\n";
    std::string response;
    std::getline(std::cin, response);
    auto got = parse_enter(response);
    if (!got)
    {
        std::cout << "Are you sure you want to quit? "
                     "Press Enter to keep playing\n";
        std::getline(std::cin, response);
        got = parse_enter(response);
    }
    return got;
}
```

Three spins for enter

Checks whether the player really wants to quit

If a player doesn't win, they can hold, nudge, or spin each reel. We can get the response like we did before and check the characters one at a time to see what the player wants to do with each reel. We can use `'h'`, `'n'`, or `'s'` for hold, nudge, or spin, respectively. Pressing Enter can mean spin all three, like it does after a win. Anything else indicates the player wishes to stop. First, we want to map a character to one of our structs, so we use a `constexpr` function and return an `optional`.

Listing 9.17 Mapping a character to an action

```
#include <optional>
constexpr std::optional<options> map_input(char c)
{
    switch (c)
    {
    case 'h':
        return Hold{};
        break;
    case 'n':
        return Nudge{};
        break;
    case 's':
        return Spin{};
        break;
    }
    return {};
}
```

We decided to accept Enter for three spins to save the player a few key presses. We map each letter, putting the corresponding option in a `vector`. Again, we use `constexpr` and return an `optional`.

Listing 9.18   Checking for holds, nudges, or spins

```
constexpr std::optional<std::vector<options>>
                  parse_input(const std::string & response)
{
    std::vector<options> choice;
    for (char c : response)
    {
        auto first = map_input(c);
        if (first)
        {
            choice.push_back(first.value());
        }
        else
        {
            return {};
        }
    }
    return choice.empty() ?
        std::vector<options>{Spin{}, Spin{}, Spin{}} : choice;
}
```

We can now check for the player's options if they didn't win on the last go using our parsing function. If the input is invalid, either empty or too long, we'll check to see if they want to quit.

Listing 9.19   Checking for options

```
std::optional<std::vector<options>> get_input(size_t expected_length)
{
    std::cout << "Hold (h), spin(s), nudge(n) or Enter for spins\n";
    std::string response;
    std::getline(std::cin, response;                    Parses
    auto got = parse_input(response);      ⟵           the input
    if (!got || response.length()>expected_length)
    {
        std::cout << "Are you sure you want to quit?\n";    Checks whether
        std::getline(std::cin, response);                  they want to quit
        got = parse_input(response);
    }
    return got;
}
```

In our original game in listing 9.10, we checked the response in the main game to see whether to spin or quit. This time, we will call the appropriate function, depending on whether the player won:

```
std::optional<std::vector<options>> choice = won ?
                                    get_enter() : get_input();
```

We now need to move the reels appropriately. Previously, we used `std::rotate` to spin all three reels. We now need to take the appropriate action based on the player's choice. Using a `variant` for the `options` allows us to use another helpful C++ feature, which is a fortuitous choice.

9.3.5   *Spinning reels with std::visit and std::views::zip*

We used an `std::variant` in chapter 5 when we wanted to add jokers to our deck of cards, and we also used `std::holds_alternative` to detect a joker. We now have one of three possible types. The `variant` header includes a method called `std::visit` that lets us supply a callable that accepts each possible type in the variant (see http://mng.bz/RmoK). We could build something ourselves using lots of `if`s and `else`s, based on `std::holds_alternative`, but it is easy to forget to add a branch for one of the types in the variant. Using `std::visit` instead means we get a compile error if we miss an alternative. The function applies a callable to one or more variants:

```
template <class R, class Visitor, class... Variants>
constexpr R visit( Visitor&& vis, Variants&&... vars );
```

The return value `R` can be `void`. The variants, `vars`, are one or more variants in a parameter pack. The visitor, `vis`, is any callable that can be invoked with the types from the variants. The callable could be a `struct`, with an overloaded `operator()` per type.

Listing 9.20   One way to provide callables for `std::visit`

```
struct RollMethod
{
    void operator()(Hold)
    void operator()(Nudge)
    void operator()(Spin)
};
```

Given a player's option, `opt`, we could then call

```
std::visit(RollMethod{}, opt);
```

and the appropriate `operator()` would be invoked. This is cleaner than building one long function checking `std::holds_alternative`, and we get a compiler error if we forget the overload for a type.

We can also use lambdas in conjunction with another variadic template for more practice. Lambdas are callable and therefore have an `operator()`. By creating a class template deriving from a lambda, we can expose the `operator()` for that lambda with a `using` statement.

Listing 9.21   Bring `operator()` into scope in a class

```
template <typename T>
struct Overload : T {          Derives from T and brings
    using T::operator();       operator() into scope
};
```

In C++17 and versions of Clang before v17, we need to provide a *template deduction guide*, which tells the compiler how to deduce the template parameters. The guide shows how to interpret a set of constructor arguments into template parameters for a class, so for our type T, we want an Overload(T) to deduce Overload<T>. Thus, we write

```
template<typename T>
Overload(T) -> Overload<T>;
```

Since C++20, we no longer need the additional deduction guide. The struct allows us to create an Overload with a lambda and call the lambda. For example, we can add an assert to the check_properties function:

```
auto overload = Overload{ [] () { return 0; } };
assert(overload() == 0);
```

By itself, an overload of a single type is not much use because we only have one function. It is simpler to use the lambda directly, but we can use a parameter pack to group several lambdas together. This will bring each lambda's operator() into scope. Again, we may need a deduction guide, and as we noted earlier, we have to think about the ellipsis for a parameter pack in three places.

Listing 9.22   The Overload pattern

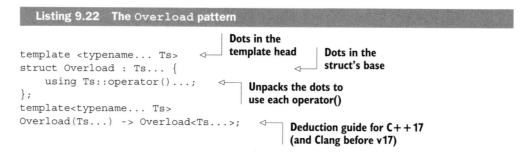

We can then create a roll method that does the right thing for each reel, using the Overload from listing 9.22 with three lambdas. Hold does nothing, and nudge moves a reel one place. Spin, like before, spins by a random amount, provided by the function random_fn. Both nudge and spin need to capture the reel used by reference.

Listing 9.23   A hold, nudge, or spin Overload

```
auto RollMethod = Overload{
    [] (Hold) {
    },
    [&reel] (Nudge) {
        std::rotate(reel.begin(),
            reel.begin() + 1,
            reel.end());
    },
    [&reel, &random_fn] (Spin) {
```

```
            std::rotate(reel.begin(),
            reel.begin() + random_fn(),
            reel.end());
        },
};
```

Now `std::visit` can use the appropriate function from `RollMethod`.

Listing 9.24   Moving the reels

```
template<typename T>
void move_reel(std::vector<int>& reel, options opt, T random_fn)
{
    auto RollMethod = Overload{
        [](Hold) {
        },
        [&reel](Nudge) {
            std::rotate(reel.begin(),
                        reel.begin() + 1,
                        reel.end());
        },
        [&reel, &random_fn](Spin) {
            std::rotate(reel.begin(),
                reel.begin() + random_fn(),
                reel.end());
        },
    };
    std::visit(RollMethod, opt);
}
```

We can now move a specific reel using the player's option. We have three reels, so we want to pair up a player's choices with the reels. We have a `vector` of reels and another `vector` of `options`. We could use an index in a `for` loop, but we can use one last new feature, ranges' zip view, instead. The `std::views::zip` was introduced in C++23, so some compilers don't support it yet, but you can use the Range-v3 library instead (see https://ericniebler.github.io/range-v3/) or a `for` loop:

```
for (size_t i = 0; i < reels.size(); ++i)
{
    move_reel(reels[i], choice.value()[i], random_fn);
}
```

We met ranges' view, `std::view`, when we first used ranges in chapter 2. We used `drop_while` and `filter` to take a *view* of a single collection. After including the ranges header, we can `zip` up the two `vectors` using

```
std::views::zip(reels, choice.value())
```

The zip view gives us tuples of items from each `vector`, without making copies. If we zip two containers and iterate, the tuple moves over both vectors, giving us an item from each vector. The vectors are not joined, but rather, the iterator moves over each input collection, as shown in figure 9.4.

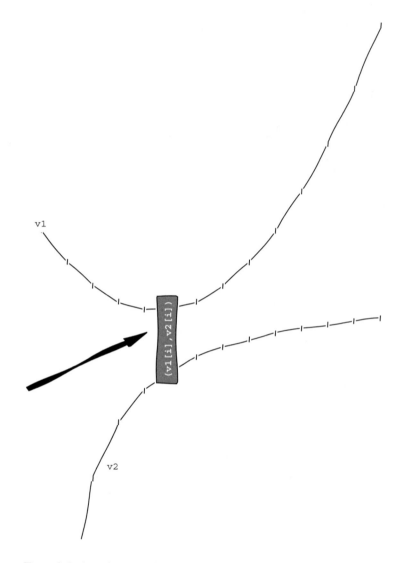

Figure 9.4   Iterating a zip view for two collections shows us a pair of items.

We can zip up more than two collections if we want. Iterating the zipped view of reels and choices gives us a tuple of two references, which we can use in a loop to move the reels. We can use structured bindings to name the two items in the tuple and move the reel appropriately, using the move_reel method from listing 9.24:

```
for (auto [reel, option] : std::views::zip(reels, choice.value()))
{
    move_reel(reel, option, random_fn);
}
```

Pulling this all together gives our final game.

Listing 9.25   An improved triangle number machine

```cpp
void triangle_machine()
{
    constexpr int numbers = 20;
    constexpr size_t number_of_reels = 3u;
    std::random_device rd;
    std::mt19937 gen{ rd() };
    auto shuffle = [&gen](auto begin, auto end) {
                        std::shuffle(begin, end, gen);
                   };
    std::vector<Reel> reels = make_reels(numbers,
                                    number_of_reels,
                                    shuffle);

    std::uniform_int_distribution dist(1, numbers - 1);
    auto random_fn = [&gen, &dist]() { return dist(gen); };
    int credit = 2;
    while (true)
    {
        show_reels(std::cout, reels[0], reels[1], reels[2]);
        const int won = calculate_payout(reels[0][0] % 10,
                                         reels[1][0] % 10,
                                         reels[2][0] % 10);
        credit -= 2;
        credit += won;
        std::cout << "won " << won << " credit = " << credit << '\n';

        std::optional<std::vector<options>> choice = won ?
                        get_enter() : get_input(number_of_reels);
        if (!choice)
        {
            break;
        }

        for (auto [reel, option] :
                std::views::zip(reels, choice.value()))
        {
            move_reel(reel, option, random_fn);
        }
    }
}
```

Setup as before

Shows reels as before

An improved payout

Charges more for this game

Enter for a win; otherwise hold, nudge, or spin

Moves reels appropriately

We call our new game from `main` and have a greater chance of gaining some credit. An example game may start with no matching rows:

```
  28   21 171
-105    3  36-
 153  136  45
won 0 credit = 0
Hold (h), spin(s), nudge(n) or Enter for spins
```

If we hold the 105, spin the middle reel, and nudge the last reel to move up the 45, we will have at least two matching last digits, so we win at least 1 credit, although we have to pay 2 for the turn:

```
hsn
  28   36   36
-105 120   45-
 153   45    1
won 1 credit = -1
Enter to play
```

We then have to let all the reels spin because we just won something:

```
  66 136 153
-  1  66  10-
   6 105  21
won 0 credit = -3
Hold (h), spin(s), nudge(n) or Enter for spins
```

Our credit ticks down, but again we can hold, spin, and nudge:

```
hsn
  66   21   10
-  1    3   21-
   6  136   91
won 1 credit = -4
Enter to play
```

We have a better chance of winning, so the game is more engaging. We also learned even more C++.

We haven't covered every new feature in C++, and as the language continues to evolve, there will always be more to learn. Starting with a vector and finding some small games and projects gave us plenty of practice. We now are in a good place to keep our skills up to date. Use CppReference, and help others by adding missing examples you spot. Experiment with the Compiler Explorer and C++ Insights. Watch the ISOCpp website for recent news, articles, and podcasts. Keep learning and practicing, and above all, have fun!

Summary

- Use std::iota to fill a container with sequentially increasing values, starting with a chosen value.
- Many algorithms support an execution policy, giving a straightforward way to request parallelization. This is a request, which may not be possible, and in such cases, execution falls back to a sequential policy.
- We can flag a lambda as mutable to allow it to modify the objects captured by copy and to call their non-const member functions.
- Using a concept instead of the raw typenames in a template means we are likely to get clearer diagnostics if we don't provide a suitable type when we use the template.

- We can use `constexpr` for almost anything, including `std::vector` and `std::string`, since C++20. Evaluation might happen at compile time but does not need to. We can test `constexpr` code with a `static_assert`.
- A variadic template is a template with at least one parameter pack, indicated by an ellipsis.
- We unpack parameter packs using ellipsis again. We used `(... + tail)` in listing 9.11 to unpack the tail, and we can also put a parameter pack into an initializer list, which we did in listing 9.12 using `{ static_cast<int>(numbers)... }`.
- We can use `std::visit` to call a function for an `std::variant`, which ensures we have an appropriate overload for any possible type held.
- One way to employ `std::visit` is the `Overload` pattern, which uses a parameter pack to bring `operator()` into scope, allowing us to package up lambdas for each type in an `std::variant`.
- Finally, we used `std::views::zip` from the `ranges` library to pair up two collections. We can zip more than two collections and can then iterate over the tuple of elements in the view.
- Keep learning and practicing, and above all, have fun!

appendix
Further resources

This appendix contains a list of resources mentioned in each chapter for ease of reference.

Chapter 1

- Some details on Working Group 21 (WG21) of the International Organization for Standardization (ISO) are available at https://isocpp.org/std.
- The IncludeCpp group has a discord server and often holds a stall at conferences (https://www.includecpp.org/).
- The ISOCpp website has an FAQ section (https://isocpp.org/wiki/faq) that provides an overview of some recent C++ changes and big-picture questions.
- C++ Insights (https://cppinsights.io/) transforms code, making things the compiler does for us visible.
- Matt Godbolt's Compiler Explorer (https://godbolt.org/) supports a huge variety of different compilers, allowing us to see how each behaves without the need to install them.
- CppReference has a list of compiler support for each of the new features (https://en.cppreference.com/w/cpp/compiler_support).

Chapter 2

- A good list of free C++ compilers is available at https://isocpp.org/get-started.
- We used `std::format`, but you might need to use the `ftm` library (https://fmt.dev/latest/index.html) if your compiler does not support that format yet.
- We used { } to initialize variables, but initialization is a big topic and can get complicated. Nicolai Josuttis' talk "The Nightmare of Initialization in C++" goes into detail (see https://www.youtube.com/watch?v=7DTlWPgX6zs).
- In his Guru of the Week problems, Herb Sutter told us to almost always use `auto` (https://herbsutter.com/2013/08/12/gotw-94-solution-aaa-style-almost-always-auto/).

- Jason Turner discussed the pros and cons of `emplace` versus `push_back` on C++ Weekly (https://www.youtube.com/watch?v=jKS9dSHkAZY).
- Thomas Becker blogged about rvalue references back in 2013 (http://thbecker.net/articles/rvalue_references/section_01.html).
- You can experiment with the `fmt` library directly in Godbolt using https://godbolt.org/z/Eq5763.
- Herb Sutter and Andrei Alexandrescu suggested preferring algorithm calls to handwritten loops in their book *C++ Coding Standard: 101 Rules, Guidelines and Best Practices* (Addison-Wesley Professional, 2004).
- If your compiler doesn't support ranges fully, you can experiment at https://godbolt.org/z/YrnsTGbfx.
- We looked briefly at the core guidelines, which suggest we should not try to avoid negative values by using `unsigned` (https://isocpp.github.io/CppCore-Guide lines/CppCoreGuidelines#Res-nonnegative).

Chapter 3

- We used `random_device` to seed random number engines (https://en.cpprefer ence.com/w/cpp/numeric/random/random_device)
- Angelika Langer and Klaus Kreft wrote a book titled *Standard C++ IOStreams and Locales: Advanced Programmer's Guide and Reference* (Addison-Wesley Professional, 2000).
- Copying a lambda to an `std::function` can be inefficient. Scott Meyers gives full details in "Item 5: Prefer auto to explicit type declarations" in his book *Effective Modern C++* (O'Reilly Media, Incorporated, 2014).
- We mentioned a proposal to introduce an `std::function_ref` as an alternative to `std::function`, overcoming the performance problems (https://www.open -std .org/jtc1/sc22/wg21/docs/papers/2022/p0792r10.html). The Open Standards group collects various proposals and papers relevant to C++ in the WG21 directory.

Chapter 4

- Howard Hinnant's "Meeting C++" talk from 2019 gives background for the design of `std::chrono` (https://www.youtube.com/watch?v=adSAN282YIw).
- The whole-value idiom has roots in Ward Cunningham's CHECKS pattern language (http://c2.com/ppr/checks.html) and is further explored by Martin Fowler's Quantity pattern (https://martinfowler.com/eaaDev/Quantity.html).
- If your compiler does not fully support the C++20 `chrono` features, clone Howard Hinannt's date library (https://github.com/HowardHinnant/date) to include its `date.h` and use its definitions instead (e.g., `using date::operator<<;`).
- ISOCpp's core guideline SF.7 tells us not to write `using namespace` at global scope in a header file (http://isocpp.github.io/CppCoreGuidelines/CppCore Guidelines#Rs-using-directive).

- Jason Turner's C++ Weekly episode 34 gives an introduction to reading assembly language (https://www.youtube.com/watch?v=my39Gpt6bvY).
- Rainer Grimm's website has instructions for compiling and using the date library (https://www.modernescpp.com/index.php/calendar-and-time-zone-in-c-20-time-zones), which you might need for time zones, as do Howard Hinnant's GitHub pages (https://howardhinnant.github.io/date/tz.html#Installation).
- Howard Hinnant has written a list of examples and recipes for `chrono` (https://github.com/HowardHinnant/date/wiki/Examples-and-Recipes).

Chapter 5

- For details on ISO deliverables, including C++ technical specifications (TS), see https://www.iso.org/deliverables-all.html.
- There is a TS for compile time, or static, reflection (see https://www.open-std.org/jtc1/sc22/wg21/docs/papers/2020/n4856.pdf). It is on its way, and you can vote for it in Visual Studio via https://developercommunity.visualstudio.com/t/implement-the-c-reflection-ts/826632.
- For extra details on creating a `variant`, `optional`, or `any` variable, see https://www.cppstories.com/2018/07/in-place-cpp17/.
- Stephan T. Lavavej explains that when you need a random number, you should not call `rand()`, and especially do not say `rand() % 100` (https://learn.microsoft.com/en-us/events/goingnative-2013/rand-considered-harmful).

Chapter 6

- For a recap on hiding, see "Item 33: Avoid hiding inherited names" in Scott Meyers' book *Effective C++* (Addison-Wesley Professional, 2005).
- We met the rule of zero for when we do not user declare or define any of the six member functions (http://isocpp.github.io/CppCoreGuidelines/CppCoreGuidelines#Rc-zero).
- For a reminder of how the public, protected, and private access modifiers behave, see CppReference (https://en.cppreference.com/w/cpp/language/access).
- The Simple and Fast Multimedia Library (SFML) is relatively easy to use for multimedia (https://www.sfml-dev.org/index.php).
- The rule of zero means avoiding user declaring any of the special member functions, and the core guidelines even tell us to avoid defining defaults if possible (http://isocpp.github.io/CppCoreGuidelines/CppCoreGuidelines#Rc-zero).
- Peter Sommerlad suggests deleting the move assignment if a destructor is defined. He calls this pattern DesDeMovA: *Des*tructor => *De*lete *Mov*e *A*ssignment (see https://www.youtube.com/watch?v=fs4lIN3_IlA for his talk or https://github.com/boostcon/cppnow_presentations_2019/blob/master/lightning_talks/Rule_of_DesDeMovA__Peter_Sommerlad__cppnow_05062019.pdf for an overview).

- Howard Hinnant has given a talk titled "Everything You Ever Wanted to Know About Move Semantics" (https://www.youtube.com/watch?v=vLinb2fgkHk), and http://howardhinnant.github.io/classdecl.html offers a succinct overview.
- There is a proposal to extend C++11's random number generators (see https://wg21.link/P1932), which gives further details on the limits of the current engines.
- See https://www.modernescpp.com/index.php/std-weak-ptr for further details on `std::weak_ptr`.

Chapter 7

- Tim van Deurzen's gave a lightning talk on structured bindings at Meeting C++ in 2019 (see https://www.youtube.com/watch?v=YC_TMAbHyQU)).
- For further details on `std::string_view`, see https://www.modernescpp.com/index.php/c-17-avoid-copying-with-std-string-view.
- Nico Josuttis' book *The Standard Library, Second Edition* (Addison-Wesley Professional, 2005) is an excellent reference book to find out more about containers and algorithms and more.
- Donald Knuth's book *The Art of Computer Programming*, Volume 3 (Addison-Wesley Professional, 2008), gives thorough details on rebalancing binary trees.

Chapter 8

- The boost library has many useful features, including `hash_combine` (https://www.boost.org/doc/libs/1_55_0/doc/html/hash/combine.html).
- WG21 has discussed hash combination functions (see https://www.open-std.org/jtc1/sc22/wg21/docs/papers/2014/n3876.pdf).
- For more details on coroutines, see https://lewissbaker.github.io/2017/09/25/coroutine-theory.
- Andreas Fertig's book *Programming with C++20: Concepts, Coroutines, Ranges, and More* (Fertig Publications, 2021) has a chapter devoted to parsing a byte stream with coroutines. He published an overview in *Overload* in 2022 (see https://accu.org/journals/overload/30/168/fertig/).

Chapter 9

- For more practice with algorithms, see https://en.cppreference.com/w/cpp/algorithm.
- Anthony Williams' book *C++ Concurrency in Action* (Manning, 2012; https://www.manning.com/books/c-plus-plus-concurrency-in-action-second-edition) is an excellent resource if you want to learn more about parallel algorithms and concurrency in general, and you can find many of his talks on the internet.
- Bartlomiej Filipek wrote a detailed blog about the use and limitations of `constexpr` vectors and strings (https://www.cppstories.com/2021/constexpr-vecstr-cpp20/).
- For further details on fold expressions, see https://www.foonathan.net/2020/05/fold-tricks/.

index